THE STORY OF
CARDIFF

THE STORY OF
CARDIFF

NICK SHEPLEY

First published 2014

The History Press
The Mill, Brimscombe Port
Stroud, Gloucestershire, GL5 2QG
www.thehistorypress.co.uk

British Library Cataloguing in Publication Data.
A catalogue record for this book is available from the British Library.

ISBN 978 0 7509 5447 1

Typesetting and origination by The History Press
Printed in Great Britain

CONTENTS

INTRODUCTION

How do you tell the story of a city? Is it possible to find a narrative that conclusively summarises two millennia of experience? I don't think that this is possible: the idea of a story is an inherently biased, partial and politicised notion. In order to tell the story of a city one must tell it from a particular point of view, and to honestly reflect that the narrative has its own biases. None of us is an impartial observer of history, and we inevitably take a stance on the past to make sense of it all. I want to write this book from the point of view of the people who have lived through Cardiff's history, both the ordinary people who are listed in parish registers, county assizes and in the records of armies and navies around the world, and the famous and infamous who visited Cardiff or made their home there.

What is the value in doing this? Other than owing it to the victims, victors and bystanders of the past to understand even a glimpse of their world, we can come to really understand the character, the soul of a city by being aware of its scars. Listen to the suffragettes, soldiers, slaves, martyrs, rebels, pirates and priests, and in the testimonies of each and every one you will find a number of prescient truths about Cardiff.

Cardiff has been on the frontline of Anglo-Welsh history, a place where the hammer blow of the past has periodically fallen hard. Because of her location and her Anglicised nature, Cardiff was devastated during the Despenser War (1321–22) and in 1404 by Owain Glyndŵr. Her location meant Cardiff was again on history's fault line during the Second English Civil War in 1648, stuck rather reluctantly between Royalist West Wales and an unforgiving Parliamentary England. Because she found great wealth as the world's pre-eminent coal port, she was later on war's frontline again and eventually faced devastation from the air.

In each of her stages of being, Cardiff's strategic or economic purpose has evolved, and there have been winners and losers: vagrants locked up in the Cockmarel prison in the sixteenth century, the callous exile of Franciscan and Dominican monks in 1538 following the dissolution of the monasteries, slaves in Cardiff in the eighteenth century. Seismic changes in the ownership of wealth have continually coursed through the city, in their wake leaving the drama and often the tragedy of history.

Cardiff has been a city of identity crises. The Welsh capital, for much of its life it has been closely associated with England, an object of suspicion, mistrust and envy to much of the rest of Wales. An international city, it has been multi-cultural for far longer than most cities in Britain. It is a city where the stresses of modernity and the challenge of new political ideas spawned communist, fascist and neutral responses to the problems of the 1930s.

To understand Cardiff's rich and often chaotic past we have to question a powerful myth that seems to resonate most loudly when we walk through newly redeveloped parts of the city. Walk past the Wales Millennium Centre, or the Sennydd, and you would be forgiven for thinking that the future has arrived, the past is over and we have escaped history itself. Walking through St David's 2 Shopping Centre and looking at the high end brands and expensive eateries, we might be forgiven for thinking that there was no past, that we have always been living in a glamorous and endless 'now'. But there was a past, and it still lingers on all around us. Many of the roles that Cardiff had as a city while questions of identity hung over it have returned to haunt her. Just as Cardiffians wondered what was going to happen nearly a century ago as the docks became less profitable, those who work in the financial and service sectors that the city has come to rely on will now be asking 'What next? Where do we go from here?' The answer to this question is far from clear, but it is certain that whatever the future holds, it will be built, as ever, on the efforts, ingenuity and hard work of Cardiffians. Once the product of Welsh, Norman and Saxon culture, the city has been made and remade by Irish, Somali, Chinese, Cape Verdean, Jewish, Arabic, Norwegian and West Indian people, all of whom have merged together into a cohesive and dynamic culture, one that whilst not completely devoid of ethnic strife, has for the most part distinguished itself with its friendship, solidarity, integrity and fortitude.

Nick Shepley, March 2014

All contemporary images are taken by Kate Whittaker.

Archive pictures reproduced by kind permission of the Glamorgan Record Office.

one

EARLY SETTLEMENT

A t St Lythans, about 5 miles from Cardiff, lies a clue about the origins of the first people to occupy these lands. A burial chamber, some 6,000 years old, is situated here. The simple ancient burial structure, known as a dolmen, stands about 5ft feet high and is built from three large stones capped with a roof stone. It sits at the end of an 88ft barrow, a long submerged burial chamber where the remains of an ancient people lie. To put the age of the barrow into perspective, it was built about a millennium and a half before Stonehenge or the Great Pyramid at Giza, making it one of the oldest man-made structures in Britain, and perhaps one of the oldest man-made structures in the world.[1]

The land here 6,000 years ago was probably wooded all the way up to the banks of the Severn Estuary. The antlers of ancient stags have been found buried in the mud of the estuary near Cardiff in the last few decades, deer being animals that prefer woodland. The lowlands of Glamorgan, the Bro, was gradually cleared over millennia as hunting nomadic peoples settled and adopted farming as a way of life. The first immigrants were probably from the Iberian peninsula. Other Mesolithic peoples had travelled across the land bridge that connected Britain to the continent about 10,000 years ago, some of whom may have migrated as far as Wales, but the Celts were a southern European people who sailed to Wales as the sea levels rose following the end of the last Ice Age. The early Stone Age settlers who had come from Central Europe, probably following migrations in deer and other animals, seem to have mingled with the new southern colonists who had knowledge of working bronze and later iron. Around Cardiff and the Vale of Glamorgan there is plenty of evidence of successful Bronze Age and Iron Age communities. These early peoples were the Silures, one of the three Iron Age tribes of Wales. Roman accounts of the Siluric people dismiss them as barbarians, dressed in hides, and cannibals. This, of course, is propaganda, and similar descriptions were often applied to the Germanic tribes and the Gauls, all of whom the Romans conquered and enslaved, and for whom convenient myths of uncivilised cultures had to be invented to justify imperial conquest. The accounts, whilst surely exaggerated, indicate a people whose culture had been influenced by the harshness of nature. As with the Romans, the Silures worshipped many different gods of nature: they saw spirits and deities in every aspect of their world, in the forests, mountains and rivers. Their gods were violent, vengeful and bloodthirsty, and they demanded sacrifice. It is not known whether human sacrifice took place in the areas now dominated by Cardiff, but the practice was an integral part of Silurian culture.

This is not the full story, however. The Silures, the original inhabitants of South Wales, had a complex and rich culture. They were fiercely independent and fought against Roman occupation.[2] The oldest settlements in the Cardiff area have been identified at Wenvoe and Dinas Powys. At Dinas, some 5 miles east of Cardiff, a Neolithic axe head was discovered in 1949 (this now has pride of place at Cardiff Museum). The Silures also built a hill fort at Dinas, the site of which was later adopted by the Normans for a castle. An excavation by Leslie Alcock of this Iron Age fort uncovered evidence that this was the seat of a powerful chieftain. The works of various skilled craftsmen were discovered, and it also appears that a very experienced jeweller lived or worked there, making finery for the ruling family with gold and glass imported from the Germanic tribes on the continent. Across the Cardiff area numerous examples of skilfully worked Bronze Age craftsmanship have been discovered, including examples of early horse harnesses, indicating that the Siluric people had sufficient wealth and a stable agrarian system to allow a sophisticated level of animal husbandry. A number of axes and spear heads dating from the Bronze Age have also been dug up, strongly suggesting that some manner of military structure existed amongst the tribes.

Tacitus records that the Silures were a Mediterranean-looking people with swarthy features and dark curly hair, not dissimilar to the Iberian tribes of Spain. They proved fearsome warriors when they encountered the Romans. A fierce and warlike people, they adopted this place because it was natural farming land – this is why the Romans eventually contested it. In ancient times the density of settlements was greatest in the Glamorgan area, because the land could sustain more people there, and thinned out towards the west (on the Pembroke to Anglesey coast). Long before a Welsh identity had been established, those who occupied this land probably had allegiances to their neighbours in south-western England and connection with them in terms of culture, trade and worship; they were more than likely a part of a regional civilisation that had Stonehenge in Wiltshire at its heart. A lively trade system also flourished during the Bronze Age in the Severn Estuary and the Irish Sea. Early Cardiffians were almost certainly part of this process, and for the next two millennia access to the Severn and the Irish Sea determined the viability of a settlement at Cardiff: again, this was something that the Romans were eager to take advantage of. The Iron Age Celts, the real Silures, built the various hill forts that dominated the pre-Roman landscape of the Cardiff area, perhaps suggesting a growth in warfare at this time. In the Cardiff suburb of Caerau there are the remains of just such a fort. Situated at the end of today's housing estate, there are earthworks and the remnants of ditches and ramparts; with a little imagination it is not hard to see where buildings stood. These forts were extraordinary efforts in engineering and construction, probably not built by volunteers or even by free men. Evidence suggests that around a hill fort there were extensive agricultural estates, maintained by slaves or serfs. Caerau is also the site of other ruins, particularly the undated, but possibly early medi-eval ringwork foundations of a castle belonging to the diocese of Llandaff, perhaps in place for similar strategic reasons.

two

ROMAN DEVELOPMENT

I n the *Notitia Dignitatum*, the Roman Empire's Domesday Book, a chronicle of the Eastern and Western Empires, there is no mention of Cardiff despite hundreds of other Brittanic settlements being mentioned. The *Notitia* is considered to have been up to date in 420, and there had been a fortress in Cardiff since the year AD 74, as Cardiff served a vital strategic role for the Romans.

The fortress is clearly a later Roman construction, and occupies a place on the coastline for two reasons. First, raiders from the sea were a continual danger, and unsecured coastlines could cost the Roman occupiers dearly. These seaborne raiders were most probably from Ireland, known to the Romans as the Scoti, and the existence of a larger garrison at Caerleon tends to suggest that Glamorgan was quite intensively militarised by the Romans. Cardiff's first maritime use was as a port for Roman ships, and it is likely that the fort was at the centre of a system of coastal defences that stretched along both sides of the estuary. Carausius, the Roman emperor of Britain and North Gaul who usurped power in 286, is likely to have first militarised Cardiff. The dangers had clearly not abated a century later when Theodosius added to the garrison at Cardiff, reinforcing the buildings and the number of ships. As Cardiff operated at this time in tandem with northern naval ports at Carnarfon and Anglesey, this meant the Romans could dominate the Irish Sea and its valuable trade routes.

The second reason for the fortress is that the Blaina, or the highland regions of Glamorgan, were impassable and dangerous, so the coastal plains were an essential transit route from east to west. Through this the Romans could control access to the rest of South Wales. The large Roman garrison at Cardiff had great strategic importance; that a powerful position was chosen is clear from the fact that the Normans, nearly a millennium later, were content to build their castle on the same site. The outer walls of Cardiff Castle are the only remnant of the Roman fort.

Roman rule in Wales traditionally relied on forts to blockade access between valleys, pinning down the local population to specific geographical areas and forming a barrier against the Silures, who had been forced off the coastal plain and further north into the mountains. The Romans' largest fortress in South Wales was Caerleon, the military and administrative hub that the satellite forts, including Cardiff, revolved around. Caerleon was home to the feared Second Legion, South Wales' army of occupation, and was one of the three main bases of military power in the British Isles. The countryside was also patrolled, and as a result the first roads were built by the Romans, connecting the fort of Cardiff with outlying villages and settlements in the south-east of Wales. These allowed troops to move in order to quell trouble, and Historian Gwyn Alf Williams

Clock tower. Burges designed the clock tower to be in keeping with the rest of the medieval building, but it is unmistakably a late Victorian folly.

called them the backbone of an amorphous society, serving as a skeleton for future societies. As we shall see, it was often Cardiff's good fortune to be situated on such roads, and sometimes her misfortune, as it placed her at the very heart of historical change and sometimes conflict.

Looking at the arrangement of fortresses in South Wales, from Cardiff to Usk, Caerleon and Abergavenny, and comparing them to similar fortresses in other parts of the Roman Empire, it appears that the subjugated people of South Wales were more than likely a troublesome and rebellious bunch. Siluria, as the kingdom of central and eastern Wales was called by the Romans, represented a threat to the strategically important Severn Estuary and the trade routes to the continent.

The original name of the fort that the Romans built at Cardiff is unknown, but the name of the settlement that grew up around it is a reference to the fort, Caer Dydd, or Castle on the River Taff (Dydd being a translation of Taff). The seventh-century 'Ravenna Cosmography' points towards the name Tamium, but opinions are divided: the anonymous nature of the document casts doubt on its veracity.[3] The fort is described thus by the archaeologist R.G. Collingwood:

> Cardiff is a rectangular, almost square, fort with angular corners and polygonal bastions. Its walls are 10 feet thick at the base, reduced by offsets to 8 feet 6 inches, and have an earthen bank behind them. The fort measures about 650 by 600 feet (7¾ acres internally) and has a single gate, with projecting towers, at each end, and perhaps a postern in the middle of each side.

There were at least four Roman forts built on the same site at Cardiff, each replaced by another of greater strength, indicating that the strategic importance of Cardiff was growing. The first fortress was the largest, housing all its successors within a large defended enclosure: a perfect square measuring about 1,000ft on each side and covering over 24 acres. It was built on the site of an existing Siluric settlement, a tried and tested Roman strategy for pacifying an area of strategic importance.

The original structures were vexillation fortresses, which housed a large contingent of battle-experienced troops, mainly legionnaires and cavalry. The original fort was a quickly built centre from which war on the local area was waged, and once the campaign to crush resistance had been successful it was replaced by a smaller structure. The first fortress was built in AD 74–8 and was most likely demolished some time in the second century, when the garrison left, perhaps to defeat an uprising elsewhere in the country. The local inhabitants who lived in and around the fort would have made good use of the ruins after the Romans had gone, but the fort was rebuilt in the next couple of decades. It was later, in about AD 260, that the Romans built the first stone structure here, creating a fort that would act as a template for all subsequent castles on the site.

The civilian settlement of Cardiff probably began in the second century, after the Roman reoccupation. Roads, military security, trade routes that were free from piracy and a garrison of men to trade with, all combined to give the new Cardiffians, Romano-British and Celtic alike opportunities to build homes, to farm, trade and to travel across the economic region, from the West Country to Ireland. This was the model for Cardiff for the next millennium and a half: trade and farming.

One of the many relics that the Romans left behind is a Roman villa at Ely. This stands between Cowbridge Road West and the River Ely, and one can imagine the value of this location to its builders in the second century: within sight of the fortress but sufficiently far away to take advantage of the rich farming land and the river, as well as serviced by a road that ran to Neath, just 100 yards or so from the villa's front door. This villa is a clear indication of wealth here, and shows that the Romans had become comfortable enough by the second century to settle, probably with the intention of farming.

However, the later stone fortifications to Cardiff Castle tell a different story, one of an empire under threat. These are similar to a Saxon Shore fort. The Saxon Shore, the coastline of Kent and Sussex, was vulnerable to invasion from European barbarian tribes, and the Romans reinforced it as they had done the northern border with Hadrian's Wall. That they saw fit to apply the same level of defence to Cardiff suggests that an equivalent level of threat existed.

It seems likely that after the withdrawal of Rome in the fourth-century Cardiff either diminished in size or was abandoned. The people here must have started to feel dangerously exposed to their wilder neighbours in the north and to other visitors from the sea, first the Irish and later the Vikings. The sea in ancient times wasn't the obstacle it is perceived as now, but was a powerful conduit that enabled small settlements to access foreign trading opportunities. It also meant that foreign opportunists could visit too.

After the Romans left there is little evidence of a continued settlement, suggesting its abandonment or its destruction by raiders. Perhaps a less dramatic fate is related to the fact that without a Roman garrison there were fewer economic opportunities – less need for farming, horse rearing, tanning and leatherworking, metalworking, brewing and carpentry. The Romans created opportunities for settlements purely by dint of their presence, so when the garrison departed the settlement that was completely dependent on it vanished as well.

three

THE MIDDLE AGES

L ittle is known about Cardiff in the 500 years between the Romans and the invasions of the Normans into Morgannwg. All that historians can do is make educated guesses about what Cardiff might have been like and if it was inhabited at all.

One repeatedly important feature of Cardiff's history is her vulnerability to coastal attack. It is also likely that Saxon invaders threatened small settlements like Cardiff, crossing a land route from what is now the West Midlands. The likelihood is that the settlement was abandoned, for at least some of this time. Cardiff thrived when there were powerful military occupiers, be they Norman or Roman, who understood the value of an estuary port that could be militarised. When the settlement lacked sufficient might to protect her, she may well have been temporarily overrun or sacked. It is also possible that insecure early Cardiffians packed up and moved inland. Possibly a small colony remained or possibly not; there is no first-hand evidence. The rest of the region was inhabited at this time, and an advanced society under the kings of Morgannwg existed until the Normans arrived. There is a wealth of information about the rest of the kingdom, but nothing about Cardiff – suggesting that the coastal region was uninhabitable.

Perhaps Cardiff's greatest treasure, and certainly its most resilient structure, is Llandaff Cathedral, founded in 1120 on the site of a small religious community that was established in the sixth century. The point at which the Roman road to Caerleon crossed the River Taff was an ideal location for St Dyfrig to found a small community and for his protégé, St Teilo, to build a church in 1107.

The kings of Morgannwg seem to have come under the influence of Anglo-Saxons in the ninth century, owing to the predations of their neighbours in North and West Wales. This perhaps gives us a clue about the historical causes of the gradual Anglicisation of Glamorgan.

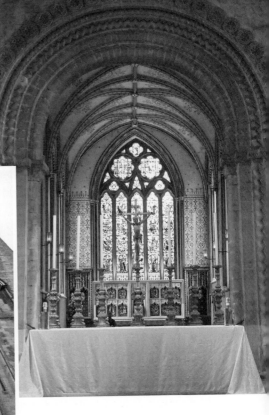

Llandaff Cathedral (*right and below*) Bishop Anthony Kitchin has the distinction of surviving Henry VIII, Edward VI, Mary I and Elizabeth's reformations, counter reformations and settlements. He died in office in 1563.

The cathedral was all but abandoned when Henry VIII dissolved the monasteries, banned pilgrims from visiting Llandaff and took away Church lands and other sources of revenue.

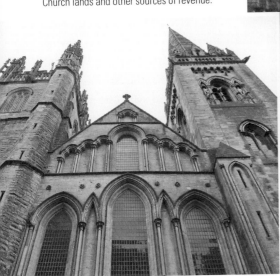

In 1067, William Fitzosbern, one of William the Conqueror's chief warmongers, took possession of the borderlands and was given the title Earl of Hereford. This was no random appointment: it was directed at the people of south-eastern Wales. There must have been a sense of resignation, helplessness and panic. Chepstow and Monmouth quickly became Norman garrisons, but for Fitzosbern the real prizes lay further east. He had to conquer Morgannwg to eliminate any threat from the borderlands, and to give his nobles, hungry for land and titles, rewards for their efforts.[4]

Cardiff was reborn when the Normans arrived in Wales and there are several accounts that suggest the settlement was rebuilt in 1081. This is when William the Conqueror made his first and only visit to Cardiff: was it purpose-built for his arrival? He must have seen the potential that Cardiff offered strategically in much the same way that the Romans had. As it happened, Cardiff was not the prime reason for William's visit: this was the Shrine of St David. His pilgrimage there was probably a show of strength and he must have enjoyed the awe in which he and his army were held by the Welsh kings. William was happy to visit shrines, pray to saints and give offerings, perhaps to quieten his guilty conscience. Rhys ap Tewdr, King of Deheubarth, seized the opportunity to curry favour with the new power in the land and offered his fealty to William, thus guaranteeing some degree of autonomy and supremacy over other Welsh lords.

On William the Conqueror's visit to Cardiff he ordered the construction of another fortress on the Taff, building on the site of the abandoned Roman fort. Perhaps his visit was to shore up strategic weaknesses, as he must have been mindful of how Nordic invaders could quickly alter the balance of power, having benefited, after all, from the intervention of Harold Hardrada in 1066. The new fortress was quickly constructed and wooden, but, in time, the Normans built a huge and imposing stone castle, which had strategic and symbolic purposes. Its imposing, indestructible character sent a clear message to all would-be opponents and troublemakers: challenge us at your peril.

William Fitzosbern did not live to see the country he had conquered on behalf of his master brought to its knee, as he was slain in Flanders in 1071. Inroads into Wales seem to have ground to a halt after 1075, as William the Conqueror lost interest in the subjugation of the Welsh. He marched as far as St David's, but realised he would be militarily overstretched in taking on the more rebellious and determined western kingdoms. The ease with which he had begun to crush the eastern kingdoms might stem from the fact that they had previously accepted the supremacy of Anglo-Saxon kings. Following William the Conqueror's death, still without a clear defeat of Morgannwg, it fell to his son, William Rufus, to complete the task. In the end, Robert Fitzhamon, Earl of Gloucester and a Norman 'enforcer', invaded South Wales, probably from the sea, and finally crushed Morgannwg creating from it the Anglicised county of Glamorgan. With him, Fitzhamon took twelve knights, many of whose descendants were the noble and aristocratic rulers of Glamorgan for the next 500 to 600 years. One of those knights, Sir Payn de Turberville, had descendants who called the shots in Cardiff in the eighteenth century: the Turbervilles, along with the Stradlings, another of the famous twelve, are synonymous with the history of both Cardiff and Glamorgan. An apocryphal tale has it that Fitzhamon used the dispute between Rhys ap Tewdr and the other local Welsh lords as a pretext for invading, with an army of over 3,000 men. Tewdr was defeated and as the Normans began to march for Gloucester they became embroiled in a second dispute, as Iestyn and Einion began to feud regarding the betrothal of Iestyn's daughter to Einion. Iestyn welched on the deal and Einion beseeched Fitzhamon to intervene, which he duly did at a battle where Rhiwbina stands today. Thus Tewdr came to know the full extent of Norman treachery.

It seems doubtful that a shrewd, aggressive and acquisitive man like Fitzhamon took all Morgannwg in this fashion, just as it seems unlikely that William would have approved of this haphazard conquest of the kingdom. The Normans were not the sort of warriors who intervened in disputes on an ad hoc basis, and it is more than likely that the conquest of Morgannwg was planned in great detail. The constant feuding and intriguing between Welsh lords gave the Normans ample opportunity to divide and rule, and it is this factor that is probably most important.

As with many of the subsequent Lords of Cardiff, Robert Fitzhamon appointed himself the lord of both Leckwith and Roath. These were small hamlets, renamed and Anglicised, that came under the rule of Cardiff. The church at Llandaff was granted much of the outlying lands around Cardiff[5], thus Fitzhamon owned comparatively little land in and around Cardiff, despite having conquered Morgannwg himself and having virtually *carte blanche* to claim whatever lands he desired. In England he was grateful for lands that he was granted by the king; in Wales there were no such constraints. He cast out Welsh lords and seized estates, but comparatively little of this land went to himself. One has to examine the military structure of Norman rule to understand why this was. Cardiff with its newly built fort was a military hub for the entire county. Norman models of land ownership and occupation were used to organise the castle and the community that had sprung up around it. In order to control this new territory, much of the land was given to knights, who fulfilled their feudal obligations to the patrons. The fact that this was necessary in Glamorgan on such a large scale suggests that the county was anything but pacified. In a bid to secure the realm from foes internal and external, Fitzhamon insisted that his knights build fortresses to defend that which had been expropriated. To describe the Normans as despised by the ethnic Welsh is something of an understatement.

Castles in places such as Cowbridge and Ogmore reinforced Norman rule, but the nexus of the system was always Cardiff.[6] A quick glance at the design of the Norman castle gives us some important clues about Fitzhamon's thinking. Strategically the castle was as important in the twelfth century as it had been in the fifth; the site commanded rivers and roads, the transport network that made Glamorgan passable. Inside the original compound the Normans dug

Cardiff Castle. A structure has dominated Cardiff on this site since Roman times.

a large ditch, and piled the earth that was excavated, probably by slave labour as it was in the rest of occupied England and Wales, into a huge mound.[7] On top of this they built a wooden keep, a solid and virtually unassailable centre of operations surrounded by a wooden palisade and accessed by a bridge that connected with the rest of the Roman fortress. Outside the inner bailey were houses built for the knights who were obliged to offer service to the castle. As with all Norman military architecture, the builders started with timber but eventually replaced it with stone when they had the opportunity. The moat that the Normans dug can be seen today; the earth they excavated from this was used to shore up the Roman walls. Waters from the Taff surrounded three sides of the castle, while the river provided defences on the fourth.

The Normans would not have gone to all this effort if they hadn't faced the possibility of rebellion and unrest during the twelfth century. However, the rebellion that followed the death of Henry I, caused by the cruelty and rapacity of the Norman occupying forces, does not seem to have affected Glamorgan and there is no evidence that Cardiff came under siege in any way, although it would have been a crucial centre of operations. This might have been because the Normans were so well established in the county that there was little prospect of a successful revolt: they might have dealt with possible centres of rebellion long beforehand. Even so, the highlands of Glamorgan still held some native Welsh resisters, although the Normans were often content to ignore them and concentrate on exploiting and dominating the lowlands. It might be that the influx of English settlers changed the ethnic makeup of the area to such an extent that the population was more loyal to its Norman masters, for economic reasons or through a mutual mistrust of and antipathy towards the native Welsh.

As with all overlords, Robert Fitzhamon was not deprived of wealth or status, although his status did not come from being a landowner but from being a military and feudal enforcer of the king's will. There is plenty of evidence to support this. His knights' first task was to garrison the fort at Cardiff, indicating that the Normans were concerned to establish an effective army of occupation.

Each knight was expected to spend forty days per year at the castle, fully equipped, armoured and ready for war.[8] They were required to finance the upkeep of equipment and horses themselves, which was probably quite reasonable given the vast wealth they had been given by Fitzhamon. Later, in the twelfth and thirteenth century as the risk of rebellion began to subside, the lords of Cardiff Castle began to tax the knights instead of demanding military service from them. Their second duty was both governmental and ceremonial: they were obliged to attend a county court in Cardiff called the *Comitatus*.

This was the second most important function of Norman government: enforcing the law. The chief object of Norman law was the maintenance of land ownership, and the chief legal officer was the sheriff, or shire reeve, indicating the relationship between the

Llandaff Cathedral. The Normans were prolific cathedral builders and constructed Llandaff from the year 1120 onwards. Craftsmen from all over Europe were employed in the project.

post and the new designation of Glamorgan as a shire. The seat of justice was the Shire Hall, within the castle compound. Administration of justice was its main role, but it evolved a governmental function as well. The Normans were concerned with property rights in a way that previous rulers of Glamorgan had not been, and the resolution of property disputes took up a large proportion of the time of the *Comitatus*, which met monthly. When Fitzhamon was available he rode from Gloucester to preside over the *Comitatus*, and the extent of his power in Glamorgan can be seen from the court's work. Here he raised taxes as he saw fit, traditionally a sovereign power. He made laws, adjudicated over land disputes and dispensed summary justice in criminal matters. To all intents and purposes he was a *de facto* king in Glamorgan with Cardiff as his capital, and he bestowed upon himself the title Prince of Glamorgan (no doubt he would have styled himself a king if it hadn't been for the likely accusation of sedition). As a traditional Norman absentee landlord, Fitzhamon was frequently called away to London and Gloucester to deal with other matters, and his sheriffs were more than able to step into the vacuum he left behind.

Around Robert Fitzhamon a new and eager ruling class emerged, situated across Glamorgan but drawn to Cardiff as their centre of power. These new families were exclusively Norman, and even if they spoke some English they would have had no understanding of Welsh. Parish records from the thirteenth and fourteenth centuries for areas such as Landough and Dinas Powys show small freeholders, little more than well-to-do peasants, with non-Welsh and distinctly Anglo-Norman surnames. It is unlikely that grants of freeholds would have been given to new generations of Anglo-Norman descendants 200 years after the rule of Fitzhamon; it is far more likely that a colonising class of nobles and knights granted land to their subjects from England and from Normandy. Wales, like Scotland, was dubbed a land for younger sons by the Normans, who saw it as a convenient place to defuse dynastic disputes. A Norman noble with two sons, not wanting to divide his lands between them and thus start the dissolution of the family's wealth, would ship the younger one off to the Celtic peripheries.

Robert Fitzhamon met his death in the time-honoured Norman way, in battle. He was dealt a fatal head injury from a lance whilst laying siege to Robert of Normandy, the king's brother, at Falaise in 1105, and lingered on in a vegetative state until his death in 1107.[9] He left only a daughter, Mabel, to inherit his titles and lands, and Glamorgan and Cardiff were retained by the king, Henry I, until she was married to the king's bastard son Robert, Earl of

Cardiff Castle and clock tower. The clock tower was a late Victorian addition by the Butes, designed by celebrated architect William Burges.

Gloucester and the largest landowner in the country.[10] Robert the Consul, as he was known, continued the works of his predecessor: where Robert Fitzhamon had built with wood, Robert of Gloucester replaced with stone. It is not hard to see why that other great builder of Cardiff, the 3rd Marquess of Bute, honoured Robert with a mural in Cardiff Castle in the nineteenth century. The marquess, whose life's work was building Cardiff's docks, was perhaps mindful that an even greater engineer had come before him, and wanted to draw parallels between them. Like Bute many centuries later, and just like his late father-in-law, Robert the Consul was an absentee landlord. He was a key member of court in London and was often required in Normandy as well. The rebuilding of the castle in stone was part of a wider consolidation of Norman power across the country, as there was now time and wealth to invest in stone. Robert built the imposing stone curtain walls that protect the keep, which was twelve-sided and also stone.

What does Cardiff owe to the legacy of Robert Fitzhamon? Like the Butes 800 years later, Fitzhamon appears to have been a larger-than-life character: a powerful, ruthless and determined ruler. What he started through military

Cardiff Castle Animal Wall. Architect William Burges designed the Animal Wall, which features animals sculpted by John Nicholls in 1890. Developers in 1970 planned to demolish the wall altogether.

This leopard (*right*) is a later addition, sculpted in 1931 by Alexander Carrick.

conquest he finished by building a feudal state in Glamorgan, centred on Cardiff as the military, judicial and political centre of the county. Stability and the rule of law (however brutal) amid good farming land, allowed the settlement to become established.

A town had been growing around the walls of the castle from the end of the eleventh century. Many of the Anglo-Norman settlers whose descendants were mentioned in parish records centuries later were the first to start building houses and cultivating common lands in the shadow of the castle. In 1111 a palisade was built around the settlement, giving the town a more distinct structure, offering the inhabitants a degree of security and a sense that Cardiff was a separate entity, not simply a collection of huts. Outlying villages such as

Roath supplied the town's markets with milk, cheese and hides for tanning, and Leckwith, the other acquisition of Fitzhamon, was prime arable land. Cardiff's network of rivers and streams teemed with fish, and it is likely that fish made up more of the diet of early medieval Cardiffians than meat did.

In the same year that Fitzhamon died, Llandaff was recognised by the Normans as a bishopric. A man named Urban was appointed first Bishop of Llandaff and began the construction of an enormous stone building. The creation of Norman churches was one of the engineering marvels of the early Middle Ages, one that required expertise from across Norman Europe. Stonemasons, architects, carpenters and others flocked to projects like Llandaff, contributing much-needed skills and expertise. The process of building began in 1107 but further additions were made over the next 200 years. Urban came from the parish of Llancarfan, near Cowbridge, and was from the kind of background that the Norman Lords of the Marches were likely to trust: minor clerical nobility. It is interesting that the Normans chose a South Walian priest: perhaps they wanted someone with local ties who was able to speak directly to the Welsh peasants. Urban seems to have been Anglicised enough to appeal to the tastes of his patrons, having been schooled in the diocese of Worcester, and this would have been comforting and reassuring to the English settlers who had begun to make Cardiff their home. It is interesting to note that the Bishop of Llandaff was a title dreamt up by Urban himself; he was originally elected Bishop of Glamorgan in 1107, but by 1115 he had assumed the new title. He designated Llandaff as his see and worked to ensure that it was raised above other dioceses in terms of its religious significance and prominence. Part of this was gaining permission to move holy relics from the island of Bardsey. These relics were the bones of Dyfrig, founder of the religious community at Llandaff some 500 years before.

One of the most important medieval documents to have survived is *The Book of Llandaff*. This was commissioned by Urban and written by an unknown scribe, and it records land transfers from kings, diocese and landowners to the church, chronicling how Llandaff came to have the lands that it owned.[11] The reason for the book's compilation appears to have been Urban's disputes with other bishops, notably those of St David's and Hereford, over Llandaff's boundaries. It was a typical Norman solution to land disputes, a sort of Domesday Book for Llandaff.

In 1134 the 80-year-old eldest son of William the Conqueror died a prisoner in Cardiff Castle. Robert of Normandy had felt cheated throughout his life for having never been given the throne. He never gave up on his claim, but was sidelined by William because of his arrogance, his feuding with his brothers and his temper, all of which exploded into open rebellion in 1077. In 1100, after the death of William II, Henry seized power while Robert was away in the Holy Land on the First Crusade, and five years later he invaded Normandy to deal with his brother, who continued to plot and scheme against him. When Robert was defeated the following year he was taken back to England and imprisoned in Devizes Castle for the next twenty years. He was then moved to Cardiff, where it is thought he lived in relative comfort. He seems to have learned some Welsh while he was a captive, and his brash, impetuous character was gradually replaced by a subdued, fatalistic and deeply melancholy outlook. Although he had been spared the executioner's block, he endured what was for a Norman warrior a slow and lingering demise. It is easy to see why Cardiff was the ideal place to send the hapless duke: it was in the fiefdom of Robert the Consul, who had become one of the most trusted and loyal servants of his father, the king. There was very little chance of him betraying his oaths of loyalty to his liege, and he had also become valued for his patience, intelligence and astute judgement.

Henry I died just a year after Robert of Normandy, leaving his son, the Lord of Cardiff, at the heart of a dynastic dispute that would see the first civil war in England and Wales. Robert's half-sister Matilda, the rightful heir to the throne, was usurped by Stephen, the late king's nephew. As we have already seen, the revolt that spread across Wales after the death of Henry I does not seem to have engulfed Glamorgan. How much of this was the result of the wise stewardship of Robert the Consul is in doubt. His personal qualities might have had an impact on his ability to quell dissent, but his whereabouts during the revolt are not known.

As is often the case in history, the patient work of great men, often done quietly and over long periods of time, can easily be undone by their lesser sons who are anxious to outshine their fathers but do not have the skills or advice that guided their forebears. The rule of William, Duke of Gloucester is a case in point. Gerald of Wales, perhaps the most illuminating chronicler of the early Middle Ages, recounted the unnecessary and rash provocations that William inflicted on Welsh lords in untamed parts of Glamorgan.[12] The notorious greed for land that the Normans had, necessary in part to keep their model of feudalism operating, was a strong trait in William – and he risked the wrath of Ifor ap Meurig, the Lord of Senghennydd, when he tried to annex Ifor Bach's (as he was more commonly known) land. Thirty years after the confrontation that was to come, in 1188, Gerald of Wales heard the story of Ifor Bach's daring raid on Cardiff Castle, an event that has now passed into folklore legend. Leading a small band of warriors, Ifor Bach scaled the walls of the castle. Some 120 armed men were supposed to be inside, and one supposes that Ifor Bach had some sort of assistance to break into the castle. Given the arrogance and foolishness of William, one of his retainers might have wanted to teach him a salutary lesson. Ifor Bach kidnapped William, his wife and son, and rode them deep into the forests of Glamorgan. There he exacted a reversion of the land grab that William had perpetrated, having the lands of Senghennydd restored to him.

Opposition to William later came from further afield, from the Welsh princes to the west whose power had not been diminished to anywhere near the same extent as the Welsh lords of Glamorgan. The inability of William to use his judgement or rule through flexibility and consent led to revolt, and it was the treaties and charters that ended these revolts which delivered the first real liberties and privileges to the people of Cardiff. The failure of informal government and the subsequent revolts led to more formal relationships, enshrined in law, which were created between ordinary people and their overlords. Many of the Lords of Glamorgan over the following decades came to an understanding with the crown, and even fought for the king in Normandy.

William had ordered hostages to protect himself from revolt, including from Morgan ap Caradog, who had skilfully dominated the Glamorgan highlands. When revolt came, William, renowned for his cruelty, had the hostage blinded. This gave Morgan ap Caradog an abiding hatred of William and so he launched a powerful offensive on William's death in 1183.

The rising that followed William's death was far more serious in Glamorgan than the rising that had been the result of Henry I's death. Again, this points towards William's rule as being the key factor that precipitated years of anger and resentment. During the revolt the west of the county was a target, but Cardiff also came under attack, a sign that in the most settled, well-defended and prosperous part of the county matters had got out of control.

The Normans threw themselves into a vigorous military and engineering defence of Cardiff. Supplies of building materials flowed across the Bristol Channel, and from as far as Chepstow. The castle was reinforced with men too: Glamorgan's Anglo-Norman nobility rallied to the defence of the town. The keep was designed to withstand sieges, not to be a pleasant place to live, and so conditions within the walls of the castle were no doubt unbearable – cramped, cold, damp, and surrounded by human sewage. Many Cardiffians would have flocked to the castle during times of unrest, adding to the overcrowding.

The offensive after the death of William was not mere opportunism. It was coordinated, and had clear strategic objectives: to reclaim the entirety of the Bro Morannwg, the lowlands that had been so attractive to generations of invaders. Whilst some modest gains were made by the Welsh rebels, by the time the revolt had petered out no serious harm had come to Cardiff. The castle remained an imposing military presence throughout the Norman era.

The town that was now emerging around the castle was drawn together by the ability of the Normans to protect it, and also by the town's charter. This document gave certain exemptions from the myriad of feudal dues and taxes that had been imposed on Wales and England by the Normans. Obligations were limited, meaning that wealthier householders who paid a certain level of taxation (an annual levy of 12*d*) no longer had to provide service, labour or military duty to the Lord of Cardiff Castle. This illustrates, as does the issue of the ending of compulsory military service for knights in return for taxation, that amassing wealth had become more important than building. Much of the Norman infrastructure was built at this point, and expensive foreign ventures like the Crusades were bleeding the coffers of every town and borough in Norman Wales. The burgesses of Cardiff were in an advantageous position because of the charter: they were exempted from paying market tolls (a small levy imposed on market day), and they could buy and sell property without having to pay duties to the castle. Most importantly, monopolies held by the lord on key industries such as brewing, tanning and milling were lifted, giving Cardiffians the ability and the right to make these goods for themselves or to take them to market. In all, this charter was the most positive aspect of William of Gloucester's rule in Cardiff and it set the town apart from many others in South Wales. In the following decades there was a growth in entrepreneurial business, as people became more able to make a living. It appears that the granting of this charter was a turning point, making the town a small hub of trade, commerce and enterprise, something that enriched the Normans more than excessive taxation. If we take into account that the charter was updated with each successive lord, until by the time of Henry VIII it was issued as a royal charter, then we can begin to see why security and stability helped prosperity to flourish.

When William died without an heir (his son had died in 1166), his great estates were inherited by John, son of Henry II through his marriage to Isabel, one of William's daughters. John, later crowned king, lived up to his reputation of pantomime villain by eventually divorcing Isabel and retaining the Lordship of Cardiff for himself in 1199. John died in 1216 and Isabel, on her third marriage, died a year later with no clear heir. Cardiff passed to her nephew Gilbert de Clare. In thirteenth-century Welsh and English history Gilbert was an important actor, along with the rest of the de Clare family. In 1215 he rose against the king at Lincoln in the first Barons' War, which culminated with the signing of the Magna Carta that same year (de Clare and his father were signatories). Two years later he was taken prisoner by William Marshal, who was acting as regent while the new king, Henry III, who was still a child, making him in effect a *de facto* king. Gilbert married Marshal's daughter, and offered loyal service to Henry III as the boy grew to adulthood, working tirelessly as a dedicated warrior for the king. The de Clare family maintained the lordship of Cardiff for a century. The sons and grandsons of Gilbert de Clare also took an active role in national events, especially in the long struggle throughout the thirteenth century to establish the rights of the barons in England and to bring an end to absolutism.

Gilbert's grandson, Gilbert the Red, had a pivotal role to play in the struggle of rebel leader Simon de Montfort, and also in his downfall. Gilbert the Red was knighted by de Montfort on the eve of the Battle of Lewes. De Montfort fought to hold King Henry III accountable to the Magna Carta during the second Barons' War and all but defeated the king. To all intents and purposes he was running England and parts of Wales; however, he was to be betrayed by his most trusted knight, Gilbert de Clare.

In 1264, Gilbert was excommunicated by the Pope for his involvement in treason. Being declared a rebel in the middle ages was a religious indictment as much as it was political, for a king was put in place by God, according to the popular hierarchical idea of the Great Chain of Being. Therefore to rebel against a king was to sin against God. As punishment all of Gilbert's lands, Cardiff included, were deemed forfeit. This must have been a very difficult and dangerous time for Cardiffians, for if they came out directly in support of their liege, the city could have been razed to the ground in revenge if he lost. However, it is unlikely that Cardiffians would have supported the Crown over their own lord, because the Earls of Gloucester had such enormous autonomy in Glamorgan. People would have looked to them for leadership, law and protection, not to a remote and unpopular king in England.

When Gilbert changed sides during the war, after having disagreements with de Montfort, he destroyed de Montfort's chances of escaping England for Wales by demolishing the bridge at Gloucester and burning his ships at Bristol. Had de Montfort crossed the Bristol Channel or ridden west from Gloucester, would he have arrived in Cardiff? It seems unlikely that Cardiff could have avoided the impact of having de Montfort's army in such close proximity and so perhaps this act of treachery spared Cardiff from becoming a battleground in the second Barons' War. It certainly doomed de Montfort, and also any chance of progressive change in England and Wales for centuries.

Gilbert joined Prince Edward, the king's son, at the Battle of Kenilworth, and then at Evesham, where Simon de Montfort was slain. Later, having repented and been absolved of his part in the revolt, Gilbert was given the lands of Abergavenny and the castle of Brecknock as a thank you.

When the deeper reasons for Gilbert's treachery are examined, once again Cardiff features as a pivotal factor. Gilbert had indeed supported parliamentary reform, but he was afraid of the Welsh prince Llewellyn ap Gruffudd, who disputed Gilbert's claims to lands in Glamorgan. In 1265, months before his death, de Montfort had made generous arrangements with Gruffudd, virtually allowing him to rule Wales and entitling him to any disputed Glamorgan lands. Caerphilly Castle was built in response to Gruffudd's territorial claims, indicating how great the potential risk was to Cardiff. It was this threat that led Gilbert to make his secret deal with Henry.

When Henry III died, Gilbert took a lead role in securing the throne for the king's son, Edward I, who was away in Sicily. He swore fealty to the new king *in absentia*, and then rode to London with the Archbishop of Canterbury and proclaimed Edward's right to take the throne immediately, bypassing the need for another interim ruler or monarch. It is interesting to note that as he rode into the city he proclaimed peace to all Christians and Jews living there. He perhaps referred to the Jews because of the guilt of his actions towards them during the second Barons' War: at Canterbury in 1264 he had killed the town's Jews, unprovoked savagery and violence that was repeated by de Montfort at Leicester.

Gilbert the Red continued to wage war on behalf of the new king, this time against the Welsh. Gruffudd was now officially a traitor, as he had sent troops to fight on behalf of De Montfort, and Gilbert was not about to let a critical advantage like that go unexploited. Llewellyn ap Gruffudd was severely punished for his opposition, and with him vanished the last real independence of the Welsh.

In order to fully understand the antipathy between the two men, we have to understand that the de Clares had been progressively Anglicising the county of Glamorgan. In earlier times, immediately after the Normans arrived, English migrants had come to Glamorgan and settled at Cardiff, probably as individuals as there is no evidence to suggest that there was a settlement policy. Under the rule of the de Clares, however, a policy of major demographic change seems to have been in existence. From 1183 onwards they moved English migrants to Glamorgan, from the start facing stern opposition from Welsh lords. Robert the Consul had ruled with a degree of consent and grudging acceptance from the Welsh nobility, but the de Clares had no such cordial welcome.

There were frequent raids of English and Norman settlements across Glamorgan, and it was Gilbert the Red's father, Richard, who crushed opposition, added swathes of new territory to the family holdings and built new defences, such as a castle at Llantrisant. It is easy to see how these mounting tensions between the de Clare dynasty and the Welsh nobility culminated in a showdown. Even before the coronation of the new king, Edward, who would eventually lead the most crushing invasion of Wales, Gilbert was anticipating his defeat of Llewellyn: he could not attend court in 1268 as he was busy preparing his outlying castles for war. He went through the motions of arbitration with Llewellyn, but in reality he had made up his mind that war was desirable and necessary. It seems that Henry III was anxious not to ignite war in Wales, and sent one of his bishops to take custody of Caerphilly Castle, a key piece in Gilbert's battle plan. When Gilbert used deception to regain control of the castle, Henry was impotent, once again showing how autonomous Glamorgan and the rest of the Marcher lordships had become.

When Edward launched his invasion of Wales, it was Gilbert who demanded the right to lead the assault in the south. He claimed that he knew the land and the people, and that this would be advantageous to the battle, but in reality it was his own agenda that drove him. Unfortunately it drove him to a humiliating defeat. William de Valance, the 1st Earl of Pembroke, took over from the disgraced Gilbert, and the fact that Gilbert's poor leadership had led de Valance's son to his death must have made for a difficult handover. The campaign was successfully concluded, and Llewellyn was defeated at Builth Wells. Throughout the campaign, and the subsequent rebellion in Glamorgan, Cardiff Castle was the military headquarters of Gilbert, and of the king's rule in South Wales.

When Gilbert died in 1295 he left behind a violent legacy, but one in which the Norman model had reached its logical conclusion. English law had been imposed forcefully on Glamorgan, the Welsh had been defeated conclusively and Cardiff had been defended; it had also prospered as a town.

From the 1260s to the end of the century Cardiff's net worth had almost doubled. Tax revenues were nearly twice as high in the mid-1290s than they had been in the 1260s, and as there was no significant increase in the rate of taxation one can only conclude that the size of Cardiff's economy had grown significantly. The population was probably around 2,000, and this remained stable for the next 350 years, until the Civil War.

The end of the de Clare line came with the death of Gilbert's son, also Gilbert, at Bannockburn in 1314. The last of the de Clares had grown up without a father, Gilbert the Red having died when his son was 4. He was invested with the Earldom of Gloucester when he was 16, and seems to have had the favour of the new king, Edward II. The focus of events had moved away from Wales, as the Welsh kings had finally been defeated, and so centred on Scotland. Although Gilbert's interests lay in Wales, he spent more time at war in Scotland. Military matters were most dear to him, but he took some interest in politics – and like his father was at the heart of disputes that raged across England and Wales regarding the powers of kings and barons. However, fighting was what inspired him, and this was the cause of his untimely demise. Various accounts have him charging on horseback into the Scottish army; although others suggest that he was abandoned by more cowardly companions, the tone of these indicate embellishment. It is most likely that after years of leading from the front and relying on 'shock and awe', Gilbert's luck ran out. There is some suggestion that he was not wearing his livery and so was not recognised as a wealthy nobleman where he would have been worth more to the enemy alive than dead (he could have been ransomed to his family if captured).

There was unrest at the news that the Lord of Cardiff had been killed. There had been a cordial arrangement between Gilbert and the last Lord of Senghenydd, Llewellyn Bren, who was granted lordship over the village of Whitchurch. For all his hawkishness, and perhaps because of his lack of interest in domestic politics, Gilbert had been quite relaxed when it came to the administration of his own lands. On Gilbert's death, Payn de Turberville, a descendant of the original Turberville, was given the job of administering the estates until it was decided who would inherit them. He made the same mistakes that William of Gloucester had made, behaving with contempt towards the local population. Glamorgan and the rest of South Wales was facing a famine at this time, because of poor harvests and bad weather. Although this was a Europe-wide phenomenon, the peculiarly vindictive Turberville, who imposed hefty fines and taxes on a starving and impoverished people, made matters worse.

Unsurprisingly, he was greeted with a revolt. The history of the 250 years after the Norman invasion of Glamorgan seems to hinge on the judgement, or lack thereof, of whichever feudal overlord was governing from Cardiff Castle. Llewellyn Bren lost the titles and lands that had been gifted to him by Gilbert, and an able, intelligent and charismatic man was forced into following a path that led to direct confrontation. Llewellyn suddenly had nothing to lose. He asked the king to intervene in the dispute and demanded that he do something to curb Turberville's excessive behaviour. The king was impassive, and gave his unconditional backing to Turberville. Although we are often led to believe that Edward was weak and indecisive, the weakest of monarchs are capable of the greatest reaction: feeling impotent in the face of opposition, they order savage reprisals instead of skilfully managing the situation. It is possible that Edward relished an opportunity to display royal might in Wales, following repeated criticism of his weakness in the Scottish campaign. He summoned Llewellyn to London to face trial for treason, and execution if convicted. The outcome would have been a *fait accompli*, and Llewellyn wisely turned down the summons, opting for open revolt instead. In 1316 he presented the biggest threat to Cardiff that it had encountered in two centuries when he attempted to repeat what he had done in Llantrisant, where he took the castle and town and slaughtered the inhabitants. His marauders destroyed more than twenty of only about 400 houses and the people of Cardiff took refuge inside the town's walls. These were strong enough to keep the rebels at bay. It was probably the inability of Llewellyn to take Cardiff that caused his revolt to fail, and it bought time for the king to prepare a response. An army was quickly assembled, and over 2,000 men were mobilised at Cardiff to fight Llewellyn. It must have seemed a savage irony to Edward II that a 'pacified' region like Wales had exploded in revolt, almost as a direct result of his attempts to pacify the Scots.

In a bid to relieve the garrison at Caerphilly, also under siege from Llewellyn, the royal force marched from Cardiff, only to be intercepted at Cefn Onn. The battle, which was fought across what is now Thornhill, ended with the defeat of Llewellyn at Castell Morgraig, the ruins of which are close to the Traveller's Rest pub. From the moment when it became clear that Cardiff would not fall, Llewellyn must have known he was fighting a lost cause. He eventually surrendered, and was imprisoned first at Brecon and then in the Tower of London. He gained immense credit with his captors, Roger Mortimer of Chirk and Humphrey de Bohun, Earl of Hereford, when he insisted that only he should be held accountable for the revolt, not his followers. Mortimer interceded on his behalf, citing the provocation that he had endured and the reckless and cruel actions of Turberville. Llewellyn spent two years in captivity, and the king seems inclined to have granted him mercy, which tends to suggest that even by medieval standards Turberville had behaved with exceptional cruelty and folly.

Llewellyn might have survived had it not been for the rise of Hugh Despenser, Lord of Cardiff Castle. This sealed Llewellyn's fate, in a process that sheds a great deal of light on the king and his reign. Despenser went from landless knight to one of the most powerful magnates in the kingdom in a short time. His story of social advancement has few parallels in the medieval era. He married Gilbert's sister, Eleanor de Clare. Considering that she was unlikely to inherit the estates of Gilbert the Red (unless something happened to her brother), it was a match that was probably in keeping with Despenser's status at the time. Edward I, Eleanor's grandfather, was indebted financially to Despenser's father, and the marriage was seen as a convenient way of discharging this debt.[13] The size of the material prize on offer was huge: the total income from the Glamorgan estates was £1,415 4s 11½d a year. However, there was an obstacle between Despenser and this wealth: Gilbert's widow, Maud. She claimed that she was pregnant, and if the child was a boy any possibility of Despenser claiming the wealth of Glamorgan would be snatched away from him. The pregnancy seemed to go on and on, however, and long after nine months had elapsed there was still no sign of a baby. Despenser was anxious to take the matter before the courts, but all those who had examined Maud seemed convinced she was with child. When a further eighteen months had elapsed, Despenser appealed to the king. In typical fashion, Edward II vacillated, hoping that the whole unfortunate business would go away. During this time, of course, Glamorgan lay in the hands of Turberville, who was fuelling revolt. Despenser was not particularly well known at court at this point, and in the eyes of the law he was treated like everyone else, so his petitions were dismissed. It also suited the king to keep the revenues from Glamorgan and the rest of the de Clare estates flowing to him. Eventually, after the other de Clare sisters had been married off, and with the pretence of the pregnancy wearing thin, Despenser got his way and was made Lord of Glamorgan.

The stewardship of Glamorgan was finally handed over to Despenser, and not to his wife. Suddenly, the debt owed to the Despensers seemed to have been repaid several times over, and with this new-found wealth came political influence and a relationship with the king that still causes controversy amongst historians today.

It seems to be agreed that the new Lord of Cardiff Castle and the king were lovers. At the time this was suspected by those close to the king, though in 1318, perhaps before any relationship between the two men had begun, the nobility surrounding Despenser seemed to accept him. Perhaps this was unwise when dealing with a man who distinguished himself in the fields of deception and ruthlessness. He was made chamberlain to the king in 1318, which coincided with a general clear-out of the king's entourage in which previous favourites were dismissed and banished. It was an environment in which an ambitious man could thrive. The role of chamberlain involved attending to the king's needs and keeping his living chambers clean and tidy, and also being in the king's confidence. This role kept Despenser close to the king (and probably never in Cardiff), and over time he became intimately trusted. Many royal honours and grants were bestowed upon him, and by 1319 he was in a position to rival the barons for power in court. By now they deeply distrusted him, and realised how naïve they had been.

It was in this climate that the fate of Llewellyn was decided. Despenser persuaded Edward to transport the rebel leader back to Cardiff for a gruesome public execution. Just as William Wallace had been dismembered thirteen years before, so was Llewellyn. Hugh Despenser had a gallows built by the Black Tower, the medieval prison for rebels and traitors in Cardiff. There Llewellyn was hanged, drawn and quartered, his severed head afterwards displayed outside the castle gates for passers-by to see. Despenser didn't miss the opportunity to take Llewellyn's lands, which might have been his motivation. Some historians dispute that Despenser ever got permission to execute Llewellyn, and if he did it is not recorded on any surviving official documentation. It is likely that he illegally executed Llewellyn even though other rebels had been pardoned and allowed to hold onto their lands. As the likes of Mortimer were sympathetic towards Llewellyn, perhaps Despenser wanted to break a potential alliance there. There could also have been nothing more irksome to a power-hungry chancer like Despenser than having a known rebel living in Glamorgan and owning land there.

Following the execution, Llewellyn's body was interred at Greyfriars. The death sparked fury amongst Mortimer and his friends, who became committed enemies of Despenser, a man they elevated in their own minds almost to a satanic figure. The other Marcher lords quickly came to loathe him, following a dispute over the ownership of the Gower. When they tried to claim ownership of this strategic region, with the lucrative port of Swansea, Despenser, using his royal influence, delivered royal troops to back his claim. This was perceived by the Marcher lords as a gross violation of the rules and customs of the Marches and of the quasi-independent nature of the eastern part of Wales, which dates back to the Norman invasion.

Hugh Despenser's runaway greed, his cavalier disregard for any rules of gentlemanly conduct, and his seemingly unassailable position of favour with the king sowed the seeds for war with the nobility and with the other Marcher lords in particular. A revolt against the king's favourite, however, was an attack on the king himself. One by one the Marcher lords withdrew from the court. Without fear of rebuke, Despenser began to call them traitors; that they had sought to grab land in the Gower without the king's say was in his mind treason. Ignoring the enormous hypocrisy of such claims, it was astonishing to many nobles to see this young upstart speaking on the king's behalf.

Panicked, Edward II forbade any separate assemblies of the nobility, mindful of the risk of a noble revolt. These orders were ignored, and a meeting was convened at Hereford with one issue on the agenda: the death of Hugh Despenser. When Edward was presented with a list of potential conspirators, he noted the names of Mortimer and his brother on the list. Mortimer was dismissed as Justiciar of Wales and relieved of Chirk Castle, being replaced with one of Despenser's men, Ralph Gorges.[14] Edward sent Roger de Wodehouse to Cardiff, Swansea, Neath and all other royal Welsh towns to make sure they were effectively garrisoned, as he expected a series of long sieges. Then he rode to the Welsh borders. Preparing for trouble himself, Despenser wrote:

> We are informed by several of our friends that all this plotting on the part of certain magnates is planned to begin and to do damage to us in our said lordship, in order to cover themselves that this is not done against the king, and with the intent that he shall interfere in the matter, and thereby take sides. We therefore rely upon you to take all the necessary steps to safeguard us, for we have sufficient power, if we are well arrayed and carefully served, to guard against our enemies, and it cannot be, when tales are growing daily, that there is nothing in them.[15]

Before hostilities began, the king made a last-ditch attempt to reason with the Marcher lords. He wrote to them from Gloucester, asking them not to participate in seditious activity. They replied that they would be satisfied if Despenser was delivered to their custody for a full trial before Parliament. The king, faithful to his servant, said that the Magna Carta did not permit him to limit the freedoms of Despenser. Thinking this was the end of the matter, Edward returned with Despenser to London, but they were deeply mistaken. Ten of Despenser's Welsh castles fell to the Marcher lords, including Cardiff. To give their attacks the veneer of respectability they raised royal insignias as they sacked Cardiff Castle, indicating that their action was taken on behalf of the nation in general, and to take the sting out of Despenser's accusation that they were traitors. By contemporary standards the army that the Marcher lords raised was huge: some accounts put it at over 10,000 men, with at least 1,000 men at arms, or professional trained warriors, an army far greater than anything Llewellyn Bren had commanded. The greed and cruelty of Despenser in Glamorgan meant that few Welshmen were inspired to defend him. An indication of the violence and ferocity with which Cardiff was attacked comes from the 'Calendar of Close Rolls', one of the most illuminating accounts of the Despenser War:

> They [the armies of the Marcher lords] stayed there in his lands for five days in order to destroy the lands completely, within which time they made by force all the greater part of all the country swear to be of their accord, and they imprisoned and held to ransom those who refused, and burnt their houses and goods, of his peers or by the law of the land.[16]

This savage explosion of violence was completely unexpected, and Despenser's property across Glamorgan, and especially in Cardiff, was devastated. Shocked by the powerlessness of the crown to do anything, he handed his properties to the king, assuming that this would safeguard his holdings as surely nobody would attack royal property. The fact that attacks continued must have been an ominous sign for the king.

Ordinary Cardiffians were ruthlessly exploited and robbed. A high premium was set upon their loyalty, and they were expected to contribute food, livestock and money. The Marcher lords justified themselves by saying that this was simply wealth that would have gone to Despenser. The behaviour of the Marcher lords towards the people of Cardiff and the rest of Glamorgan gives them no greater moral legitimacy than Despenser.

The revolt that had engulfed Cardiff was a revolt against the king as well as Despenser. Possibly he began to realise his folly in backing the arrogant Marcher lord so wholeheartedly, but if the rest of his reign is anything to go by he probably didn't. The focus of Edward's advisors seems to have been on avoiding an all-out civil war, but events slipped out of their control as the Marcher army invaded England. By midsummer they were camped outside London, a trail of destruction behind them. The lords demanded the exile of Despenser and his family, and Edward's queen, Isabella, begged the king to see sense before he was deposed. Finally Edward acquiesced, and sent the terrified Lord of Glamorgan and Cardiff Castle into exile.

Recorded in the medieval *Life of Edward II* is this description of Despenser: 'Confident of the royal favour, he did everything on his own authority, grabbed everything, had no regard for the authority of anyone whomsoever, set traps for his co-heirs; thus, if he could manage it, each would lose his share through trumped up accusations and he alone would obtain the whole earldom.'[17]

This was not the end of the saga. A trial of Despenser was heard *in absentia*, and one of the key issues to be raised was the fate of Llewellyn Bren. It might well be that the rebel leader's unlawful execution at Cardiff was not the primary reason for the Despenser War, but it was important enough to be raised at the hearing, showing that the events in Cardiff were not insignificant. Mortimer, amongst others, angrily accused Despenser of usurping royal authority by having Llewellyn killed: it was a good illustration of Despenser's cruelty, and pinned a charge of treason on him at the same time. Despenser, in the meantime, was living on the south coast of England, where he had the protection of the barons who controlled the Cinque Ports, and in typical fashion he went on to a career in cross-Channel piracy. It is clear that he was also still meeting Edward in secret at Gravesend, no doubt plotting to undo the Marcher lords. It was eventually Queen Isabella who brought about the end of Edward and Despenser, and cornered them just miles from Cardiff. She and her lover Roger de Mortimer, nephew of Roger Mortimer of Chirk (whom we have previously discussed) had built up an army in France after escaping from England in 1323. Mortimer had been imprisoned in the Tower of London for fighting on after the end of the Despenser War for a further year. The army, sent with the blessing of the French king, pursued Edward from London after landing in Suffolk. Eleanor, Despenser's wife and Gilbert's daughter, was given custodianship of the Tower of London, inside which were Mortimer's children. Fleeing the capital and travelling north to Oxford, then west to Gloucester,

Edward must have realised the end was near. The small force that Isabella landed with was swelled massively by former royal loyalists who had turned their allegiances away from the king. When he reached Tintern Abbey, Edward sent troops ahead of him to pacify the Marches and to find the disloyal and punish them – perhaps not a wise strategy.

Weeks later, Edward and Despenser were unexpectedly in Cardiff when, having set sail from Chepstow possibly to get to Bristol, bad weather forced them to put ashore. They rethought their plans and rode for Caerphilly where Edward, now clearly quite divorced from reality, tried to rally support amongst the Welsh. He asked the supporters of Llewellyn Bren to aid him in his struggle, most likely with Bren's murderer at his side. They may have realised their doom when Depenser's father was cornered at Bristol Castle and hanged. Now that most of the rest of the country had not so much fallen to the rebels but willingly joined them, Edward's son, Edward III, was recognised as the new ruler of England and Wales.

Edward and Despenser planned their last stand at Caerphilly Castle, knowing full well it had been designed to withstand armies of Welsh rebels, though it is hard to imagine they believed they had a chance. In a final bid to outsmart their enemies they rode for Neath Abbey, hoping they would be able to negotiate, but on the way were betrayed and captured at Llantrisant Castle. Upon his capture, Despenser was taken to Hereford, where he was paraded through the streets on a donkey with a crown of nettles and a tabard with his coat of arms turned upside down, a ritual humiliation. He was put on trial in the town's marketplace and found guilty of treason. Dragged by horses to the walls of Hereford, he was hanged from 50ft gallows, then taken down and disembowelled over a roaring fire. It seems strangely apposite that Despenser should have died in a manner not dissimilar to Llewellyn Bren. As for Edward, he is largely believed to have been murdered the following year at Berkeley Castle, though the prurient tales about the manner of his death, burning pokers and the like, are probably invention. It is most likely that he was suffocated by an agent of Isabella.

The Despensers were eventually rehabilitated. Eleanor, Hugh's long-suffering wife, remarried and when she outlived her second husband, William Zouche, her eldest son, Hugh, Lord Despenser, gained the Lordship of Glamorgan. The trials and tribulations that his father had caused the Despenser family did not leave the young lord unaffected: he had spent four years in prison because of his father's scheming. As was common in dynastic struggles in the Middle

Ages, the families of the winners and losers were eventually reconciled. The new Lord of Cardiff Castle was welcomed back to the court of Edward III, and distinguished himself in wars against the French, particularly at the battle of Crécy. Like most of Cardiff's feudal overlords, however, he took little interest in its affairs. As a thriving medieval market town, it was more than capable of taking care of itself.

Religious Life

The centre of ecclesiastical Glamorgan was the diocese of Llandaff, which seems an appropriate place to begin an examination of the religious life of Cardiff and Glamorgan. We have already noted the ancient roots of the diocese, but the beginnings of medieval Llandaff can be found with the arrival there of a man whose name is synonymous with our understanding of medieval Wales – as well as much of the British Isles. Geoffrey of Monmouth was an early chronicler of the lives of kings, but there is very little recorded about him and his time as Bishop of Llandaff. Almost certainly he was Norman or Anglo-Norman. He seems to have been born in Monmouth, probably in about 1100, and his parents probably came directly from Normandy as some of the first Norman inhabitants of Wales, and part of William and William Rufus's colonising mission. Their social status is unknown, but as they were able to send their son to be educated at Monmouth Priory they were unlikely to have been from the toiling poor. It is likely that he was deeply Anglicised as he spent many years in England, at Oxford's Collegiate church of St George, one of the embryonic parts of the later university. He taught there for twenty years before returning to Wales in 1147 to become Archdeacon of Llandaff.

It is for his historical writings that Geoffrey of Monmouth is best remembered and probably earned him the prestigious position of archdeacon. He appears to have been a skilled political operator, well aware that his ability to write was highly prized. In writing his *History of the Kings of Britain* in 1136, he made the astute move of dedicating it to Robert the Consul, and it is not hard to see why he came into favour shortly afterwards.

It is hard to overstate the extent to which Norman culture was based around church building; they were active pioneers in religious architecture in all their conquered territories. Cardiff, barely secured as a Norman forward command post, was the site of just such a construction in 1100. Priests from Tewkesbury

Abbey, the spiritual home of the Earls of Gloucester, were sent to Cardiff by Robert Fitzhamon to establish a church, probably because of the emigration from England to Glamorgan, and the fact that many of these new migrants had made Cardiff their home. St Mary's church was built in what is now St Mary's Street, at the opposite end to the castle. An examination of John Speed's map of Cardiff, completed in 1610 and probably the best indication of what the town looked like for much of the Middle Ages, has the church at the edge of town, close to the Norman stone walls. It stands in what would have been one of the few patches of unspoilt greenery and whether there was an adjacent graveyard is unclear. The church appears to have a stature in the town that was second only to the castle itself.

About eighty years later there was an explosion in building activity: by 1175 St Mary's church was being expanded and enlarged and St John's church, which survives today, was built from about 1180 onwards. St John's, which stands in St John Street, was built as a chapel of ease. The parish of Cardiff was centred on St Mary's; the chapel of ease was built for people who were unable to access the main church, which indicates that the population was expanding rapidly and that church capacity was insufficient. Perhaps the most important reason for this increased building activity was the fact that in 1180 the parish of Cardiff was placed in the care of Benedictine monks from Tewkesbury Abbey, an establishment that seems to have had a far greater hold over Cardiff than Llandaff Cathedral in the early Middle Ages. From this date, St Mary's is referred to as a priory, not just a parish church but a spiritual community.

Llandaff Cathedral. The site of the cathedral has been a place of Christian worship since long before the conquest of Wales by the Normans. Much as with Cardiff Castle, the cathedral has been rebuilt several times and has had a number of different roles throughout its various incarnations.

As the town continued to grow, St John's church gradually became more autonomous. In 1242 a debate

St Mary Street and Castle. St Mary Street is now the main thoroughfare, along with Queen Street, through the city centre. It takes its name after the medieval St Mary's church and can be seen on John Speed's Cardiff Map.

over the future of St John's church was passed all the way to the Vatican for adjudication. The Archdeacon of Llandaff, one William De Christchurch, was so impressed by the church's growing popularity that he wanted to create a parish for it. Perhaps not the best thought-out idea, this would have meant fewer parishioners for St Mary's and a division in the churches' revenue. Pope Innocent IV, at the same time negotiating with Mongol hordes to prevent them sacking all Europe, was compelled to intervene, and ensured that St John's remained a dependency of St Mary's for the rest of the Middle Ages. The popularity and wealth of St John's began to eclipse that of St Mary's, as is indicated by the enormous tower which was built between 1453 and 1473, a gift from Lady Anne Neville. No doubt the priests at St Mary's looked on in bitter envy, realising that whilst they had won a battle against the upstart St John's, they would inevitably lose the war.

In the Middle Ages three friaries were established in Cardiff: Black (the first, in 1242), Grey and White Friars (the Carmelites). It was Richard de Clare who first granted land to the Dominicans (Black Friars) and the Franciscans (Grey Friars), named after their patrons St Dominic and St Francis of Assisi, who established monastic orders at the start of the thirteenth century. All were located in dangerously vulnerable positions outside the town's walls. Whilst the risk of uprising diminished throughout the Middle Ages, and the threat of sacking was less of a worry, it was not completely prudent to ignore the protection of the city walls. The White Friars' house, according to Dugdale's *Monasticon*, was probably destroyed during the rebellion of Owain Glyndŵr in 1404. Certainly it had disappeared before the Dissolution of the Monasteries, but both Blackfriars and Greyfriars remained. Greyfriars was built outside the castle walls in 1284, and fell victim to Thomas Cromwell and the opportunistic Glamorgan gentry in the sixteenth century. The fact that Cardiff had monastic orders a couple of decades after Rome granted their right to exist is interesting. It demonstrates that the spread of monasticism across Europe was rapid, and also that Cardiff and Glamorgan were far from being backwaters. This, as well as the fact that the Pope intervened in a religious dispute in the parish, indicates that Cardiff had some importance.

Chantries emerged in Cardiff throughout the Middle Ages. These were abolished by Edward VI and his uncle, Edward Seymour, but there is evidence to suggest that alongside the guilds, the chantries and the friaries provided some kind of rudimentary social welfare. One of the key features of this was the treatment of lepers. The Spital, Cardiff's first hospital, can be seen on John Speed's map of 1610, just to the left of the castle. Built to quarantine lepers from the rest of Cardiff, by the end of the fourteenth century it was forced to diversify as the prevalence of leprosy had dramatically decreased. In the same way that Cardiff saw a brief period of accountable democratic rule, before the rise of the guilds in the later Middle Ages, so it seems that modern ideas about social welfare can be seen in the town long before the sixteenth century and the birth of the modern state. The hospital was eventually developed by its chaplain, Simon Worgan, as an almshouse for the poor. Attitudes to poverty ranged from Christian charity and sympathy to harsh indifference. In the contemporary mind, the poor were poor because the hierarchical Great Chain of Being had determined it thus: social mobility undermined God's celestial order, and was considered a blasphemy. By 1393 the hospital was helping Cardiff's poor, and it continued to do so until 1536. The site is now completely obscured by the Capitol Centre on Queen Street.

Cardiff's monks lived in a bustling, chaotic town that had evolved a life and momentum of its own, and yet they sought out lives of tranquillity, contemplation and silence. The Franciscans were strictly forbidden to engage in any form of idleness, to own any property or to engage in idle conversation with women. They dedicated their lives to God and abandoned all earthly pleasures. Dominicans lived in a similar way. Their friary stood to the west of the castle, near the West Gate, and its ruins are in Bute Park. The first friary, built on lands bequeathed by Richard de Clare, was probably nothing more than a rudimentary timber building, but this was replaced by stone. The deeply intellectual St Dominic and the gentle and kind St Francis had different attitudes: the Franciscans had a greater following amongst the poor, whereas the Dominicans were seen as more aloof. The poverty of the Franciscans, who felt this was closer to godliness, casts much doubt on the accusations of Thomas Cromwell some 200 years later. He alleged that the monastic orders were hoarding vast wealth for themselves and the glory of Rome, but this was certainly not true of the monasteries of Cardiff.

Bute Park. Another one of the Bute family's gifts to the city, Bute Park is the largest space for leisure and recreation in the city.

An indication of the success of Cardiff's monastic houses is that one of the monks went on to become the Bishop of Llandaff. Just after the insurrection of Owain Glyndŵr, John de La Zouche, descendant of William Zouche, successor to Hugh Despenser, was made bishop, reigning until 1423.

The spread of churches across the Cardiff area tells us about the development of settlements outside the castle walls. Outlying communities all gained chapels of their own, which lessened the dependence on St Mary's and St John's and also gave villages like Llanishen and Roath a sense of their own identity. During the religious upheaval of the sixteenth and seventeenth centuries, attitudes and beliefs in these parishes contrasted starkly with more mainstream worship in Cardiff. Initially chapels were far from grandiose: without the financial backing of the Earls of Gloucester, nothing as impressive as a medieval Norman church was likely to grace a small hamlet. The chapels were modest single-storey affairs, probably made from timber and plaster. Tewkesbury Abbey and Margam Abbey were both granted lands and rights in many villages, and it seems probable that parish churches near Cardiff were built thanks to the wealth of Tewkesbury Abbey. This gave the abbey and its patrons total control over the spiritual life of these communities.

Administration

Cardiff was the political and judicial centre of all Glamorgan, so their running cannot be separated. The absentee lords of Cardiff devolved power into the hands of a sheriff. From the beginning of the Norman era and for centuries afterwards, he was the most important legal and political figure in the region. His chief duty was to preside at the *Curia Comitatus*. Whilst men like Robert Fitzhamon were happy to ride from Gloucester each month to dispense justice, adjudicate over land disputes and hear the grievances of tenants, by the time the de Clares ruled Cardiff this power had been almost completely devolved. This was not necessarily to do with the indolence of feudal overlords (although this cannot be completely ruled out) but was thanks to the changing nature of noble obligations in the Middle Ages. The estates that the de Clares and their descendants presided over grew in size, location and diversity, often scattered around Normandy, Ireland, Scotland, Wales and England. In addition, as families rose in prominence they were required to visit Westminster or wherever the king was holding court. There were also crusades. It became increasingly difficult for noblemen to take a direct role in the day-to-day administration of government and justice in their baronial seats.

The fact that the *Comitatus* took on an extra, quasi-political dimension is brought home by the fact that it was sometimes referred to as a *Parliamentum*. Hearing grievances and petitions of commoners was an important part of its work, and legislating in order to address or resolve those grievances was also within its remit. The sheriff was assisted by bailiffs, who collected fines and enforced common law throughout Glamorgan, and even across the border into lordships such as Caerleon and Monmouth. It is clear that the power of Glamorgan in the Middle Ages meant that whilst there were independent rival marcher lordships, Cardiff's *Comitatus* was a dominant legal institution. Fees, fines and other charges were also banked in the town, but these would have been administered by separate officials: perhaps the lords of Cardiff didn't think it prudent to give the sheriff that degree of political and financial power at his disposal. As a legal officer the sheriff frequently witnessed the charters and other documents that were binding legal agreements between the Earls of Gloucester and individual peasants. It is likely that having a sheriff as witness made both parties more likely to abide by the agreement. This sort of grass-roots accountability was at odds with the absolutism of later Norman and Angevin kings.

The role of sheriff was normally given to a knight in the service of one of the Earls of Gloucester. As we have already seen, the ties of obligation to the lord of Cardiff Castle by Glamorgan's knights began to change during the later Norman period, as there was less need for constant military service.

The chief financial officer in Cardiff was the receiver. He was accountant in general for the whole county. As the Lords of Glamorgan grew in power and stature, and as their lands grew, so must the role of Receiver of Cardiff have become more complex. When Gilbert the Red gained control over Usk in 1289, the rents from the estates there flowed directly to the receiver. They lay outside the jurisdiction of Glamorgan, as they were the property of the de Clares, but there was still an outflow of money from Gwent to Cardiff. Glamorgan was enriched to the detriment of other parts of Wales, as money was quite literally exported to the region. The office of receiver was eventually replaced with the exchequer, run by a treasurer. This trend of increasing complexity can be seen in almost all areas of governmental life over the following centuries, reaching its height in the Tudor period.

The real legal powerhouse in medieval Cardiff was the chancery. The Lord of Glamorgan's chancellor was responsible for writing the legislation that was discussed at the *Comitatus*, putting into written form the lord's will. Much of the development of Cardiff, its culture and character, has rested on the fact that although it has traditionally been Anglicised, it has always retained a degree of political and legal autonomy, sometimes leaving the town with a curious identity crisis, arguably neither Welsh nor English. The de Clares took this autonomy from the crown to its height. In administrative and legal terms they were almost completely independent from the crown. The king retained the final say as supreme feudal overlord, but was unable to intervene in the running of Glamorgan. Some cases heard in Cardiff would have been heard in a royal court in England. Cardiff was almost a private fiefdom for the Lords of Glamorgan, and they dominated the law. Evidence from several key legal disputes suggests that the lords vigorously protected their legal independence.

Cardiff Charter II (1340) BC/1/2 granted by King Edward III.

The de Clares actively used the courts to extend their land rights, which translated into wealth. Henry II, Henry III and Edward I all seem to have been quite happy to endorse this. In 1278, when a commission was assembled by the crown to try to create a unified system of law across the Marches, Glamorgan was not required to attend – and the de Clares also seem to have had virtual immunity from lawsuits from other Marcher lords. In 1281, Gilbert the Red's bailiff, Robert le Veel, was charged with assaulting the Lord of Gower, William de Braose. Gilbert claimed that the matter did not come under the jurisdiction of the crown, and that it was a matter for the earl's court to deal with. Only if de Braose could prove that he had not been shown justice in Cardiff would the matter be tried in a royal court. Gilbert's argument was dismissed, as de Braose had been given his title by the king and was therefore a royal subject, making the assault a crime against the crown. Gilbert protested that the matter had to be proved first in his own court, because the Marcher lands of Glamorgan had not been gifted by the crown but taken by force. It is unclear if this was resolved in favour of Gilbert or de Braose, but it is clear that the Marcher lords were not afraid to stand up to the jurisdiction of the crown and fiercely defended any encroachment on their legal sovereignty. The importance of this is magnified when one considers the fact that the Marcher Lords of Cardiff, particularly the de Clares, seem to have been almost constantly involved in low-level banditry against other Marcher lords, stealing cattle, chattels and land in Caerleon, Usk and Chepstow.

In one important regard, the power of the Lords of Cardiff was curtailed by the crown: the power to annex the lands of the Bishopric of Llandaff if the seat was vacant. When Bishop William de Braose, a relative of the aforementioned Lord of Gower, died in 1287, Gilbert and a coalition of Marcher lords seized the bishop's lands, which stretched far beyond the diocese across South Wales. Gilbert then refused to hand the land back. Edward I proved legally that the lands of the bishopric did not have the same status as other lands in Glamorgan, and the Bishopric of Llandaff had the same status as other dioceses across England and Wales, which meant it reverted to royal control if the seat was vacant. Gilbert was guilty, and he backed down before the king was forced to punish him. In an act of magnanimity uncharacteristic for Edward I he eventually granted all rights over these lands to the bishopric for life. Clearly the ownership of the land was not his bone of contention; it was a question of royal supremacy.

The perennially warlike Edward was well served by having good relations with Cardiff. Throughout his reign, forces were regularly raised in Glamorgan, their central marshalling point being Cardiff Castle, to fight in West Wales, Flanders and Scotland. As the de Clares and Hugh Despenser controlled the raising of forces in the county, it was imperative that the king treat the Lords of Cardiff reasonably: they owed no formal military service to the crown so all military service given to the kings of England was offered voluntarily by Cardiff's lords. A direct snub to the king, especially when he was marshalling forces to fight the Scots or the French, would have been political suicide, so both sides had to consider their powers and prerogatives very carefully indeed.

A new office emerged after the Despenser War, that of constable of Cardiff Castle. This position superseded sheriff and placed yet more administrative and political power in the hands of one individual. The constable was in effect the lord's steward. This role merged with that of mayor, and in later years one individual held both offices. This office of mayor was one that the later Glamorgan landed aristocracy feuded over, as they attempted to get 'their man' in place and by doing so control the town.

In 1340 the charter that William of Gloucester had produced was updated and renewed in order to reflect the growing prosperity of the town. It enshrined

Cardiff Charter III (1358) BC/1/3
granted by King Edward III.

Cardiff Charter IV (1359) BC/1/4
granted by King Edward III.

Cardiff Charter V (1396) BC/1/5
granted by King Richard II.

in law what was most important to the medieval Cardiffian, rights to common land and annual fairs. The issue of common land became a battlefield that the ordinary folk struggled over in the coming centuries. It is most likely that grazing on common land, on the two heaths, was common practice, but what Cardiff's burgesses probably wanted most from the constable was clarification of these rights: they wanted some kind of permanence. The annual fairs were ideal opportunities off the calendar, on Midsummer's Day and on the Feast of St Mary, to trade, to sell cattle and to celebrate. The other rights that the new charter gave to the people of Cardiff was the right of *habeas corpus*, or freedom from arbitrary arrest when it came to most offences (meaning it became impossible to imprison someone without a trial). At this time a town hall was built. Burgesses were allowed to select a shortlist of candidates for the offices of town bailiff and provosts, but the final choice was the constable's.

Cardiff was increasing in prosperity at this time, and wealth afforded people the luxury of rights. The town's autonomy from England, the lack of a native Welsh threat (and permanent stone walls, something local people would have seen as a sign of their safety) and the fact that the Lords of Glamorgan took a relatively hands-off approach to administration, perhaps allowed for a greater degree of freedom than in many other towns and boroughs. Within 100 years, however, the charter had been effectively undermined, and by the 1420s the open, fair and democratic government that had existed in the previous century had been swept away. The rule of the town's aldermen and the gentry class deprived ordinary Cardiffians of their rights for nearly half a millennium. Dennis Morgan describes these men as 'a self-perpetuating oligarchy'[18], a judgement that seems to be fair and accurate.

The focus of Cardiff's life in the Middle Ages was trade, and the oligarchs of whom Dennis Morgan spoke more often than not came from the new guilds of merchants that began to establish themselves in the fourteenth century. In 1324 the first guild, for cordwainers and glovers, was made an official body by Edward II, when he renewed the charter. This recognition by the crown, followed by the establishment of other guilds, had far-reaching implications for the town's economic structure. Cordwainers and glovers were leatherworkers, and their being granted an official status meant they held a monopoly of the tanning and leatherworking trade. The guild had something of a dual purpose: it kept the trade concentrated in a few hands, prohibiting non-guild members from participation, and there was a quasi-religious element; they had a shrine at St Mary's church until the Reformation.[19] Hugh Despenser, when making his proclamation to the town in 1340, reinforced the rights of the guild: 'Nor shall anyone keep an open stall of any merchandise, nor a shop ... unless they lot and scot with Our aforesaid Burgesses and [he] be received in the Guild of their liberty. Also We have granted unto Our same Burgesses that they and their heirs may make a Guild among themselves, at what time and whenever they will, for their own profit.'[20] The charter that recognised the Cordwainers' legitimacy was witnessed by most of the leading churchmen in England and Wales, including the Archbishop of Canterbury, and the list of rights and privileges it conferred was extensive. It offered harsh financial penalties for anyone who disrupted the guild's trade:

> Also We grant to Our Burgesses aforesaid that no forestaller or any other person or persons whatsoever of the Crafts aforesaid shall set up any shop, booth or standing within seven miles compass of the Town of Cardiff, unless it be in a borough town at any time or times, or anywhere as in villages or churchyards or by church doors on Sundays or saints' days or offering days or any other times, for to annoy the Town and Market of Cardiff, upon pain of forty shillings every fault, the party being warned. And for every time that every booth-holder or forestaller or any other shall be warned and not obey Our orders, he or they shall lose every month forty shillings.[21]

It is small wonder that the cordwainers, and the other guilds that followed them into legal respectability, came to dominate the politics of Cardiff for much of the Middle Ages, and only faced a serious challenge by Henry VIII. The cordwainers were probably the most powerful guild in the town, and although their records are the only ones to survive it seems likely that there were also guilds for weavers, metalworkers, brewers, bakers and other skilled professions. As the Middle Ages wore on, these guilds would have announced their social and economic supremacy with a mixture of religious devotion, public pageantry and almost Masonic secrecy. The cordwainers worshipped at St John's, and are recorded leading processions to mass through the town's streets.

The guilds were sometimes the only source of charity within the medieval town. They would have made sure that their own members were looked after, and the membership contributions would have been redistributed in the form of pensions for elderly or sick members.

High Street was the location of the trading hall. Records show that it was probably completed in about 1331: the first quarter of the fourteenth century was a period when the town's economic fortunes were improving. The building reflected the times in which it was created, as its functions merged the political and legal with the mercantile. It dominated the town centre, a large, two-storey building in the middle of the road, clearly announcing the rise in power of the mercantile classes. On the first floor there was a meeting house for merchants, town aldermen and magistrates, with the Cockmarel, a dirty and oppressive prison, below it. A telling detail is that this was a prison for debtors, superseding an important function of the castle. Dynastic disputes were at an end, so traitors and rebels did not have to be locked away in the castle; instead disputes over money were taking centre stage, and to be imprisoned in a building that was dominated by the new guilds had some significance. The Cockmarel eventually moved to larger premises, but the public nature of punishment was maintained by the introduction of stocks outside the prison, so miscreants could be ritually humiliated and abused by passers-by.

In the charter of 1340 the first moves towards a degree of trading standards were made, with the constable appointing not just bailiffs but also beertasters. Several brewers guilty of watering down ale found themselves imprisoned in the Cockmarel, and were then left in the stocks to the tender mercy of the Cardiffians to whom they had sold unfit ales. Drunkards also found themselves confined in the High Street stocks.

A flavour of the exotic was added to the biannual market days in Cardiff, held within sight of the Market Cross. From the early Middle Ages onwards, as Europeans began to build trade routes to the east and a trade in spices, the tastes of the Middle East, Mediterranean and North Africa would have flowed into fairs and markets all over Wales and England. Cardiffians might have tasted ginger, cinnamon, dates, figs and cardamoms for the first time. It is hard for us to imagine what this explosion in variety would have done for medieval Cardiffians.

Alongside such exoticism, there were farmers and traders from nearby. Parishes such as Roath and Llandaff were the breadbaskets of Cardiff; it was upon small traders that the town depended for its food. Smaller markets were held twice a week, and vast twice-a-year events usually lasted a fortnight or so. Cardiff became synonymous with its hostelries on these days, and even as late as Queen Elizabeth's reign there was concern of a disproportionately large number of ale houses and taverns for the size of population.

The traders who came to Cardiff on the biannual market days knew that they would probably leave with a tidy profit. As the population of the town boomed

Cardiff Charter VI (1401) BC/1/6 granted by King Henry IV.

Cardiff Charter VII (1421) BC/1/7 granted by King Henry V.

and the size of the markets increased, the revenue generated became a valuable income for the Lord of Cardiff. Gradually the growth in the power and wealth of traders, and their evolution into a middle class, in some instances into minor gentry, saw Wales and England evolve by the sixteenth century from a medieval feudal society into an early modern state.

We know little about Cardiff in the fourteenth and fifteenth centuries, but it is more than likely that the town was not dissimilar to market towns in England of an equivalent size. The buildings would have been largely made of timber with a plaster-like render made of a mixture of clay, lime and horse hair. Thatched roofs and (later) slate tiling would have completed the building, all sloping, to deal with the notoriously rainy climate of South Wales. Commercial property doubled as residential and homes were quite literally built on top of shops and businesses. It is highly likely that for much of its medieval history Cardiff had constant sanitation problems, as no system of public drainage existed. There must have been an omnipresent fear of disease, even before the Black Death. As houses were built progressively closer together, people and animals shared a decreasing amount of living space and there were enough people coming in from outside Cardiff to spread communicable illnesses. It would have been remarkable if the town did not suffer from one kind of epidemic or another.

Cardiff was connected to the wider world through the seas. From the fifteenth century onwards a wide variety of new people came to Cardiff, bringing a variety of opportunities with them. The small, medieval wooden quay was eventually replaced with a more robust stone structure, which fell to the Lord of Cardiff to maintain – and he pocketed the tariffs levied on ships and supplies going to and from the quay. Royal whims impacted heavily upon the port, and the king of the day could dramatically help or hinder the town's economy. Edward II was very well disposed to the port. He granted the town the honour of becoming a staple port for wool and hides, unusual as Cardiff was not a royal borough. The cordwainers must have been delighted. As the king could not collect revenue from Cardiff, why did he allow the port a virtual monopoly in South Wales on the export of the most valuable commodity of the age? Perhaps his devotion to Despenser clouded his judgement as this was an opportunity for the Lord of Cardiff to reap enormous rewards from the wool trade. In 1332 the charter was revoked and Carmarthen, a royal borough, was granted a monopoly on the trade instead, thus ensuring a steady stream of wealth for the crown.

There are no records that tell us anything about Cardiff and the Black Death. What we do know is that no town or village escaped the ravages of the most lethal epidemic that the country has ever known. The bubonic plague that swept across Europe was carried by flea-infested rats and may have had its origin in China, so the opening up of trade routes to the east brought the plague back. From 1348 to 1350 a third to half of the British population died. In Bristol, Gloucester and Swansea at least half the people succumbed, and it is possible that Cardiff suffered similarly. It had the perfect conditions for a mass epidemic. The population had boomed for about 200 years, but the fear of rebellion kept the townsfolk packed tightly within Cardiff's walls. There was a quay, and the town was close to marshland, often associated with the spread of the disease. The Carmelites, Franciscans and Dominicans probably suffered disproportionately, given their commitment to alleviating the suffering of the poor and sick. [22]

The Later Middle Ages

Was the enthusiasm for backing Owain Glyndŵr based around the massive social changes that transformed Wales in the aftermath of the Black Death?[23] It seems unlikely that Glamorgan would have been exempt from these changes, given that deep and grinding poverty was widespread in the highlands of the county. In the half-century up to 1404 there was a transformation across Wales, with the beginnings of a squirearchy or gentry class, and the origins of yeomanry, private volunteer-based armed forces that were at the disposal of the landed aristocracy.

Land ownership was of fundamental importance. Already highly Anglicised in Glamorgan, in fifty years all vestiges of Welsh custom, along with the open field system and strip farming, vanished. Later we shall examine the transformation that enclosure had on Cardiff, but the practice began before the start of the fifteenth century. Enclosure was normally part of the process of switching land from low-level arable to intensive pastoral use, invariably to profit from the wool trade. Cardiff must have benefited dramatically from this: as a port it became an important link with England, with tons of wool and leather being shipped every year to the lucrative markets in Bristol and beyond. An abundance of cheaper wool probably explains the growth in prosperity in the town in the late fourteenth and early fifteenth centuries, and indicates why the cordwainers continued to be so wealthy and powerful.

The Welsh population boomed in the last part of the fourteenth century, as did social mobility when serfdom, as it had been known across much of Wales, ceased to exist. The free peasants were divided into two groups: aspirant small farmers who eventually evolved into gentry squires, and subsistence or landless poor. This division sowed the seeds of conflict that Owain Glyndŵr later exploited. Were Cardiffians aware of what was happening? Doubtless the social changes in Wales as a whole were not lost on Anglicised Cardiff, partly because the noble landowners who dominated Glamorgan were also heavily represented in the town. Whether or not the increase in disenfranchised and socially marginalised peasants was recognised by the Lords of Cardiff as a danger is debatable, given the fact that the rebellion they were the footsoldiers for was only the second to breach the town's walls. Certainly they could have had little idea of how big the rebellion would be.

At this time Welshmen frequently fought England's wars, especially as archers; Glamorgan was famed in English poetry as a source of excellent fighters.

Cardiff Castle, the military and administrative focal point for the region, was doubtless where men from across Wales amassed periodically to fight in France or Scotland.

The eventual fate of Owain Glyndŵr is unclear. By 1408, with dwindling support from France and with a better understanding of tactics on the part of the English, the rebellion had all but failed. Harlech Castle, the home of the Glyndŵr family, fell, and Owain vanishes from the pages of history. Perhaps he succumbed to illness, famine or random accident or possibly lived for years in obscurity. What is clear is that with him died Wales' last great rebellion, one that was particularly threatening to Cardiff because the rebels saw the town as a bastion of foreign oppression.

Richard Beauchamp, Earl of Warwick inherited the Lordship of Cardiff. When Despenser was executed in 1400 his daughter Isabel, born six months after her father's death, became the rightful heir to his estates. By marriage she handed them to Richard Beauchamp, the Earl of Worcester. He was killed in France in 1422, and his widow married his cousin the following year: he was also Richard, this time the Earl of Warwick. It was the second Beauchamp who added significant fortifications to Cardiff Castle, particularly the castle's octagonal tower.

Beauchamp, the thirteenth earl, had proven himself in battle against the enemies of the king decades earlier. In one of the first near defeats for Glyndŵr, the Battle of Mynydd Cwmdu, Beauchamp temporarily routed Glyndŵr's men before charging headlong into an ambush prepared by the retreating army. He was known as a man of piety and had taken a pilgrimage to the Holy Land in 1408. Beauchamp was another of Cardiff's absent lords, a man who was profoundly influential at court and very useful as a diplomat. On his death in 1437 his son Henry inherited his estates. He ruled for just six years before his death in 1445, and the titles passed to his sister Anne. Through marriage they passed to Richard Neville, the next Earl of Warwick. Records kept since the 1450s and published by the Corporation of Cardiff in 1920 give a fascinating insight into life in Cardiff at this time. These are the Lordship of Leckwith's yearly rents and accounts, which were recorded in detail by one Patrick Crispy (a name of Norman descent, but Anglicised perhaps).

Most of the records deal with the issue of tenures, giving very detailed instructions from the Lord of Leckwith, who was probably Neville. Many of the decisions seem to have been made by the lord of the manor himself, which tends to suggest that Neville was probably less of an absentee lord than his predecessors. The accounts show that people were granted rights to build new homes on the west side of the River Ely. Although they were to be financed solely by the people themselves, the lord of the manor found them timber to use, probably meaning they had access to the lord's woodlands to fell trees. A type of inheritance tax seems also to have been employed[24]. There are at least six pages of detailed records of the various duties, entitlements and taxes upon ordinary Cardiffians. By the Middle Ages a complex system of administration was in place. This should not be confused with modern bureaucratic government, as it was simply a codification of feudal rights and dues. One of the beneficiaries was St John's church, now the remaining church in Cardiff. It is a sign of the amount of destruction that was wrought upon the town by Owain Glyndŵr that it took until the 1450s to start the rebuilding of the church, which was all but destroyed by the attack. The tower was rebuilt, and would have had all but skyscraper status in the 1470s.

Neville was a supporter of the Yorkist cause during the Wars of the Roses and campaigned successfully across the Welsh Marches for Edward IV. By the 1460s he was the richest man in England and Wales with the exception of the king. The unpopular and incompetent Edward IV soon found an enemy in Neville, who schemed against him and began a rebellion in Yorkshire which led to him imprisoning the king in the Tower of London until 1469. Neville was slain at the Battle of Barnet in 1471, and his body was displayed in St Paul's Cathedral. Because of his treachery, the king divided the forfeit estates between his two brothers, Clarence and Richard, Duke of Gloucester, the future King Richard III. Clarence was awarded the chamberlainship of England and the lieutenancy of Ireland, while Richard was given the title of Admiral of England and Warden of the West March. Clarence was given the earldoms of Warwick and Salisbury, and so inherited Cardiff. When Richard of Gloucester married Neville's younger daughter Anne in 1472 (she had been widowed by the demise of Prince Edward), a bitter feud erupted between the princes over the rights to the Beauchamp and Despenser inheritances. A settlement was finally reached and the land was divided, but this did little to appease Clarence. In 1477 he plotted again to destroy his brother Edward and take the crown and the disputed lands for himself. This time the king could no longer act with lenience, and the next year the Duke of Clarence was executed. Another Lord of Cardiff had plotted against the king and lost.

As the Middle Ages drew to an end there was one last act in the long and turbulent history of the town as it passed from dynasty to dynasty. This was

Church Street. The bustle and pace of Cardiff's Church Street today; it has been a thoroughfare to Cardiff's various markets for much of the last 1,000 years.

the story of Richard, Duke of Gloucester, perhaps the most infamous Lord of Cardiff. Cardiff Castle bears lasting evidence of being the property of Richard III, though his reign was brief. There is a stained-glass window of Richard and Anne in the entrance hall, alongside the ill-fated Duke of Clarence. This window was placed in the castle by Victorian architect William Burges at the behest of the Butes. Near to Richard and Anne is a stained-glass window that depicts his nemesis, Henry Tudor, the victor of Bosworth and subsequently Henry VII.

four

THE TUDOR AGE

Henry VII

The Tudor age in Britain began with the death of Richard III at the Battle of Bosworth in 1485. The first Tudor Lord of Cardiff was Jasper Tudor, uncle to the new king Henry VII and a man without whom there would probably have been no Tudor dynasty in England and Wales for the next century. Cardiff's sixteenth century was a time of religious change, but more gradually and subtly there was social change. As in the rest of England and Wales the medieval period was coming to an end.

Cardiff was pivotal in the period after 1485 in the forging of an Anglo-Welsh state. Wales was the focus of Tudor ambitions for an integrated kingdom, far more so than Ireland or Scotland, because territorial ambitions by Tudor monarchs were thwarted in both kingdoms throughout the sixteenth century. Ireland in particular resisted any attempts at religious reformation, whereas in Wales, particularly in Glamorgan and therefore in Cardiff, there was very little opposition. Perhaps this was due to a general feeling of anti-clericalism that was prevalent in much of Wales at this time and would have probably been stronger in Cardiff because of the high number of churches, monastic houses and a nearby cathedral. Many of the priests and monks were of a low calibre by the sixteenth century, often poorly educated and commanding little respect among their congregations.

When considering the political changes that shaped Cardiff and Glamorgan in this period it is important to exercise a little caution. It would be premature to think of the political union of Wales and England that took place in 1536 as the beginning of a British state, but certainly these changes had enormous significance for Cardiff. As we have seen, since Roman times the town had been on a historical fault line. It existed partly as a shock absorber between Welsh nationalism and English hegemony, being reinforced and devastated periodically as the tides of war, dynastic dispute and revolt washed over her. Cardiff resumed her traditional role of being in the front line of cross-border change, partly because the town was economically valuable, being on trade routes from east to west, but mainly because of its strategic value to those wishing to control the important lowlands of Glamorgan. Later, in Henry VIII's time, it was a staging post for the militarisation and domination of Wales, so that it could not become a back door to European invasion.

Jasper Tudor was made lord of much of South Wales in 1486, being the Earl of Pembroke and Lord of Glamorgan, Abergavenny, Newport and Haverford; he was also the Lord Chief Justice of South Wales. The Lordship of Glamorgan as such was abolished and the properties of Lady Anne Neville were confiscated and given to Jasper. By now, any Lord of Cardiff was almost a full-time member of the royal court, and as Henry VII had few other advisors (having come from France to unseat Richard without much of an entourage or any real wealth), his loyal uncle was often at his side. Inevitably Jasper spent much of his time in England. He was one of a growing class of 'London Welsh', a group made up of aristocrats and the newly emerging gentry class. Jasper appears to have been a relatively beneficent lord in Cardiff until his death in 1495, having provided a tower at Llandaff Cathedral and several generous bequests to the friars of Cardiff.

Llandaff Cathedral (*above and below*). What the Normans began, the early Tudors contributed to. Jasper Tudor, uncle of Henry VII, built a north-west tower to the cathedral.

The Bishops of Llandaff during the Reformation were some of the key figures in the ecclesiastical drama, including Catherine of Aragon's own personal priest George D'Athequa and the later spendthrift Anthony Kitchin.

Cardiff most likely benefited simply by having Jasper's patronage as he was the king's most important representative in Wales. Though notionally Welsh himself, Henry VII seems to have had only a peripheral interest in Wales; the problems of 'Pretender' plots and rebellions kept him occupied. In general his policies were beneficial to the country as a whole, and it is hard to imagine that they wouldn't also have benefited Cardiff. His chief interest was the maintenance of law and order, achieved through the Council of Wales and the Marches. Throughout his reign, trade between England and Wales improved – this primarily consisted of the trade in finished goods brought from the south-west of England across the Bristol Channel and the export of commodities such as wool, leather, grain and beer to England from West Wales and Glamorgan through Cardiff. The Navigation Acts also benefited the small but important port. The town's market days, and her hostelries, got busier.

Before Cardiff became a coal port she was a wool port, her principal competition in South Wales being Carmarthen. There is evidence to indicate that via this wool trade Cardiff became integrated into a wider British and European economic system.[25] When Henry IV removed excise duties on finished cloth from Wales, woollen goods from Cardiff made their way to Bristol, to Marches towns such as Ludlow and Hereford and as far as Southampton, to be shipped to Florence. Wool shipped to Bristol was sent from there to France, Portugal, Iceland and Scandinavia. Germanic traders from the Hanseatic ports on the Baltic also bought Cardiff wool. In the relationship between Cardiff and Bristol, which became increasingly important to the development of both cities, Bristol continued to have the upper hand because of the size and development of its port. In comparison, Cardiff's docks, effectively sprouting from the end of St Mary's Street, only had the capacity to ship goods up and down the Bristol Channel. Cardiff wool merchants who wanted to take their goods to market in Europe had to sell their wares to larger trading concerns in Bristol.

In the Tudor Age the whole of Britain underwent a century of economic and social change as the structures of feudal society faded: the stage was set for the ascendancy of gentry and mercantile classes over the next 300 years. Cardiff was at the forefront of this change and the town was characterised by growing trade, mercantilism and early capitalism. It was becoming a modern settlement. Trade was the driver of change and Cardiff became progressively wealthier. However, the town also had to weather the religious turbulence that was not fully resolved until the eighteenth century.

St Mary Street is a centre for post-rugby celebrations and commiserations, but the density of bars and clubs offering cut-price drink deals has ensured it continues to attract national and international infamy.

There were, however, rumblings of darker times to come. By 1495 there had been an increase in population across England and Wales that indicated the demographic collapse caused by the Black Death was well and truly forgotten. However, surplus population in a time where work was gradually becoming less labour intensive, combined with factors such as the enclosure of common lands, and later, in Henry VIII's reign, growing inflation thanks to feckless spending, saw the problem of vagrancy emerge – and Cardiff's Cockmarel no doubt meted out punishments to vagrants. The town was ideally suited to attract the wandering poor, as it stood on a vital east-west route. The poor themselves were seen as a danger because of the potential for civil unrest and because they were more likely to communicate disease. Cardiff of the early Tudor era, relatively prosperous, though later in the sixteenth century suffering from prolonged economic troubles, fiercely loyal to the crown and unified around the rule of a small group of guildsmen, would not have been a welcome place for the hungry and desperate. Perhaps the friaries were the only source of poor relief. These institutions were to be devastated by the arbitrary whims of a king in the 1540s as the town was plunged, with the rest of the country, into a century of religious turmoil.

Henry VIII

In 1542 two events took place that shaped Cardiff during the reigns of Edward VI and Queen Mary. The first was the declaration of the town as a free borough; it had already become the county town for Glamorgan in 1536 when Glamorgan was incorporated into a shire. This meant that Cardiff could return MPs to Parliament, and became more likely to build cultural and political ties with London and Westminster, the heart of the Tudor dynasty, so that it would not be a backwater during the sixteenth century. The second event was more dramatic: the execution of Thomas Capper of Cardiff.

With the failure in 1529 by Thomas Wolsey to arrange the king's 'Great Matter', his divorce from Catherine of Aragon, the impetuous and wilful Henry VIII initiated the break with Rome, installing himself as the head of a new Church of England. Before this, however, a more radical European Reformation had been developing as the fundamental principles of Catholicism started to be called into question by an increasingly literate population. The martyrdom of Thomas Capper is only known because of the notes left in a bailiff's journal that refer to the cost of his imprisonment and burning. Whilst Henry was head of the Church of England, he hadn't brought about a doctrinal break with Rome, just a political one, and was as harsh on heretics as his daughter Mary. Thomas Capper's crime was to espouse the radical religious idea that transubstantiation was a myth, and this was enough to have him burnt at the stake. Before his incarceration he was held in the prison of Cockmarel.

Even though Cardiff eventually accepted the Reformation with relatively little bloodshed, before Edward VI it remained a bastion of religious conservatism. Whilst the parish of Roath later produced some of Wales' most famous Puritan firebrands, the fate of martyrs in the town and the lack of public outcry is a clear indication of the lack of interest in change. Perhaps the eventual acceptance of change has more to do with a sense of loyalty to the crown than a widespread and ardent belief in Protestantism.

Cardiff's martyrs were buried according to Protestant rites, largely out of respect but also to prevent further religious disturbances.[26] This also suggests a degree of pragmatism and an ability to compromise, the need for which might have been given fresh urgency following the horrific public spectacle of a man being burned to death. It is unclear whether Puritan attitudes towards work and play were the official policy of the constable and his bailiffs, and whether they were shared by the increasingly embattled Catholic monastic houses.

Whatever the case, it appears that there was little formal opposition in Wales to the king's actions. Cardiff's clergy were quick to recognise the king as the legitimate head of the Church, and this was by and large the picture across the country. One possible explanation for this attitude is probably linked to the town's evolving nature. Rebellions like the Pilgrimage of Grace were limited to communities that were dependent on monasteries for their livelihood, and Cardiffians were not because of the growing commercial strength of the town.

The obvious local target for the king, as part of a mission to restock his depleted treasury, was Llandaff Cathedral. After Henry VIII had finished with it the building fell into ruin for at least 200 years. Existing in a rather precarious position at the time was Catherine of Aragon's chaplain George de Athequa, a Spanish Catholic who was Bishop of Llandaff, although he seldom visited the diocese (this was standard practice for most high-ranking churchmen). De Athequa refused to betray his mistress when England finally broke with Rome and so would not take the Henrician Oath of Supremacy.[27] Perhaps he could see the writing on the wall in 1536, when he was criticised by the king for failing to stop seditious preaching in the diocese of Llandaff. It is unlikely that there was a secret hotbed of religious radicalism, and the 'sedition' might have been exaggerated to put pressure on an unpopular priest. His unpopularity mirrored that of Thomas Wolsey in 1529: both men (de Athequa more so than Wolsey) resisted immense pressure to have the king's marriage to Catherine of Aragon annulled. De Athequa was left vulnerable and without a patron when the queen died in 1536, and he was finally arrested when he was trying to board a Flemish ship bound for Spain. Imprisoned in the Tower of London, he was rescued after an intervention by the Spanish ambassador and returned to Spain, where he died a year later.

After the imprisonment and flight of de Athequa, inspectors were sent by Thomas Cromwell to Llandaff to look into religious dissent in the diocese. Adam Becansaw and John Vaughan reported to their master that there had been a woeful lack of enforcement of the king's decrees, and that de Athequa had done very little to expound the Act of Supremacy. Vaughan stated that there was much work to do in Llandaff, and that the previous bishop had been a malign influence on the people: 'People were never so far out of frame concerning the spiritual jurisdiction by reason of naughty bishops and worse officers.'[28] As well as religious crimes, de Athequa seems to have been guilty of a general level of administrative and managerial negligence: 'The Bishop and his archdeacon [are] guilty not only of great ruin and decay of their mansions

Llandaff Cathedral. Both St Dyfrig and St Teilo, the original founders of the cathedral, have their tombs at Llandaff.

but of other great faults.' De Athequa's actual crimes were probably relatively trivial[29], as we must remember that Thomas Cromwell was an arch-propagandist who thought nothing of using his functionaries to besmirch reputations if it suited his purposes. A greater prize than royal supremacy was up for grabs: the material wealth of the monastic houses.

An indication of what was to come was one of de Athequa's final tasks; he must have been left feeling suspicious and anxious when he was asked to stocktake Llandaff's ecclesiastical wealth in 1535. Cromwell, determined to seize the wealth of the monasteries, needed to know where the money lay in each diocese. Quite why he wanted de Athequa to lead the team of inspectors is unclear: as a member of Catherine of Aragon's inner circle de Athequa must have been distrusted for at least five years. The gentry, who were the main beneficiaries of the Dissolution, were probably more than happy to participate. By this date, de Athequa's refusal to cooperate with the king was common knowledge, so it is hardly surprising that the information gathered in Llandaff is patchy and insubstantial when compared with other dioceses in South Wales.

Perhaps Cromwell expected a lack of cooperation, and was giving de Athequa enough rope to hang himself with.

In Cardiff the two houses of the Franciscan Friars were dissolved in 1538. Sir Richard Ingworth, himself a former friar, was sent by the Crown to Glamorgan to ensure that they were closed, and that the wealth of the friaries made its way to the king's treasury. By the time he arrived, the two friaries were in a rather desperate condition. Four years after the Act of Supremacy was signed and two years after the Dissolution of the Monasteries had begun in 1536, the Franciscans and Dominicans in Cardiff were bankrupt and heavily in debt to the townspeople, so much so that they had begun to pawn their wealth, such as the communion chalices. These had never been wealthy monastic houses in the first place, and much of their wealth was routinely redistributed back to the community through alms to the poor and the education of poor children. The number of friars was depleted as well, to just sixteen across the two friaries. Ingworth took a careful note of his plunder, including candlesticks and vestments from the church and everyday living utensils from the monks' living quarters and kitchen. They were given a deed of surrender, which they had no choice to sign, putting all their belongings into the hands of Ingworth and the king, and then they were sent out into the world when the friary was closed, without any recompense. Following this official looting an unofficial plundering took place: at Greyfriars, now Greyfriars Road in the city centre, the townspeople carried away the building materials. This was sometimes met with legal action by the Crown, which had assumed full ownership of all assets; the Court of Augmentations saw several prosecutions of Cardiffians. One can only imagine how distressing this process was for the friars, who had devoted themselves to a life of service to God and were now homeless in an apparently hostile town that was loyal to Henry VIII. All the high value items that were surrendered were sent directly

Llandaff Cathedral. The cathedral is supported now in large part by donations and monies raised by The Friends of Llandaff Cathedral.

to the treasury to be melted down for currency, to deal with the king's growing debt crisis, but most of the other assets were auctioned on the spot. Stained glass, lead piping and slates from the roof were all sold in the street to the highest bidder. The two friaries were stripped down to their foundations and the Greyfriars was built upon in the 1960s.

There were other pockets of land near Cardiff that were owned by the three abbeys of Glamorgan: Margam, Neath and Ewenni. These lands were surrendered, and the main beneficiaries were the Glamorgan gentry, with families such as the Herberts and the Mansels gaining valuable property. The Diocese of Tewkesbury still owned land in and around the town, particularly a manor at Roath, Llandough. This went to Sir George Herbert of Swansea, who also purchased the remains of the looted friaries. The men who had the money to buy large amounts of land were the elite amongst the Glamorgan gentry. Very wealthy men to start with, they left their contemporaries behind after the Dissolution, a process that only cemented their loyalty to the crown.

The bishops of Llandaff who followed de Athequa had mixed fortunes. Given the scale of the changes Henry VIII had introduced, the bishops of Llandaff were often placed in a very difficult position when the townspeople of Cardiff expressed rebellious sentiments.

De Aquetha's direct successor was Robert Holgate, a Yorkshireman who had a rather liberal temperament. He was only in office for a year, but appears to have demonstrated a competence for administration and was assigned to Cromwell's Council of the North. Following Holgate, another short-term appointee was John Bird, who in 1539 was sent to be an ambassador to the king in Germany. For six years following Bird's departure the diocese had no bishop, but this was finally rectified with the appointment of Anthony Kitchin. He came to the diocese late in Henry's reign, in 1545, and has subsequently been regarded as a rather craven individual who, like the proverbial Vicar of Bray, changed his opinions and loyalties as conflicting religious winds blew across Wales in the sixteenth century. The historian Eamonn Duffy wrote of him: 'In less than a year Elizabeth I had undone all Pole's and Mary's reforms. She had outlawed the Mass and deprived and imprisoned the entire episcopate, with the craven exception of the turncoat Henrician conformist Anthony Kitchin of Llandaff.'[30] Indeed, Kitchin was the only bishop to take the Oath of Supremacy, which recognised Elizabeth as the rightful head of the Church of England.

A contemporary account is that of Bishop Godwin in 1603, who called Kitchin 'the calamity of our estate.'[31] His enemies and critics accused him of selling the diocese's lands for a pittance during his time as bishop and bankrupting the cathedral and its lands. Doubtless this had dire implications for the people who lived in Llandaff at the time, as community life and its economic activity were centred around the cathedral. The most notorious incident, in which even an impartial observer would suspect some degree of corruption, was the sale of Llandaff Manor to Sir George Mathew. These expansive and valuable estates, which accounted for a large portion of the wealth of the diocese and even included the bishop's castle, was leased in perpetuity at a nominal

A copy of the Court Roll (1734) (Rumney). The courts by the eighteenth century reflected the growth of trade but also of crime and disorder in an expanding Cardiff.

rent, virtually giving away hundreds of acres for next to nothing.[32] Mathew had married into the family of William Herbert, one of the Cardiff gentry who was appointed to manage Llandaff during the plundering of the parishes by Edward VI. It clearly paid to have friends in high places; both Mathew and Herbert had a patron in the Earl of Northumberland. Perhaps Kitchin had no choice but to part with the lands, but it is unlikely that he put up much of a fight. Although he had dabbled in religious dissent earlier in his career (as a monk he had been caught in possession of Protestant books, and it is clear that he was part of the supply chain of such literature), he recanted when he was caught. It seems that he earned favour from Henry VIII for being amenable to reform.

Perhaps the greatest religious change to come to Cardiff in the Tudor age was not the Reformation and the dissolution of the two friaries, but the introduction of the English Book of Common Prayer. The real reformation came to the town in the guise of Edward VI and the *de facto* ruler of England and Wales, the Earl of Somerset. It was in 1548 that the traditional practices of Catholicism, potentially idolatrous images, ceremonies and mass, were banned. Later, altars were abandoned for tables. It is likely that the advent of the English Book of Common Prayer was less of a shock to Cardiffians when its use was enforced from Whitsunday 1549 onwards because of the already bilingual nature of late medieval and early modern Cardiff. By 1551 the book had been translated into Welsh, and by 1552 Cardiff congregations were being preached to through the second Book of Prayer, a far more radical Protestant book.

The next wave of action against the Church, from 1548 onwards, was an attack on the chantries, of which there were several in Cardiff. This meant a pillaging of all institutions connected to them, even if they were educational, such as the poor school at Llandaff Cathedral. Documents of the asset-stripping of St Mary's parish dating back to 1548 show that the king demanded in rents the stipends of John Thomas, the parish priest, and Nicholas Penllyn, a priest at the altar of St Nicholas at St Mary's church. Audits were taken of the parishes of Michaelston-super-Ely, Llanishen, Sully and Cardiff itself. Whilst some of this might have been motivated by the new evangelical passions of the new king, mostly it was a raid on the last pockets of wealth as the country lurched into crisis once more in the late 1540s and early 1550s. After the chantries had been dissolved large quantities of plate and jewels were shipped off to London, and the priests were given a meagre pay-off of approximately £4. Again this was a bonanza for the wealthy Glamorgan gentry, who took land from the chantries at Llandaff, Cardiff and Llanishen.

In the late Middle Ages, chantries performed much the same task that charitable foundations do today, everything from the relief of the poor and the elderly, the education of poor children and the upkeep of public amenities such as Cardiff's dock. One of the biggest losses was the financial wherewithal to keep the dock maintained, and to repair the bridge over the River Taff, but this paled into insignificance when the plunder of the parishes got under way. At the end of Edward's life in April 1553 the county of Glamorgan was divided into four districts or hundreds. In Cardiff's district were Cardiff, Llandaff, Caerphilly and Dinas Powys. The ever loyal Glamorgan gentry were appointed as administrators of the audit of each parish for valuables previously belonging to the church. Edward's logic was simple: since the second Book of Prayer outlawed the ornate splendour of Catholic worship, the churches had no need for the finery that went with it. One of the most valuable items to be removed, and it is hard to see what this had to do with the functioning of the Catholic mass, was *The Book of Llandaff*, the twelfth-century register of the history of the cathedral and the diocese.

These changes were intensely unpopular with the people of Cardiff. They had been prepared to stand by King Henry, partly because he had only replaced

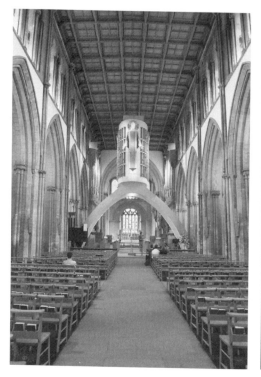

Llandaff Cathedral (*above*). The cathedral was desecrated by Parliamentary troops during the Civil War; it came under attack from the puritan iconoclasts in Parliament's armies opposed to High Church Anglicanism.

Christ in Majesty by Jacob Epstein (*above, right*). Epstein, the son of New York Polish-Jewish immigrants, became one of post-war Britain's most celebrated sculptors and created *Christ in Majesty* in 1955, a few years before his death. The sculpture is proudly displayed in the cathedral.

the Pope as the head of the Church and had not altered religious doctrine, but primarily because they had benefited from the closure of the two friaries. Edward's Reformation was a different matter altogether for the Cardiffians and people of surrounding parishes found their communities poorer, and strange, unfamiliar doctrines imposed upon them.

The sixteenth century in Cardiff was a time of decay and decline for several reasons. All the towns across Glamorgan seem to have suffered a fall in population in the previous century, and in 1544 Cardiff, Swansea and Cowbridge were all mentioned in an Act of Parliament as being 'decayed and in need of rehabilitation'. It seems symptomatic of a wider malaise in Wales at the time. As we shall see, however, Cardiff's status as a town protected her in the sixteenth century from the extremes of rural poverty. During the Lay Subsidy of 1543, the first great Tudor tax assessment of Wales, there was a taxable revenue from Cardiff of £42 3s 8d, as opposed to £18 collected from the whole hundred of Cardiff. This statistic suggests that the town was capable, even in an economic downturn, of amassing wealth, most likely through trade. During the years of the mid-Tudor Crisis, following the death of Henry VIII, currency was debased, inflation was rife and the country faced bankruptcy but inhabitants of Cardiff, whilst not rich, were insulated against the worst of the economic storms that battered the country. The town had become a diverse centre of economic activity. Cardiff's geography saved her and saw her prosper for a century to come, by making her a marketplace for county-wide trade, and more importantly a port for goods from inland Wales, predominantly wool and leather but gradually also coal.

Feltmakers, weavers, dyers, cappers, hatters and a variety of other tradesmen were reliant on the wool trade. Much of the growth of government in the sixteenth century had been to monitor and tax key industries like wool, but Cardiff's wool merchants and tradesmen appear to have paid scant attention to the requirements of the law, particularly with respect to paying tax. In similar

Llandaff Cathedral (*left and below*). The cathedral's stunning stained-glass windows and the various important works of art kept there, including *The Seed of David* by Dante Rosetti, require constant maintenance and upkeep.

Bombs dropped during the blitz devastated much of the restored cathedral. A parachute mine in 1941 caused an explosion and extensive damage.

manner, the leather and tanning industry was a key part of the economy of Tudor Cardiff, and the guilds for these industries wielded a not inconsiderable amount of power.

Coal, eventually to make Cardiff a global city and power Britain's Industrial Revolution, became a notable industry in the second half of the sixteenth century; however, the centre of the coal and later the iron industries lay to the west in Neath and Swansea. Only in the 1560s did iron begin to establish itself as a small industry in Cardiff, after laws against deforestation were passed by Queen Elizabeth. Acute deforestation in England and resultant laws to prevent further loss of trees led to enterprising iron producers to look towards Wales for three reasons: abundant wood for charcoal, iron stones and limestone. Even Henry VIII had not been blind to the importance of creating an iron industry, and in 1531 had seen Llantrisant as an ideal spot for smelting iron and lead. There was clearly an understanding in governmental and mercantile circles in the sixteenth century that the iron industry was strategic, and would be of growing importance. The Mathew family of Radyr, one of the most established and wealthiest dynasties of the sixteenth century, had a key interest in building the iron industry in South Wales, constructing the Pentyrch ironworks.

In 1564, probably in Radyr or Pentyrch, Sir Henry Sidney established a forge and furnace. Accounts of the enterprise that have survived seem to indicate that it was operating on an industrial scale that had not previously been seen in Cardiff. Miners, fillers, founders and charcoal burners were all employed. Skilled labour such as the master founder commanded comparatively high wages, and industrial principles such as division of labour and specification of skills are clearly in evidence.

The chimneys of a rival iron foundry across the River Taff would have been visible from the Radyr site. They stood at an ironworks at Tongwynlais, established in 1560 by Hugh Lambert of Tunbridge Wells. There were English Tudor iron magnates throughout Glamorgan, attracted by the opportunities that the industry represented. Despite these promising beginnings it was another 200 years before anything approaching the heavy industry that we are now familiar with took hold in the Cardiff area. The first faltering steps towards an Industrial Revolution began in the 1560s, but the quantities of iron produced, the lack of a coal industry and the lack of significant world markets meant that the iron industry remained a fairly small affair.

During the 1560s, Cardiff had the briefest beginnings as an iron port, as iron merchants there found buyers for the cast iron and iron plate that was produced in East Sussex. Ships from Cardiff sailed to Rye on the south coast or to Bristol and then iron proceeded overland. It was taken to be smelted into steel at Robertsbridge, but this lasted at most for a decade, and as the Robertsbridge forges lost their importance Cardiff iron began to be shipped to Ireland.

Ironworking was not new in Pentyrch, as there is evidence of ironworking there from the early Middle Ages, but it appears to have been the dynamism and the unscrupulousness of Edmund Mathew that took the industry to new heights. In the 1570s, Mathew seems to have been nothing more than an arms dealer, using Cardiff's small and probably poorly run port to illegally ship 150 tons of ordnance out of the country. He was accused of bribing the poorly paid port officials, and the crime was seen as so serious that the king's privy council was made aware of it. Mathew, in trouble and also in debt, leased part of his share of the ironworks to an equally crooked Dutchman called Peter Semayne, also involved in the smuggling of weapons and later wine. It is difficult to establish whether Mathews and Semayne were more interested in legitimate or illegal business, but the appearance of the latter in court three times before 1616 suggests that criminality was a significant part of his life. Sir John Throckmorton described him as a 'pestilent fellow, in these and suchlike businesses, making an infinite gain thereof besides the arming of all the world with our artillery against us'. It appears that Mathews had interests in the legitimate arms trade, as he shipped a well-documented forty-eight pieces of ordnance to London in 1600, mainly small cannons that were used on warships. One can only assume that they were produced at his Radyr and Pentyrch ironworks.

Cardiff Charter IX (1465) BC/1/9 granted by King Edward IV.

Later the Porth Llongau, also known as the Go Late, a small landing stage that nestled between St Mary's Street and Westgate Street before the redirection of the River Taff, was the scene of legitimate gun-running on a far larger scale. Guns were shipped to the British Army in the Americas during the American War of Independence and to the British in Portugal and Spain during the Peninsula Wars against Napoleon. These were made by the gun makers Bacon of Cyfarthfa. It is no coincidence that the largest ironworks in the country eventually supported the nascent British arms industry.

Cardiff Charter VIII (1453) BC/1/8 granted by King Henry VI.

Further corruption was revealed at the port of Cardiff in 1615 when Matthew Price and Edward Jordan, the controller of Cardiff and the controller of Swansea, were accused of taking bribes and allowing the export of cloth, wool, lead, tallow, butter, cheese, hemp and flax without the correct payment of duty. In essence, all the major commodities that Cardiff exported were slipping out of the port without the Crown seeing its rightful share. In 1618 the corruption problem still seems to have been unresolved as Thomas Williams, the former searcher of the port of Cardiff, and his brother were accused of trying to illegally export 160,000 gallons of butter to France in collusion with merchants from Bristol. The evasion of tax would have netted Williams 1s for every 16 gallons. He claimed to have a pardon for all crimes committed before 1617.

Corruption also affected Cardiff merchants. In 1622, one Edmund Morgan complained to the Exchequer about the conduct of the deputy collector at Swansea, who had prevented him from accessing the all-important customs house in that town as Morgan had been unwilling to pay the right bribes. There was a growth in graft and corruption, largely because trade was flourishing, and with it there was inevitable tax evasion.

Cardiff townspeople soon began to see that the small port had taken on a significance that was undeniable, and realised that this part of the town's economic infrastructure had to be looked after. The docks had probably been built and maintained by private investment from wealthy townspeople, and in 1552 it was revealed that the chantries had funded their upkeep.

Trade flowed from the docks predominantly across the Bristol Channel, but there were some instances of pioneering ships' captains and risk-taking merchants who sailed as far as France and Ireland, normally when Glamorgan harvests supplied a surplus. Bristol's growing population demanded more resources than the West Country could supply alone, which encouraged Cardiff business and eventually facilitated the growth of Cardiff as a market centre. During the later Elizabethan wars in Ireland there was a huge demand for grain from Cardiff: in 1600, seventy-one shipments left the docks, twenty-five to Ireland and twenty-one to Bristol. Cattle were shipped to Bristol and Minehead from Sully, while boats packed with hundreds of sheep were a frequent sight in the Bristol Channel. An indication of how big this trade had grown by the mid-seventeenth century is the claim that one South Wales cattle dealer made twenty trips in one year, taking on average 240 cattle each time. Even if this is an exaggeration it suggests that the trade was extremely lucrative, and probably employed a large number of people on both sides of the Bristol Channel. It is clearly another reason for Cardiff's ascendancy in the sixteenth and seventeenth centuries.

The Society of Merchant Venturers in Bristol appointed agents permanently in Cardiff to help manage the trade in dairy products, particularly butter and cheese. This was lucrative because markets in France, Portugal and Spain had been discovered by Bristol's merchants. The long-term significance of these new markets was a growing dependence on trade, and Cardiff's vulnerability to adverse changes in trading conditions.

On return voyages from La Rochelle in France, Cardiff's iron traders brought back two main items that were in great demand, wine and salt. Salt was vital and fetched a premium in Cardiff's markets, bought by anyone looking to cure meat, tan hides, churn butter or preserve fish. Via France, Cardiff also imported produce from all over Europe and the Near East, Ireland and, as the sixteenth century wore on, the Americas. The vessels that brought these goods in tended to be relatively small, and for the most part plied the waters of the Severn Estuary, goods from further afield having been transferred to them in Bristol and Swansea.

A threat to this new prosperity manifested itself in the late sixteenth and early seventeenth centuries. The Barbary pirates were North African raiders who terrorised shipping in the Bristol Channel and the Irish Sea. In the next chapter we shall see how fear of these pirates bolstered support for the inept Charles I, but it is worth mentioning here that at the height of their attacks on shipping, and the subsequent disruption to trade, the whole of Glamorgan was reported by the lord lieutenant to be impoverished. It does not take a great deal of imagination to fathom the knock-on effect this had on Cardiff.

One of the greatest ever feats of piracy was perpetrated by a South Walian pirate, John Callis. In 1576 he sailed a Spanish galleon up the Severn Estuary, then up the River Taff to dock at the Porth Llongau, the harbour gate in the middle of Cardiff. The residents must have been absolutely astonished. The Spanish and Portuguese plunder of the New World had seen a flow of untold wealth into Europe. The Welsh and English were anxious to take a share of the booty, and were not too fussy about how they got their hands on it. Some privateers operated with the tacit approval of the Crown, but any acts of theft on the high seas were denied. Callis was arrested after an official protest by the Spanish crown: sailing one of their ships into Cardiff was so blatant that it could not be ignored. In a desperate attempt to avoid the gallows, Callis offered to inform on the many other pirates who were operating from havens along the rugged and uncharted Welsh coast, but to no avail. He was hanged at Newport the same year. Callis has been cited by historians as the inspiration for Robert Louis Stevenson's *Treasure Island*.

Alongside national and international trade, farming continued. Cardiff's commoners were spared the scourge of enclosure during the sixteenth century, one key reason why they were not plunged into penury during the challenging economic times of the mid-century. The lands now occupied by Roath and the Heath were cultivated in small plots, as was the East Moor. It is interesting to note the degree to which supposedly urban people, living off mercantile and clerical incomes, were also deeply dependent on farming. Despite the growing economic troubles of Tudor England and Wales in the mid-fifteenth century there was still a growing demand for rural produce. In the sixteenth century there was explosive population growth, and Cardiff (a market town and port) was the perfect place to bring grain, cattle and other goods to market. Taking goods by water to Bristol was still a lot easier than any land route to England. The town was heavily reliant on its twice weekly markets, held on Wednesdays and Saturdays, and appears to have been alive with entrepreneurial spirit.

The High Street was lined with stalls selling all manner of farm produce from cloth to honey to leather. Markets for meat were held at the guildhall on High Street, and there were cattle markets twice a month from March to October. Cardiff was also a venue for county fairs. The fair was very big business, especially for the trade in cattle, though the perception was often that it was a magnet for troublesome and lawless types. Whether this was simply Tudor moral panic is unclear.

Tudor times were a golden age for tradesmen and craftsmen, largely because of the Cardiff's position as a port and marketplace. Hostelries for weary travellers, brewers, vintners, butchers, fishmongers, bakers and tanners were all numerous in the sixteenth century. There were shoemakers, weavers, dyers and saddlers, while all manner of men were involved in mercantile professions, trading tobacco, spices, cloth and wine, and there were also professional men such as lawyers and doctors. The wealth that bought many of these more expensive services and luxuries was generated by the Glamorgan gentry, who maintained properties in the town as well as their country houses.

The guild was a central facet of late medieval and early modern economic life in Cardiff. The town's medieval guild of cordwainers had a chapel to St Piran in St Mary's church, and in 1550, during the campaigns against the chantries, this was threatened with closure. As the angry guild members protested and refused to allow the civil authorities entry to the building, they found themselves facing the local magistrates. Religious aspects of the guild were suppressed, but the chapel was retained as a secular meeting house for cordwainers and glovers. Only in 1589 were the rights of the guilds to independent worship restored by Elizabeth.

Along with the expansion in trade, guilds and commerce came a growth in law. The new mercantile classes of Cardiff were governed with by-laws that were created when the town became a borough. For example, the court of great sessions prosecuted a number of Cardiff tradesmen for unlawful sale of alcohol and for using fraudulent weights and measures. The great interest that the Tudor state seemed to have in extending effective governance to all parts of the realm can be seen in these small measures, designed to allow commerce to function effectively.

Brewing in Cardiff grew during the Tudor age because larger quantities of coal, principally from Carmarthen, were available, along with large quantities of barley malt, more than likely imported from across the Bristol Channel. A saltworks in Barry is mentioned at the start of the seventeenth century in

Cardiff Charter VI (1581) BC/1/10 granted by Queen Elizabeth I.

a lawsuit. Cardiff's fishermen made a good living out of the heavily stocked river Taff. There had been an abundance of fish in the Taff for centuries, and small fishing boats were a common sight in the early Middle Ages. Cardiff's fishermen survived long after the Tudors, and the income that fishing generated was not insubstantial.

Cardiff acted as Glamorgan's judicial and governmental centre. It was here that all manner of criminal and civil matters were heard at the court of great sessions and quarter sessions. The town was also the centre of parliamentary life for the county. The second half of the sixteenth century, particularly the reign of Elizabeth I, saw the medieval town being gradually replaced with the kind of early modern settlement that was considered fashionable and desirable. The historian and writer Rice Merrick described Cardiff at the time as 'very well compacted, beautified with many fair houses and large streets'. By the mid-sixteenth century, Wales was impoverished and Cardiff in particular had clearly seen more prosperous times, but there was still an extraordinary buzz of economic activity. In the half-century that followed Cardiff was the epitome of a prosperous Tudor town.

Thomas Wolsey and later Thomas Cromwell were increasingly concerned about lawlessness in the Welsh Marches and Glamorgan. The 1534 appointment of Rowland Lee, Bishop of Lichfield as Lord President of the Council of Wales and the Marches was part of a terror campaign that gripped South Wales; and there were allegedly 5,000 hangings in five years. Cardiff seems to have been spared the brunt of this, partly because the town represented something desirable in Tudor thinking. The key to civilising the uncultured and barbaric Welsh, in the eyes of Westminster, was to enrich them and bring about civilisation through prosperity. The murderers and brigands who crossed the Bristol Channel to avoid being hanged in England tended to steer clear of Cardiff after 1536, as the stamp of effective government and law enforcement could be felt in the town as soon as it became the administrative centre for Glamorgan. The Act of Union in 1536 was bemoaned by the iron-fisted Lee, as he felt the Welsh were unfit for assimilation into English society.

Perhaps the most important reason for Lee's barbaric violence against the Welsh was the fear of Catholic Spain, as 1534 was the year Catherine of Aragon was being divorced by the king. Her Spanish family was understandably scandalised. Wales, thought Cromwell, was the perfect place to land an invasion force to defeat Henry, so it had to be tamed. As it was impossible to garrison Wales with English soldiers without risking an uprising, Wales had to be brought into line with England. If this was achieved, a lord lieutenant would stand at least some chance of raising armies from native Welshmen. It was not until after Cromwell's death that Cardiff was garrisoned in the same way that England was. In 1543 the militia system was introduced in the town, where men aged between 16 and 60 were required to meet regularly, normally at weekends, to practise military drill and be ready for call-up. It was the descendants of these men, a century later, who had to make a decision when Charles I announced the Commissions of Array in 1642, calling all able-bodied men to defend him against Parliament.

Mary I

That Wales was entering a period of civil and religious strife which would last over two years can be seen through the case of the fisherman Rawlings White. Living as a tenant on what is now Westgate Street, in front of a slaughterhouse, he was married with children. In the 1542/3 Ministers' Accounts he held a 'farm' of five 'hengis' (hang-nets) in Roath manor. Described as illiterate but possessing a good memory for the spoken word, he had memorised passages from the Bible and had converted to Protestantism. By the time he was tried for heresy, during the reign of Queen Mary, White quite openly admitted that he had practised the Protestant faith for many years, perhaps since the days of Henry VIII. White was targeted as an example to other Protestants[33], and was one of the earliest Marian martyrs. Foxe's *Book of Martyrs*, a sixteenth-century account of heretics and martyrs in England and Wales, includes a startlingly clear and revealing account of his life and death. The account is heavily biased in favour of Protestantism:

> Though the good man was altogether unlearned, and withal very simple, yet it pleased God to remove him from error and idolatry to a knowledge of the truth, through the blessed reformation in Edward's reign. He had his son taught to read English, and after the little boy could read pretty well, his father every night after supper, summer and winter, made the boy read a portion of the holy scriptures, and now and then a part of some other good book. When he had continued in his profession the space of five years, king Edward died, upon whose decease queen Mary succeeded and with her all kind of superstition crept in.[34]

Rawlings White was arrested by officers acting for the Bishop of Llandaff, and was imprisoned first in Chepstow and then later in Cardiff Castle. He refused to recant his beliefs even when threatened with the direst of punishments: 'Being brought before the bishop in his chapel, he counselled him by threats and promises. But as Rawlins would in nowise recant his opinions, the bishop told him plainly, that he must proceed against him by law, and condemn him as a heretic.'[35]

It would be easy to draw from this that the Bishop of Llandaff was active in the persecution of heretics at every level, although the truth is more ambiguous. The bishop in question was of course the much-criticised Anthony Kitchin, but he seems to have gone the extra mile to save the fisherman's life. White appears to have been every bit as stubborn and inflexible as his tormentors, and Kitchin vainly tried to reason with him. Prayers were heard for White's conversion, but to no avail. Foxe's account records him as saying: 'This is like a godly bishop, and if your request be godly and right, and you pray as you ought, no doubt God will hear you; pray you, therefore, to your God, and I will pray to my God.' After the bishop and his party had finished praying, he asked Rawlins if he would now revoke. 'You find,' said the latter, 'your prayer is not granted, for I remain the same; and God will strengthen me in support of this truth.'

It is possible that White's living conditions at the castle were not uncomfortable, because following his refusal to recant he was taken to the Cockmarel, described by Foxe as a 'loathsome prison'. He languished there for three weeks before being executed. Foxe's account of this is detailed, though how much of it is poetic licence is hard to determine:

> When he came to the place, where his poor wife and children stood weeping, the sudden sight of them so pierced his heart, that the tears trickled down his face. Being come to the altar of his sacrifice, in going towards the stake, he fell down upon his knees, and kissed the ground; and in rising again, a little earth sticking on his face, he said these words, Earth unto earth, and dust unto dust; thou art my mother, and unto thee I shall return.

Foxe records that White was defiant until the end, calling the priest who officiated at his execution a hypocrite.[36] He was quickly consumed by flames, the account by Foxe not sparing any details: White's legs were consumed quickly, and he toppled over into the fire.

The horrific death of Rawlings White took place in 1555, two years into Mary's reign. It was one of the first acts in her attempt to undo the Reformation, and there are clues in White's treatment that give us insights into her motivation. His persecution began long before the officially sanctioned campaign of burnings began, so it may indicate a process of cumulative radicalisation within Mary's reign, perhaps a goal that was long-sought and only available after the repeal of the Heresy Acts in 1554.

There is abundant evidence to suggest that savage though White's execution was, there was no small support for Mary's regime in Cardiff and Glamorgan. Mary, pronounced illegitimate in 1533 and regaining her legitimacy in 1538, was seen by loyal Glamorganites as the rightful heir to Henry VIII and successor to Edward. There was little appetite for defying the Crown on political or economic grounds, and fewer reasons for defying Mary on religious grounds. With the exception of lone preachers and the occasional Puritan martyr, Cardiff was a bastion of religious conservatism. However, there may well have been some growing religious dissent, and by the early seventeenth century parishes like Roath had clear elements of religious radicalism. Kitchin was hardly a thorough inquisitor, and as it was his job to root out heretics in Glamorgan there may well have been other dissenters who were not caught. But the majority of townsfolk probably wished to carry on with their worship without interference. This does not necessarily mean that they were loyal to the Catholic faith or that they were supporters of Philip of Spain; indeed, an ample number of Cardiffians joined the Earl of Pembroke's army to help put down Wyatt's Rebellion, an uprising that was sparked by the arrival of Philip of Spain in England to marry Mary. It seems likely that the town's religious conservatism was a reaction to the speed of Edward's innovations and his attempt to impose a radical brand of Protestantism. In typical fashion, Anthony Kitchin, bending with new religious breezes, was not opposed to the changes that Mary introduced, including the resumption of ties with Rome and the laws on heresy that would cost Rawlings White his life.

Elizabeth I

In 1559, the Elizabethan Book of Common Prayer was introduced to Cardiff, and, as if to underline its gravity, it was enforced (as changes had been under Henry and Edward) by an Act of Uniformity. Kitchin appears to have been in the first wave of protesters against the book, but unsurprisingly he soon acquiesced.

Elizabeth instituted an investigation into the parlous state of Llandaff Cathedral's affairs following a protest from the Cardiff Hundreds. A full account of the pillage of the cathedral was written in the nineteenth century:

> They stripped from the shrines of Saints Dyfrig, Teilo and Docheu the costly adornments wherewith generations of benefactors had encased the memorials of the three great bishops (especially that of St Teilo), and removed the crucifixes, images, pyxes, candlesticks, censers, &c. When these had been divided among them, they took away the vestments of the clergy and the coverings of the altars, and even went so far as to pull up the paving-stones to sell for what they would fetch. So far all went smoothly enough. But at length the Protestant Bishop, Robert Holgate, heard of what was being done (he did not reside at Llandaff, and rarely came there), and he informed Thomas Cromwell, the veteran soldier whom the king had appointed Vicar General to manage the ecclesiastical affairs of the realm. Cromwell ordered the Chancellor of the diocese, John Broxholme, to claim the stuff from the Canons Residentiary on behalf of the king. The Canons thereupon produced some silver plate, and pretended it was all they had. Broxholme suspected that they had hidden the remainder, but he gave them a receipt and took the plate

to London to the Bishop, who sold it to a goldsmith in Cheapside and kept the proceeds. Broxholme was afterwards told that Henry Morgan, one of the Canons, had delivered the rest of the plate to Cromwell, to the use of the king. A quarrel happening to arise afterwards, between Morgan and the Bishop, Morgan informed Cromwell of the Bishop's share in the plunder, but no notice was taken of his complaint. Holgate, indeed, was soon afterwards made Archbishop of York. When Catholicism was restored on the accession of Mary Tudor, a petition was sent to the Queen by the inhabitants of Glamorgan, complaining of the spoliation and desecration of their cathedral, and praying that the offenders might be compelled to make restitution. The Grand Jury of the Hundred of Cardiff presented a detailed statement of the damage done, from which it appears that Henry Morgan himself had a part of the spoil. Accordingly the Queen appointed a Commission to enquire into the facts, whose finding is fully set out with the other documents in the case. Whatever was then done in the way of reparation at Llandaff was but temporary, for the final triumph of the Reformation under Elizabeth was followed by the almost total destruction of the cathedral fabric.

This lay a roofless ruin, until the revival of artistic sentiment led to its admirable restoration in the latter half of the nineteenth century.[37]

The grinding poverty of much of Cardiff was in sharp contrast to the new wealth of the Cardiff gentry, enriched by the Dissolution of the Monasteries. Owing to the profligate spending of Henry the country had a legacy of inflation and a debased currency in the second half of the sixteenth century. Rural areas were particularly badly affected by rising prices, and diocesan lands seem to have failed in the challenge to compete economically. Poor peasant farmers are generally less inclined towards productivity when they are surrounded by the effect of plunder and theft, but the overriding factor must have been the Reformation itself: it had been more than just an economic and social upheaval but a spiritual one too.

The imperialistic focus throughout the sixteenth century was the reform and control of the Marches, which were governed quite ineptly by English Marcher lords. Cardiff was the scene of an uncommon amount of violence and bloodshed, peaking in the years 1585–7 in a series of bloody street battles between gentry households. The causes were different from the lawlessness in the Marches, where the Marcher lords governed as if they were feudal monarchs in their own private fiefdoms, and the lack of a unified legal system made it an attractive area for bandits and fugitives from across England

and Wales. In Cardiff, the Lords of Glamorgan feuded openly. The problem was caused by too many nobles vying for prestige and power, rather than the absenteeism of the Marcher lords. It was often the retainers and servants of the Glamorgan gentry who died. As an example, Roger Philip, murdered in 1585, was manservant to Thomas Lewis of the Van. He was stabbed to death at a fair held in the town during a fight between his master's men and those of the Beaudripp family.

Following the religious upheavals under Henry and Edward, Elizabeth's attempts to moderate and manage religious change appear, at least in Cardiff, to have been a success. There is evidence of a relatively smooth transition to Protestantism. Whilst the Bishops of Llandaff were living in genteel poverty, owing to the struggling fortunes of their diocese, churches like St Mary's in Cardiff adapted quickly to the new faith and busily made changes. St Mary's removed its ornate stone altar and replaced it with a wooden table, in keeping with the new doctrines.

A consequence of the impoverishment of the Bishops of Llandaff was their recourse to corrupt practices in order to stay solvent. Bishops like Bleddyn, also the prebendary at York, were encouraged to be absent from their diocese, to sub-let land to already wealthy families like the Herberts and Mansels, and even to appoint their own sons to key positions within the diocese. Bleddyn was committed to improving the condition of the cathedral in any way he could, but by 1576 he was forced to conclude that it was 'derelict and destitute of pastoral care' and 'untidy and full of dirt and almost beyond repair'. Poverty was also a heavy burden for parish priests in the diocese. It was unlikely that they were living prosperous lives before the Reformation, but after it they must have borne the brunt of the diocese's financial problems during the next half-century.

The struggle for the soul of Cardiff was not over. Whilst it may be true to say that there was a passive acceptance of Protestantism, there was the ongoing issue of recusancy throughout Elizabeth's reign. In the prison records of 1595 there is an almost casual reference to the death in Cardiff gaol of James Turberville for recusancy, one of fourteen men in the space of a month who died there, indicating the poor sanitation and conditions there. It was also documented that the gaol was crowded with Catholics. Among the lists of Cardiffians being prosecuted for crimes ranging from theft to drunkenness to murder, there was also a list of names of suspected Catholic recusants who had not turned up at court. They were being prosecuted because of their

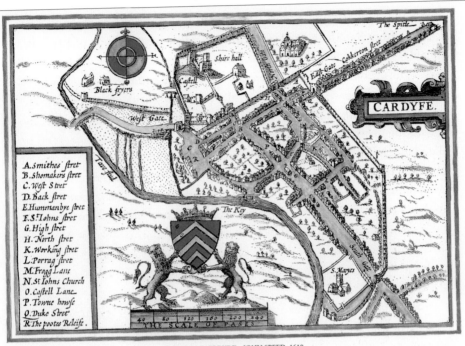

Legend:
A. Smithes stret
B. Shoemakers stret
C. West Stret
D. Back stret
E. Hummanbye stret
F. St Iohns stret
G. High stret
H. North stret
K. Working stret
L. Porrag stret
M. Frogg Lane
N. St Iohns Church
O. Castell Lane
P. Towne howse
Q. Duke Stret
R. The pootes Releife.

CARDIFF / CAERDYDD, JOHN SPEED, 1610

A map by John Speed, the most famous Jacobean cartographer of his era. His depiction of Cardiff shows a town not much changed from how it would have been during the Middle Ages; its explosive growth was yet to come.

non-attendance at Protestant church services. As late as 1616, long into the reign of James I, Nicholas Spencer died in Cardiff gaol for recusancy. In fact there seem to be precious few instances of any recusants actually surviving gaol in Cardiff. Perhaps they were facing a *de facto* death sentence or maybe they died of neglect, illness, violence or by their own hands.

In 1622 the Turberville family was in trouble again. Matthew Turberville and twenty-two others were arrested for recusancy and imprisoned, and in 1636 yet more Turbervilles were jailed, along with one William Morgan James of Llannedyrn – forty-six people in total. The date of this last is interesting as it was just on the eve of the Civil War when Charles I was accused of having Catholic sympathies, of being a recusant himself. It must be stressed that the recusants of Cardiff were a vocal minority, and it is more than likely that the majority of the people who appeared for crimes of recusancy in Cardiff's gaol and in her quarter sessions would have been from across the county. One particularly fearless priest in the diocese of Llandaff was Walter Powell, who continued to openly preach the Catholic faith long after 1558. He appears to have been ordained under Mary I and was determined to stick to the doctrine that he had initially adhered to. It was the duty of successive Bishops of Llandaff, starting with Bleddyn, to help rout out recusants and Bleddyn had at least five of his own priests put on the list by 1578. The Elizabethan government in Cardiff and elsewhere hoped that Marian priests would gradually die out, but in Llandaff this appeared to be less likely as the 1570s wore on and a new generation of young Catholic priests emerged, to be subsequently exposed by Bleddyn. At the time, he intimated that if it were not for the interference of other recusants, a list of possibly 200 names could have been produced. From this we can deduce a high possibility that Elizabeth's anti-Catholic policy had some effect in Cardiff, but it seems likely there was considerable ongoing subversion and resistance.

five

THE SEVENTEENTH CENTURY
AND THE CIVIL WAR

When discussing Cardiff at this time it is always instructive to refer to the maps of John Speed that were drawn up in 1603. They show a town that covers a narrow strip of land from the castle to the River Taff, beyond St Mary's church and out to a small dock. It was built for trade, and for most of the seventeenth century it would not have exceeded 2,000 people.

Cardiff was granted the status of a free town in 1608 by James I.[38] Henceforth the town was to be governed by a corporation, bailiffs, aldermen and burgesses. The corporation was granted the power to enforce its laws by fines and imprisonment, and to hold a court of justice – the origination of the quarter sessions. This shifted a degree of power from the Earl of Pembroke to the well-to-do merchants and craftsmen of the town, the new wealthy of the middling sort who, as a class, would decide the country's future.[39]

Historians often downplay the experience of Cardiff and Glamorgan in the Civil War, treating the struggle between Parliament and the king in Wales as something of a sideshow. However, the town's geographical position made it more and more important as the 1640s wore on. Cardiff saw more than its fair share of fighting between 1642 and 1648, and was wedged between two of the main campaigns of the war, in West Wales and at Gloucester. Cardiff people suffered the same privations of war as the rest of the country, and with the advent of the rule of Charles Gerard in 1644 the whole of south-east Wales was subjected to a violent military occupation from the very side that it had supported. The lawless and indiscriminate violence of Gerard and his men alienated the people of Cardiff and Glamorgan as effectively as they had routed their Parliamentarian opposition.

To understand why Charles I enjoyed such a healthy support from Cardiff when two of her neighbours, Gloucester and Bristol, and a sizeable proportion of the Notables of Swansea declared for Parliament, one must look closely at the legacy of the Reformation. The mid-sixteenth century was, in general terms, a very good time for the minor aristocracy of the Glamorgan area. The Dissolution of the Monasteries and the Acts of Union in the 1530s had created a class of wealthy landowners, and an ascendant gentry began to challenge the economic and social hegemony of the old aristocracy. By the time of the Civil War this new class was firmly established, and their prosperity was comparable to far wealthier English shires, such as Worcestershire. There was a concentration of wealth in Glamorgan almost ten times greater than mid-Wales.[40] Much of this wealth was generated from dairy and leatherworking, and Cardiff served the same role as a market and port for these goods as she did two centuries later for the coal industry. The new gentry consolidated their wealth and actively participated in the enclosures of commons. Frequently Oxford-educated, anglicised and economically and culturally more attuned to western England than to south-eastern Wales, they were conscious that an older Welsh landed class, living further inland, was still capable of commanding the support of the rural poor. In the Cardiff area there was a general sense of siege, and a deep feeling of insecurity marked many of their thoughts and writings. Perhaps this is why Cardiff steered a course of religious moderation in general, as they had extremists on both sides. While in England the emergence of a new gentry class saw the growth of an interconnected Puritan bloc, whose opposition to the king gradually became more coordinated and more vocal; in Cardiff the opposite occurred, with the gentry largely supportive of the king, with the exception of the incumbent aristocrat the Earl of Pembroke, who effected a transition to Puritanism after a lifetime in Charles's inner circle. If one compares Cardiff to Bristol, the difference is stark. Bristol was something of a hotbed of Puritan thinking, and later of political and religious radicalism. As Bristol was the second biggest city in Britain in the 1640s, and not much of its wealth was a result of royal charity, it was a more likely venue for printing presses, debate and politics, the right conditions to foster Puritan discontent.[41]

The new structure of local government that encompassed Cardiff and created a shire out of Glamorgan, anglicising local government, also had its benefits when looked at from the perspective of this newly ascendant class. Older feudal structures that were peculiar to the Marches and the Principality were swept away, and with them the powers of an older class. While a new mercantile Puritan class began to amass wealth, influence and political savvy at the end of the sixteenth and beginning of the seventeenth centuries in towns such as Bristol and London, in towns such as Cardiff a new agrarian class of upper middling sorts began to increase its power in towns like Cardiff. The former class began to see itself increasingly as hampered and inconvenienced by the arbitrary power of kings, whereas the latter flourished as a result of it. They both had their reasons for supporting the Reformation, but in the case of Cardiff the ruling elite benefited financially from it.

By the time of the Civil War only the Marquess of Worcester and the Turberville family were still openly Catholic amongst the nobility, and the Prices of Gellihir and the Carnes are the only two supposed Puritan families. The marquess opened a Catholic college at Cwm in 1622, and in the following decades something of a small Catholic revival began in rural Monmouthshire, thus adding to a feeling by moderate Protestants in Glamorgan that they were vulnerable to the predations of popery.

Another reason for Royalist support in the region relates to an accident of geography, and the vulnerability of Cardiff midway up the Bristol Channel. Piracy was a constant threat, as Cardiff and Glamorgan were one of the most remote, inaccessible and most poorly defended parts of the British Isles during the seventeenth century. Britain had a woefully insufficient naval presence; indeed, the only really substantial expansion in shipbuilding took place in the 1650s when Cromwell launched his quasi-messianic imperial crusade against Spain. Ever since Thomas Strafford's intimations that an army of Catholics from Ireland might be imported to 'level the nation', South Walians from Pembroke to Cardiff had feared the arrival of ungodly savages on their Western shore. Therefore the imposition of ship money, the illegal tax that was in some part meant to raise money for a new fleet, was quite well received in Cardiff. In reality it was plugging holes in Charles's leaky finances and rebranding the Stuart dynasty as something more akin to the glories of the *Roi du Soleil* across the Channel. Charles's obsession with trying to create an image of grandeur was perhaps the uptight king's way of distancing himself from his rather vulgar and promiscuous (yet hugely popular) father, and it earned him at least one high-profile opponent in Cardiff. Philip Herbert, 4th Earl of Pembroke and Montgomery and Baron of Cardiff and Shurland, was the most unlikely Parliamentarian in 1642, and his story sheds light on the failings of his king.

As a young man Philip came to the attention of Charles's father James I. Much has been written about James's favourites, and the nature of James's patronage is perhaps less important here than its extent. Unlike his son, James was an outgoing and gregarious man who was never happier than in the company of his nobles, hunting and hawking. Philip seems to have had a natural aptitude for such pursuits, and during James's rule was inducted into the innermost circle, rubbing shoulders with James's beloved Buckingham. James bestowed upon Philip the honour of Baron of Cardiff and Shurland in 1605, giving him ownership of Cardiff Castle. He also took Philip's side in disputes that occurred periodically with other members of James's inner circle; it seems likely that Philip had a fiery temper. In 1635, a decade into Charles's reign, Philip and his family were painted by none other than the Dutch master van Dyke, an indication of Philip's privileged position.

The relationship between Charles and Philip was for the most part amicable: both were patrons of the arts and both had similar aesthetic tastes. Philip was godfather to the Duke of Buckingham's son, and whilst the duke was widely loathed across Britain, in Parliament and among the nobility he still featured as the king's favourite. The question that divided the two men, however, was religion. Initially Philip was part of the embassy of Henrietta Maria, Charles's French-Catholic wife, and had accepted her Papist faith even though it had scandalised England. Throughout the 1630s he appears to have become more enamoured with Puritanism, and his sympathies seemed to lie with the Scots in 1639 when he was sent to negotiate an end to the first Bishops' War. The manner in which Charles glorified himself and his court doesn't seem to have pleased Philip, who perhaps looked upon the king as becoming increasingly Catholic in taste. Evidence of this was plentiful as Charles grew increasingly autocratic, with the prorogation of Parliament, the promotion of William Laud and the imposition of the Book of Common Prayer on the Scots. It was Charles who finally abandoned Philip, after the latter voted for the Bill of Attainder against Strafford, effectively forcing the king to kill his right-hand man. For this there was no forgiveness.

The fact that the largest landowner in Wales and the keeper of Cardiff Castle raised his standard for Parliament seems to have had little if no effect on the locals. Parliamentary support was marginal even after the earl's defection, and the net result was the end of any political influence for him in Wales.

By the start of the Civil War, Puritanism had not made great inroads into Glamorgan or Cardiff. The vicar of St Mary's church, William Erbury, formerly of Roath, was perhaps an exception to this rule. He was accused of being a Seeker and was ejected from the Church in 1638 by the Bishop of Llandaff. Contemporary accounts describe Erbury simply as a Baptist, and indeed the terms Seeker, Ranter, Anabaptist and Leveller should be treated with caution as none of these movements were unified theological or political associations.

The Levellers of the 1640s are seen as the cutting edge of British radicalism, but in some ways their views were comparatively tame compared with the Seekers, who can be summed up as turning basic Biblical precepts upon their heads. Their doctrines suggested that not only was organised religion the greatest barrier between man and God, but that it was entirely possible that God himself was a fiction.

The bishop who admonished Erbury was William Murray, previously the provost at Eton and a friend of William Laud. His closeness to Laud is probably the reason for his appointment at Llandaff in 1627, right at the start of Charles' reign. It is unclear whether the rise of Puritanism in Cardiff and the surrounding areas was a backlash against Laud's innovations or part of a trend that was sweeping South Wales.

One possible reason for the support amongst wealthy Cardiff and Glamorgan gentry for religious non-conformism was a siege mentality. The Marquess of Worcester was a fanatical Royalist and Catholic, and he dominated Monmouthshire and the Marches as far as his stronghold at Raglan. There was a constant fear of a Catholic Irish invasion and a suspicion that Catholicism was lurking in every direction. One practical reason for resisting Catholicism was the fear that the well-to-do might one day have to return lands to the Church. Equally, many were not completely sure about the Puritans either: their talk about not paying tithes could easily translate in the minds of the rural poor into not paying rents. It is likely that the wealthy families of Cardiff supported Puritanism in its demands for a root and branch purge of all traces of Catholicism, but anything more libertarian than that would not have been acceptable. Even so, in 1642 the vast majority still declared for the king.

In Cardiff on the eve of the Civil War there was a general reaction against Laudianism, evident in the demands for simplified church services, less ritual and a lack of adornment in churches, in direct conflict with the archbishop's wishes. This can be seen as far back as the 1580s, with prosecutions in Cardiff for vagrancy, working or playing sports on a Sunday, and even fights occurring at funerals as more ardent Protestants objected to supposed popery in sermons as people buried their dead.

It has been argued that Parliament had a vested interest in isolating Wales from the conflict. Forces for the king could be recruited from the relatively loyal Glamorgan gentry, and the route from Pembroke to Bristol was a vital corridor for moving troops from Ireland. It is easy to see why Cardiff increased in strategic importance as the king's plight worsened. Ironically, it was the issue of troops from Ireland that may have dealt Charles a body blow from which he could not recover.[42]

At the outbreak of hostilities in 1642, Cardiff was seized by Royalist forces. The stewards of the castle handed it over to the Marquess of Hertford, the king's man, without a shot being fired. When Charles I paid his first and only visit to Cardiff in 1645 he was a desperate man, and the town was the scene for one of his final disappointments. Marston Moor and Naseby had finally broken the king's armies, the illustrious Prince Rupert had failed the king at last and the Scots were intervening on Parliament's side. Charles appealed for men, money and goodwill from the great families of South Wales, but his appeals largely fell on deaf ears. Cardiff had been a Royalist bastion throughout the Civil War, and for Charles to be openly spurned by its people in his hour of greatest need tells us a great deal about the factors that had an impact on Royalist support.

An account of Charles's visit by Richard Symonds sheds a great deal of light on attitudes towards the king in Cardiff by the end of the war. Opposing the king was the 'Peaceable Army', a militia that had formed to protect itself from Gerard, whose rule had lasted little over six months but had been catastrophic for the king in terms of support. The other catastrophe was the discovery by the Parliamentarians of documents that revealed a plan to bring Irish Catholic soldiers to England. There was no doubt as to the route they would take: through Cardiff. Exaggerated news of atrocities in Ireland led ordinary Cardiffians to dread what might be in store for them. Whether or not this plan was a serious part of the king's design is debatable, but the revelations caused immense damage to the king's reputation.

The Royalist propaganda sheet, the *Mercurius Civicus*, reported: 'The King met 600 men in Glamorgan ... They demanded that the Papists be removed from the country ... and a governor and garrison of their own put in ... the removal of the £7,000 demand from Colonel Gerard ... The King left Cardiff that night ... Gerard was put out of command in Wales, it being the country's demand.' Symonds confirms this in his diaries. Charles negotiated in Cardiff for a day and then retired to Cefn On, where he finally acceded to the requests of the Peaceable Army. Despite these concessions, and despite the fact that Gerard had been sent to fight in England even before the meetings had taken place, the king struggled to find Welshmen willing to fight in his army. With the expertise in warfare of Gerard lost, it wasn't long before the Royalists were defeated. Shortly after the king left for North Wales, Cardiff fell to Parliament for the last time.

The Battle of St Fagans

The ending of the first Civil War was in no way the end of Cardiff's struggles. In fact it was the scene of one of the most decisive battles to be fought on Welsh soil. At the end of the first Civil War, when Jacob Astley, 1st Baron Astley of Reading, surrendered to Parliamentary generals, he said: 'Well, boys, you have done your work, now you may go and play – if you don't fall out among yourselves.'[43] He had rather astutely read the dynamics within the coalition that was arrayed against the king and there were already tensions that the king would try to exploit in 1648, tensions that led to the Battle of St Fagans. The scale of this battle, and the importance of its outcome to Parliament, was confirmed by a special day of thanksgiving being designated to it after Parliament's victory.

There was a growing anger within the New Model Army from 1647 onwards about the proposed disbanding of regiments by Parliament. Many suspected that the cash-strapped Parliament would try to dispense with the army without paying its men the arrears they were owed. There was also a fear that the war-weary troops might be sent to Ireland, that acts of brutality they committed during the war might not be pardoned and that widows would not be adequately compensated. December 1647 saw these fears realised when it was announced that all soldiers who had enlisted after August 1647 were to be dismissed without pay, and all those who had joined after 1644 would be dismissed with just two months' pay. When angry and disillusioned Parliamentary troops under John Poyer, the military governor of Pembroke for the Parliamentarians, and Colonel Rice Powell declared for the king in April 1648 and marched into Glamorgan, the landed families in the Vale and the well-to-do of Cardiff did not hesitate in declaring for Charles also. In a joint statement Poyer and Powell wrote: 'A few men ... have already gotten too much power into their hands, and want to disband us ... so they can enslave the people ... and establish taxes. We promise to protect the people from injury and maintain the Protestant religion ... as established by the law in this land. We therefore crave the assistance of the whole kingdom.'[44]

Whilst they had protested to the king in 1645, and he had lost a lot of support owing to the cruelties of Gerard, it was likely that they finally rejected the king out of pure desperation. For the rest of the Civil War Major-General Rowland Laugharne, Parliament's commander in South Wales, did not have an easy time of it, and was forced to repel several attempts to take Cardiff Castle back for the king.

In 1647 Laugharne was arrested by Parliament due to suspicions that he might be involved in Royalist plots. He was placed in custody and then on parole, which he fled. He tricked his Parliamentary inquisitors by declaring with all earnestness that he backed Parliament, before fleeing to lead the king's men at St Fagans. This duplicity earned him a death sentence after the end of the rebellion. It appears that his loyalty to his men led him to declare for the king.[45]

The threat to Parliament began when Poyer and Powell refused to disband their regiments when instructed to do so, and subsequently seized Pembroke Castle. Parliamentarian Colonel Robert Overton tried and failed to retake Pembroke, and in disarray fell back to Cardiff. Parliamentary officer Colonel Thomas Horton raised a brigade at Neath and marched to join Overton, seizing Brecon on the way. By this time a narrow corridor of land from Brecon in the north down to Cardiff and St Fagans in the south were the only areas that were controlled by Parliament; Chepstow to the east had also declared for the king. Poyer and Powell were aware that they were in a race against time. They had to crush Horton's force and take Cardiff Castle before Cromwell marched on Wales, and hoped that simultaneous uprisings in England and the intervention of the Scots would overwhelm Parliament. Their hopes were to be dashed, however, as uprisings across the kingdom were defeated one by one.

Horton placed his headquarters at St Fagans, blocking the route to Cardiff and controlling bridges across the Ely and the Taff. He was no stranger to war, having fought at the Battle of Naseby. Although he had 2,700 horse and foot, and 750 local troops (200 of which were borrowed from Cardiff Castle's garrison), Horton faced nearly 11,000 men under the command of Laugharne and was well aware of the seeming hopelessness of his situation. He wrote in a report to Parliament after the battle: 'I think it now reasonable to make known to you the straits we were in and the difficulties which composed about, we having a potent enemy lying within two miles upon much advantage of ground. Before us, high mountains, near us on the left Chepstow taken and Monmouthshire beginning to rise in our rear, besides our great want of provisions and long hard duty ...'[46] Cavalry officer John Okey, who served under Horton, wrote after the battle: 'Hither until today I could give no account of our Welsh expedition. we have had so many obstructors through unseasonable weather, and rugged ways, want of necessities and other inconveniences, that we may well say, except the lord had been with us, the armie may well have been swallowed up quick.'[47]

Horton held fast, however, despite exchanging letters with Laugharne in which each challenged the legitimacy of the other. Horton's cavalry scouts found Laugharne's army quickly at St Nicholas, marching for Cardiff Castle, and Laugharne's weaknesses must have been glaringly apparent. He had few cavalry and at least half of his men were clubmen. This was a generic term that described a number of farmers' militias that had sprung up across the country to protect local communities against the depredations of both sides. Most had never seen battle or been trained in weapons drill. Many were probably members of the Peaceable Army that had negotiated with Charles I.

Laugharne might well have opted for a war of attrition to wear down the smaller force or even starve them out, but news of Cromwell's march forced his hand. He threw his men into battle on 8 May 1648. Early that morning the main body of Laugharne's force was sighted at Pentrebane, and they were met by 3,000 cavalry. Quite early in the battle, Horton was surrounded by two pincers of the Royalist army and quickly lost his headquarters to Royalist cavalry. He resisted the temptation to fall back to Cardiff, but the inexperience of a large portion of his army was clear by the way in which they scattered under relentless cavalry charges, a tactic that gave Horton his only advantage. Eventually an encircling manoeuvre by Okey and Barton trapped the Royalist army, whose only choice was to retreat in disarray.

In a report to Fairfax after the battle Horton wrote:

On Monday morning ... the enemy advanced towards us ... we took the best ground ... About sixty men on horses charged once, but we beat them back, and after that none of the men on horses appeared again ... The enemy tell us they were 8,000. We had a sharp dispute with them for about two hours. Our men on horses charged the enemy, who were wholly routed ... Many of the enemy were slain ... We have taken 3,000 prisoners ... we have not lost many soldiers and not one of our officers.[48]

It was a remarkable success for the Parliamentarians, and a disaster for the king's cause. His duplicity and the failure of the revolt sealed his fate, and he was executed in 1649. Many of the 3,000 men taken prisoner at the battle were kept at Llandaff Cathedral, while 4,000 clubmen were sent home after swearing never to raise arms against Parliament again. Of the officers, 260 bachelors were sent to the new colony of Barbados to work out the rest of their lives as slaves. Laugharne was tried by a court martial and found guilty of treason, along with Poyer. It was decided that only one of them would be executed, and after drawing lots Laugharne was spared.

The second Civil War proved beyond a shadow of a doubt to Parliament that the king was untrustworthy, and it proved to the New Model Army that the king was prepared to ignore God's verdict in the first Civil War. In order for there to be a resolution to the wars that had torn the kingdom apart, the king had to die. Cardiff's MP, Algernon Sidney, a veteran of Marston Moor and cavalryman with the New Model Army, could not bring himself to sign the death warrant for the king: 'First, the King could be tried by noe court; secondly, that noe man could be tried by that court. This being alleged in vaine, and Cromwell using these formall words (I tell you, wee will cut off his head with the crowne upon it) I ... immediately went out of the room, and never returned.' He later recanted these views, saying that the execution

Llandaff Cathedral. The cathedral, standing as one of the major repositories of Cardiff and Wales' collective cultural and national memory, has survived through most of the country's most momentous events.

was 'the justest and bravest act ... that ever was done in England, or anywhere'.[49]

Following the Peaceable Army's rejection of the king, which indirectly served his enemies, Parliament was not about to let the people of Cardiff have freedom to reject the law. The degree of Sidney's success in pacifying the borough is unclear, and when rebellion broke out in 1648 he was adventuring in Ireland, returning only as the king went on trial. Sidney sat on Glamorgan's assessment and militia commissions until 1652, and extended his influence across Glamorgan on behalf of Parliament and later the Commonwealth – though he steadily came to view Cromwell as a tyrant.

The Post Civil War Era

The Rump Parliament and Protectorate were for the most part hugely unpopular across Wales, and Cardiff was no exception. Cromwell's reforms were seen as yet more interference in worship, and his increasingly authoritarian intrusions into the lives of ordinary people were resented.

Cardiff MP Algernon Sidney proved himself to be far from pliant. He opposed the purge of moderates by Colonel Pride in 1648, which led to the radicalisation of Parliament. When Cromwell finally expelled the remainder of the Rump Parliament, Sidney refused to be moved, and had to be carried out of the Commons. The stance that he took did not prevent the wealthier families of Cardiff from appealing directly to the new regime to intercede in personal disputes. Cromwell's son Richard, whose brief and inglorious stint as Lord Protector after his father's death, speeded up the restoration of the monarchy, interceded in the case of William Bond of Llantrisant, who submitted a bill against Dame Margaret Kemeys of Cefn Mably, widow of the late sheriff of Glamorgan, Sir Charles Kemeys. Cromwell found in favour of Bond.

In 1660 the first fully contested election in Cardiff since 1536 took place, and the winner was Bussy Mansel, scion of the wealthy and powerful Mansel family. He had been an ardent Parliamentarian during the war, commander-in-chief of military forces in Glamorgan in 1645 and a favourite of Sir Thomas Fairfax. His actions indicate that there was great capacity for compromise in the Glamorgan gentry, as he made his peace with the Stuart dynasty and served as the MP until 1661, serving again in 1681.

The story of Christopher Love, a Presbyterian minister and native of Cardiff, sheds a great deal of light on life in interregnum Britain. Love was converted to Puritanism by William Erbury in Roath at the age of 14, much to the consternation of his father, who sent him away to be apprenticed in London. This seems to have been a rash choice, as the London apprentice boys were notorious for their Puritanical instincts. Erbury and Love's mother conspired to have the boy taught at New Inn College, Oxford, where he completed his degree but refused to endorse Archbishop Laud's Innovations in 1640. At the outbreak of war Love declared for Parliament and fulminated strongly against the king's misdeeds. But as the revolution took a leftward course, he came to despise the rampant sectarianism of the army. His outspoken criticisms of the new republic were not well received. He was jailed twice for his outspoken sermons, but by 1644 he had been acquitted of treason and was serving as a chaplain to the Parliamentary regiment of Sir John Venn at Windsor. It was also in 1644 that he was ordained into the Presbyterian faith, an act that would have made him deeply suspect to Cromwell. When the Scots joined the fight against the king that year, on the understanding that Presbyterianism would become the officially recognised religion of Scotland and England after the war, many moderates in Parliament, dubbed the Peace Party, accepted this and were converted. Radicals like Cromwell were adamant that a godly kingdom would be created after the war, nothing to do with Presbyterianism and the Scots.

Following the victory over the king, Cromwell had to defeat the Levellers, who were looking for greater social change and justice for the poor, and then he turned his attention to old Presbyterians like Love. Love was arraigned for high treason in March 1650, and accused of trying to 'stir up a new and bloody war and to raise insurrections seditions and rebellions in this nation'. The case against him rested on letters from himself to the exiled former Queen Henrietta Maria in France, and meetings he held at his London home with Scots allied to Charles II. These meetings allegedly discussed the raising of money for arms amongst English Presbyterians. In June 1652, Love was charged with plotting against the government and conspiring to revive the Stuart cause. He was hanged for treason in 1652. During a two-hour address from the gallows he cryptically warned his hearers against mistaking old devils for new gods.[50] This perhaps related to the new political and religious settlement that the country had adopted. Clearly many of the dreams fostered by more radical actors in the Civil Wars had been dashed by the 1650s: Cromwell had been socially conservative and not interested in the Levellers at all, but he'd actually been a religious radical, hence his opposition to Presbyterianism. Perhaps Love was implying that there was nothing new or noble in Puritanism, that it was an old devil, the wickedness of a bygone era repackaged as something new. Love's death had an importance for the Rump Parliament. His execution ended clerical resistance to the new republic, and given the sectarian nature of seventeenth-century England and Wales this was of no small significance.

Religious war, rebellion and intrigue dominated the rest of the seventeenth century, and Cardiff was the scene of further bloodshed. The violence of the post-Reformation period continued, as memories of the savage reign of Queen Mary and fears about Catholic Ireland dominated public consciousness. In Cardiff the ghost of Rawlings White still exercised a great deal of power.

One case from the Cardiff Sessions reminds us of the degree of suspicion that still surrounded religious freedom:

> The Jurors of our Lord the King upon their oath present that William Morgan, formerly of Neath ... gentleman, being an impious, profane and irreligious person, and not having the fear of God in his heart, but moved and seduced by the

instigation of the devil and designing and intending to scandalize and vilify the true Christian religion within this realm of England received and publicly professed, as also to blaspheme the wisdom and majesty of Almighty God, the Creator of heaven and of this world, and to subvert and withdraw the subjects of our said Lord the King from the Christian faith, as also to vilify and mock the holy scriptures, on the 31st day of December in the eleventh year of the reign, &c., at Neath aforesaid, in the presence and hearing of divers of the liege subjects of our said Lord the King that now is, who well understood the English tongue, said and uttered these false, impious, blasphemous and heretical English words of and concerning the creation of this world and the holy scriptures: This world was not made by God, but was made before there was a God; nor do I believe the Scripture (meaning the holy scriptures of the old and new Testament) which is an old booke; for we are not to believe old books. And Moses (meaning Moyses, a great prophet named in the holy scriptures) was either a fool or a liar, and he made the scripture, which is but a fable, to the grievous scandal of the profession of the true Christian religion and the great dishonour and displeasure of Almighty God, and to the great scorn and contempt of the holy scriptures. In contempt of our said Lord the King that now is, his laws, &c., &c.[51]

This is a fascinating insight into the religious and philosophical radicalism in Cardiff at this time. Whilst it is impossible to say how many people Morgan influenced, and how many people agreed with him, the fact that he was saying such things openly is remarkable.

Following the brief and unsuccessful rule of Cromwell's son Richard, the Stuart dynasty was restored to power in 1660. Philip Herbert, 4th Earl of Pembroke, had died in 1650 and was succeeded by his son, also Philip, and an unbroken line of Herberts dominated Cardiff until the end of the century. Throughout that time religious strife continued to play a part in the town's story, particularly with regard to the rise of the Quakers as a religious presence in Cardiff. George Fox, founder of the Quaker movement, is thought to have preached in Cardiff in 1653, before the restoration, and though initially Cromwell was well disposed towards this new evangelical movement, the same prejudices towards radical and non-conformist faiths that had been in evidence in the late 1640s began to emerge. Magistrates started to see the Quakers as a risk to public order, as their message was deeply anarchic. Fox's spiritual awakening in 1647 had convinced him that all worldly authority, kings, soldiers or priests, was profoundly corrupting, and the only true spirituality could be found within one's own conscience. This message was always going to be far more radical than Cardiff's authorities were comfortable with. Fox had several stretches in prison across England, but whether or not he was prosecuted in Cardiff is unclear, though it is not hard to imagine him winding up in the Cockmarel for his troubles. Following the restoration of Charles II, statements about non-acceptance of the monarch's earthly authority were looked upon as verging on treason, and certainly a refusal to accept royal supremacy. It was for this reason that in 1661 one of the first Quaker churches in Cardiff was broken up.

The Quakers, ardent pacifists who refused to recognise the right of any man or woman, no matter their status, to wage war, were often accused of having poor manners. The records of Cardiff Castle show that one Quaker was thrown in jail for referring to Cardiff ministers as 'Dumb Dogs' in September 1652. There was a powerful subtext to this apparently impolite jibe. In much of Fox's writings on the scriptures he aluded to the debased nature of dogs or swine in the gospels, and for a Quaker, who would have read everything Fox had written, to make such comparisons is a direct declaration to the clergy that they are debased and ungodly, or unable to know God's will. The repression of Quakers occurred sporadically nationwide, but evidence that they thrived as a community in Cardiff can be seen in the creation of a Quaker burial ground outside the town's South Gate.

Throughout the rest of the seventeenth century anti-Catholic feelings still ran high. One factor that is more likely than any other to have ignited fear and hatred in Cardiff was the decision by Charles II's brother, James, Duke of York, to convert to Catholicism. As Charles aged and failed to produce an heir, many people realised that a Catholic monarch might be restored to the throne. Pro-Catholic sentiments carried implied threats as far as people in post-Reformation England and Wales were concerned: any king who was too pro-Catholic and too pro-French might invite an army of occupation to reignite the flames of counter-Reformation. Even before the Glorious Revolution, the crisis brought about following the birth of James's Catholic heir, tensions in many parts of the country, and clearly in Cardiff, were reaching deadly proportions. The brutal execution of Philip Evans in the Gallows Field, now the top of City Road, largely as a result of mob hysteria, underlines how volatile anti-Catholic sentiment was during the seventeenth century. The country was already in a fervent state of anti-Catholic paranoia following a plot by Titus Oates to assassinate the king and restore Catholicism to the country. Whilst this plot may have been fantasy on the part of Oates, it had dire consequences for Philip Evans.

Evans was born in Monmouth, and became a Jesuit at St Omer in France. He was ordained as a priest in 1675 and ministered to Catholics in South Wales for four years. As we saw, Monmouth remained a bastion of recusant Catholicism during the Civil War, and Cardiffians and Glamorganites in general remained profoundly suspicious of the town. There was every reason to suspect a Catholic priest who hailed from Monmouth. Evans was swept up in a frenzy of suspicion, fear and hatred after the discovery of the Oates plot, and was taken to Cardiff and imprisoned there. Where did this explosion of fear and suspicion come from? It is possible that the stresses and strains of the new economy, shifting from predictable patterns of agrarian life to the more erratic structures of trade and finance, were taking a huge toll on ordinary Cardiffians. It is interesting to note that the execution of Evans coincides with the witch hunts that were taking place across England. Wales was largely spared witch trials, but perhaps this is because the suspicions and paranoia of a people who were starting to face major upheavals in their life found a different outlet. Evans and another priest, John Lloyd, were tried in Cardiff in 1679; the argument that they had been involved in the Oates plot had been quietly dropped by this time. Even Oates avoided the death penalty when it emerged that there was very little plot to speak of. The two men were convicted of being priests, however, as Catholicism was still banned in Wales at this point, part of the legacy of Cromwell. The sentence, that the two men should be hanged, drawn and quartered, was exceptionally savage, suggesting that other fears were motivating the judges. A bounty of £200 had been raised for the arrest of the two men, an absolutely enormous sum for the times, and far greater than any other bounty raised in South Wales for a century. It appears that Cardiff's magistrates were approaching the issue of Catholic recusancy in Wales with a level of near-hysteria. The trial rested on the flimsiest of testimonies: two women, who may well have been bribed or intimidated, claimed that they had seen the priests giving mass. There were no other witnesses.

The men were hanged, drawn and quartered at Gallows Field on 22 July. They were both canonised by the Pope in 1970.[52]

The Bishop of Llandaff who was appointed in the year in which Evans and Lloyd died was William Beaw, one of the more colourful incumbents of the office in the seventeenth century. He was an avowed Royalist throughout the war and seems to have had a rapid series of promotions in the field. He was elected bishop in 1679, following time as a mercenary to Czar Alexei of Muscovy and diplomat for Charles II in Copenhagen. Some accounts say that Beaw was helped to office by the notorious Restoration rake and libertine John Wilmot, Earl of Rochester, who was a friend of his and had the ear of the king. It is more likely that it was the influence of Wilmot's less decadent son, following the death of his father, that counted.

In Beaw's memoirs important details about the condition of the diocese emerge. In the 1680s and '90s Llandaff was one of the poorest dioceses in Wales or England. During the latter half of the seventeenth century there was also a general agricultural depression, which hit poor farming communities especially hard. Beaw wrote:

> When afterwards I went to my diocese, I there lived not according to my Revenue, but answerable to my Dignity. I was free in my housekeeping; I observed no days of fasting or retiring (though I fasted myself) for entertainment some who so would. The meanest Vicar or Curate never went away hungry, if he came before, or at, mealtime. Bread and Beer were freely distributed at my doors every day. My Gates stood open to all comers and there were not a few that come for provision of that kind.

Perhaps a more concrete indication of the poverty of the era was the disrepair into which Llandaff Cathedral and Mathern Palace fell. Mathern was the traditional estate of the Bishops of Llandaff, near Chepstow, and had been since King Meurig had gifted it to them in the seventh century. From the early eighteenth century to 1821, Mathern Palace was uninhabitable, and much of the blame for this is traditionally heaped upon Beaw's head. However, there are accounts that Mathern was occupied twelve years after Beaw's death in 1717. Perhaps a more likely culprit for the decline of the cathedral and the palace is Shute Barrington, bishop from 1769.

William Lloyd, Bishop of Llandaff from 1675, was at the heart of the controversy generated by James II following the king's attempts to relax anti-Catholic penal laws in Wales and England. Seven bishops signed a letter opposing the King's Declaration of Indulgence issued in 1688. This declaration was one of the final nails in the king's coffin, one that led anti-Catholics across Wales and England to declare for William of Orange. It allowed Catholics the right to worship according to their own conscience, in their own homes, and it took away the requirement to declare an oath of loyalty to the Protestant faith before taking a job in public service. Seven of Wales and England's leading bishops, including the Bishop of St Asaph, signed the letter. Lloyd made his intention to sign it clear, although he missed the opportunity to do so, and he helped to prepare the legal defences for the bishops who were to stand trial in London.

There is an abundance of detail about life in Restoration-era Cardiff in records collated in 1666. A detailed census, or inquest of survey as it was known, shows us that the town's wards were teeming with people. One gains the distinct impression that by the end of the century the population of Cardiff was increasing again. Pressure on land, caused by the rise in population and a return to prosperity, became a burning issue in the coming century, alongside an increase in disputes over land ownership. This is revealed in the records: 'And that the said corporation of the said town are to have forever free common pasture, furze and turf upon the commons near the said town, called the Great Heath and the Little Heath … And that adjacent parishes of Roath, Llanishen, Whitchurch and other Parishes do daily intrude on the said liberty of the commons pasture for many years past, to the great wrong and detriment of the said corporation.' In another example, Thomas Lewis of Llanishen did the town a 'great wrong' by enclosing 60 acres of land upon the Great Heath, where he and his son had illegally built several cottages and other buildings. As punishment they were to be 'utterly disenfranchised of their liberties'. Collective action to preserve common grazing rights and common ownership of heathland was clearly a powerful force in Cardiff, though the outcome of the case against Lewis is not listed; whether he and his son relinquished their annexed land is unknown. Land enclosure was an issue largely avoided by Cardiff in the sixteenth century, but tensions like this inevitably made it more likely in the seventeenth century.

Another legal matter dealt with by the town council was what to do with the ill-gotten gains of 'waifs, strays and felons'. Their 'goods, treasure trove and goods of persons outlawed and fugitive' were to be made the property of the Lord of Cardiff, and this was to be enforced by the town's bailiffs.

Henry Morgan

The story of Henry Morgan is intimately connected with the birth of the British Empire. The man who was known as the 'Sword Of England' and in West Indian sea shanties as a 'bloody buccaneer' was one of the first great Welsh pirates, but also a loyal servant of the Commonwealth and later the Crown.

Morgan was born in Llanrumney, a manor that was then part of Monmouthshire, now a suburb of Cardiff. There are two alternate stories of his life, one more heavily mythologised than the other. The first version, which reads a bit like *Treasure Island*, states that Morgan was sold into slavery by his parents, abducted whilst in Bristol or voluntarily became an indentured servant. None of these was uncommon and there were certainly white slaves in the Caribbean before there were black. Morgan surfaced in Barbados, setting sail from there in 1655 and gaining his freedom in 1662. An alternate theory is far less romantic but more plausible. At the height of his puritanical zeal, when ideas such as sending an army to destroy Rome were being mooted, Oliver Cromwell decided to attack Catholicism on the high seas. His Western Design was a plan to seize a Spanish island in the Caribbean and use it as a base from which to attack Spanish ships, cut off Spain from her South American colonies, weaken a Catholic grip over the New World and weaken the Spanish crown at home. It seems plausible that Morgan was an officer on this expedition. His family had a tradition of military service to the crown: one of his ancestors, Thomas Morgan, had fought overseas for Queen Elizabeth and another, Sir Charles Morgan, had been a privy councillor to Charles I. One branch of the Morgan family held Tredegar House, which stands on the outskirts of Newport; this does not seem like a dynasty that would sell one of its own into servitude. Likewise, those who agreed to work as indentured servants were usually the vagrant poor, thrown off the land by enclosure and struggling to survive. If the young officer story is more plausible, then the campaign Morgan volunteered for was a fiasco.

The expedition to the West Indies was originally designed to capture Hispaniola, the island currently divided between Haiti and the Dominican Republic. A huge fleet sailed over 7,000 men to the island, but when they landed the men were poorly supplied and poorly led, and diseases like malaria claimed far more lives than the Spanish cannon. They withdrew and occupied Jamaica instead, a far simpler task but not what Cromwell had wanted. Henry Morgan made Jamaica his home, and if the accounts of early historians of Jamaica are to be relied upon, he appears to have been to the Caribbean what Robert Clive was to India, a patient, cunning and ambitious man who saw a way to make himself extremely wealthy and inadvertently laid the foundations of the British Empire. Both men used the military power of the crown for private ends, and that same power also seems to have used Morgan when it saw fit. Unlike the other colonisers and military adventurers who were, according to Charles Leslie, author of *A New and Exact History of Jamaica* in 1710, 'debauched' and 'reduced to the lowest shifts by their lavish expenses', Morgan began to save his money. This also suggests that he had been an army officer because he had an income to save. He lived in modest circumstances, bought his first ship, and was involved in a legal form of piracy. This was exactly what Cromwell had hoped for, that raiders would sail across the Caribbean and attack Spanish ports. Piracy had become official government policy, and Henry Morgan of Llanrumney was its greatest pioneer. He profited immensely from these raids. When an official peace was declared in 1658, most privateers from both sides saw fit to ignore it, as piracy was too lucrative.

Henry Morgan's fame spread, and he started to be mentioned back home. With the restoration of Charles II, one of Henry's royalist relatives, his uncle, Edward Morgan, was made lieutenant-governor of Jamaica as a reward for his support. This is another indicator that Henry Morgan was from wealthy stock. Henry married his cousin, Mary Elizabeth, in 1666, by which time he was clearly at the heart of Jamaica's colonial government.

By 1662 Jamaica existed in a state of near-siege, an English outpost surrounded by Spanish Florida, Cuba, Hispaniola and Mexico. Only far-off Barbados could offer any support. After a raid on Santiago in Cuba in 1659, which ended with the sacking of the town and the capturing of the governor, the English were determined to attack again. They did so in 1662, with Morgan as captain of his own ship. They successfully sacked Santiago's fortress with few losses, and the following year raided the Spanish Main, or Mexico. In 1665 an even more ambitious raid was carried out by Morgan, along with another Welsh captain, John Morris. This took Morgan to Mexico, Honduras, Granada and Nicaragua. The (flimsy) legal justification for Morgan's actions was a letter of commission signed by Charles II that gave privateers the right, for a certain period of time, to carry out actions against Spain and profit from it, as long as the Crown saw its share. The following year Morgan was made a vice-admiral, largely because of the previous year's expedition, and over time he seems to have become less of a buccaneer and more of a colonialist, creating an English Caribbean. It was a grand vision: to export an Anglo-Welsh model of civilisation. Morgan eventually became governor of Jamaica, and eventually banned privateering outright. In 1680 he passed an edict that privateers would be hanged if they continued to raid Spanish ships and ports; the cost of constant war with Spain was taking its toll. This theme seems to have dominated the history of the British Empire: the cost of defending imperial possessions very often outweighed the profits that could be accrued from them. Jamaica was struggling with huge debts, and the future of the colony could only be guaranteed by trade, not plunder.

In later life Morgan became a rum-drinking alcoholic, suffering from cirrhosis of the liver and probably tuberculosis. In his dying years he still courted controversy, launching a libel action against Johan Esquemeling, one of his crew, who had written a biographical account of his life entitled *A History of the Buccaneers*. Morgan was very sensitive about his origins or exploits, and his lawyers set out to prove that Esquemeling was a liar. Eventually Morgan was awarded £200. This was a legal precedent, the notion that you could be awarded money in compensation for false or damaging claims that were published about you had never been seen in English law before.

Within three years, in August 1688, Morgan died aged 53. He was buried with full military honours and a cannon salute on his Jamaican estate, also called Llanrumney.

six

THE EIGHTEENTH CENTURY

Cardiff's fate in the seventeenth century was determined largely by her strategic location, and location in the following century was also crucial as the seas opened up, creating opportunities for Cardiff's radical economic change. The Glorious Revolution, the creation of a Bank of England, the Act of Union between England and Scotland in 1707, the growth in the Atlantic slave trade and the colonisation of North America all made the Atlantic world into the centre of Cardiff's interests. These factors influenced her politics and spelt the rise of a radical Toryism in the town, lasting a century.

An entry in a 1687 Cardiff baptism register shows the name Joseph Potiphar[53], listed as a 'Black' and belonging to Sir Rowland Gwynne. Here is primary documentary evidence that slaves reached Cardiff and is possibly the first record of black people in Wales, although as Cardiff had been a busy port throughout most of the Middle Ages it is highly unlikely that Africans or people from the Middle East hadn't already set foot in the town. It is very likely that Joseph Potiphar was Sir Rowland's manservant; considering the short lives of black slaves on plantations in Barbados and Jamaica, this was one of the few chances a slave could have of a reasonably secure existence. It was nearly a century before Lord Mansfield created the legal framework for slaves to emancipate themselves, in 1772.

In April 1765 a John Thomas was laid to rest in the cemetery of St John's church, and he is listed in the parish register as being black. Whilst there is some possibility that he was a free man, before 1772 this is far less likely and he probably made his way to the British Isles as a slave.

Another revealing insight into Cardiff's role in the slave trade comes from the diaries of Thomas Thistlewood, an estate overseer in Jamaica. He wrote about the constant fear of slave revolts and the savage violence and torture with which disobedient slaves were treated for even the slightest infringements:

Tuesday, 3rd September: Mr Cope says Cardiff, who was burnt at the Bay told him and many others present, that multitudes of Negroes had took swear ... that if they failed of success in the rebellion, to rise again the same day two years, and advised them to be upon their guard; and was going to make further discoveries, but accusing Col Barclay's Tackey & others, put the Col in a rage, so that he called the Marshall 'Villain' for not making a fiercer fire, &c. A sad mistake.[54]

How had an African man, transported to the West Indies, come to be called Cardiff? We can only guess. The greatest likelihood is that he or his parents belonged to a slave-owner who originated in Cardiff. It is reasonable to suggest that Cardiff benefited from the slave trade, and this legacy has yet to be fully confronted.

The story of William Wells shows us how deeply Cardiff's merchant adventurers were involved in the slave trade. Wells moved from Cardiff to St Kitts with his wife, and after her death took a number of slave women to be his consorts. Wells was far from a rags to riches story, as he already had ample money to spend when he established his plantation: the wealth of Glamorgan and Cardiff was actively invested in plantation enterprises that were calculated to make huge returns. The almost insatiable appetite for sugar, coffee and tobacco in England and Wales made plantations a safe financial bet. Wells's son, Nathaniel, inherited his father's estates and continued to manage them in the same brutal and rapacious manner. There is no evidence that he was a soft touch towards the slaves, even though he was half-black. He would certainly not have been feted by the establishment for leniency, and he seems to have craved acceptance and approval from his white peers rather than his black captives. It was vital for men like Wells to be seen as a reliable pair of imperial hands. Nathaniel lived in style as a pillar of the establishment in Chepstow until his death, solely on the proceeds of the suffering of his mother's people.

The economies of the West Indies and Cardiff were becoming linked in other regards. The merchant trader Henry Cunniff of Cardiff was by the end of the century an exceedingly wealthy man, his interests extending into the sugar and tobacco businesses. If he himself wasn't a slaver, he certainly benefited from the trade. There were other wealthy business interests in Cardiff who were willing to invest in slavery. The diary of William Thomas, the greatest South Walian chronicler of his day, implicates two men in particular, Thomas Edwards and Bartholomew Greenwood, while the son of Richard Priest, the most popular Bristol Channel ferryman of his day, lost his only son on a slaving voyage to Guinea. It appears, therefore, that Cardiffians were involved in the slave trade at every level: there were men who financed it, who ran and owned plantations, who sailed to Africa in search of slaves, and even slaves who bore the town's name. It is likely that this involvement is overlooked because of the far great notoriety of Bristol. For much of the eighteenth century, Cardiff (with a mid-eighteenth-century population of 2,000) was still an economic satellite of Bristol and a political suburb too, as we shall see later. By 1750, Bristol had a population twenty times that of Cardiff, and whilst Swansea began to gradually exploit the natural resources of coal at her disposal, it was not until the nineteenth century that Cardiff experienced the same explosive growth that catapulted it into the epicentre of the Industrial Revolution.

Part of Cardiff's economic marginalisation came from the fact that there were very poor transport links to the town. It could be reached from Abergavenny and Brecon via the valleys, or along the banks of the Severn on a road that ran from Bristol through Gloucester. The only other route was across the Bristol Channel. Both roads were hard to navigate in the summer, ideal for cattle drovers but difficult for anyone else; they were muddy in the autumn and cracked by frost in the winter. Even in a period of relative peace, and at a time of growing opportunities for commerce and trade, issues such as this could result in Cardiff being an economic backwater.

Cardiff's success as a market town in the sixteenth century contributed in part to its later stagnation. The Glamorgan gentry fell into a trap that in the coming centuries country squires the world over would fall into, namely complacency. The economic and social status quo had benefited them for the previous 200 years and the local economy, based mainly on agriculture and cottage industries like weaving and leatherworking, still produced reasonable returns. It was these gentry who, for all their loyalty to the British crown, were casually mocked in the London society circles they aspired to for their comparative poverty and clumsy provincial ways.

Cardiff was behind the times in another way in the eighteenth century, and that is regarding enclosures. Enclosure of common land was a process that had been taking place since the early days of the seventeenth century. The practice of landlords and wealthy farmers fencing off commonly grazed or tilled land by Act of Parliament was late coming to Wales in general. In Swansea the process had been completed in 1762, but it was not until the 1790s that Cardiff had been completely enclosed, though the process had begun a century earlier, when 2 square miles of heath and common land were taken out of communal ownership and intensive farming began.

Enclosure within the confines of the town was completed in 1801, as the *Farmers Magazine* of 1804 details:

This waste was the property of the Burgesses of Cardiff; but by negligently suffering everyone to graze it, they lost this right in great measure and it became free to all the country. It was an area of great extent; but it became no one's property and was seized by all. When a poor man could scrape enough to buy a cot, there he sat down; and, by enclosing a fresh piece of garden every year, many have come to farms of a considerable extent. it had become a plantation of cottagers whose dependence for a living was on keeping two or three horses to carry coal or iron and they were so numerous that they starved each other. About twenty four years ago the neighbouring gentlemen put a stop to their further increase, by drawing down all new encroachments; and, two years back in consequence of an act of Parliament already mentioned a certain proportion was sold for surveying; making new roads, etc, etc.; another part to the amount of near 300 acres was allotted to the town of Cardiff, with liberty to improve or sell; a third portion was for the lord of the Manor and what remained was divided among the brinkers or those whose estates joined the commons in proportion to the extent of their estates.

This is an extraordinarily revealing document, giving us insights into the politics and conflicts of land ownership in the eighteenth century. It is clearly written from the standpoint of the Glamorgan and Cardiffian gentry class, the notion of free grazing land being decried as negligent. The picture that the article paints of life on the common lands is one that is familiar to anyone who has studied Britain's eighteenth century, one of rural poverty. The population of the commons appear to be involved in subsistence farming, using horses to haul coal and iron, literally any pursuit that could guarantee survival. The article also hints at the intense pressure the land was coming under, because of the numbers of people who were forced to use it: it suggests that the horses were so numerous they were 'starving each other'. Finally the article indicates a more fundamental feature of the enclosures, the fact that they were ratified by an Act of Parliament. The close association of the Glamorgan gentry with London and the ruling classes of the rest of Britain clearly yielded results. Without this largesse, perhaps such acts would not have been given the veneer of legality. The article does not indicate the fate of the people who were dispossessed, but in a time of increased poverty, hardship, vagrancy and social distress one can only imagine that this was bleak.

Gentry families dominated Cardiff for the first half of the eighteenth century: the Windsors and the Herberts dominated the town, with the Windsors controlling the castle. While the Herberts had a raft of political and civil powers, the Windsors could appoint a constable who presided over the elections of bailiffs and aldermen, who were also members of the Glamorgan gentry class.

The early eighteenth century saw the rise of national political parties in the guise of the Tories and the Whigs. Before this the politics of Cardiff was largely factional, and the gentry in the countryside had favourite townsmen they could call on to support their interests within the town. Glamorgan families such as the Stradlings, Kemys and Mansells had within their factions a wide variety of people with conflicting political, philosophical and ideological views, and their enemies had an identical mixed bag of political persuasions, suggesting that fealty to family was more important than a commitment to a national political party or ideology: feudalistic thinking was not quite extinct in Cardiff even in the early eighteenth century. One could argue that this quasi-feudal political allegiance was intimately linked to the quasi-feudal economy. As industry began to develop, modern political ideas followed suit.

A dispute that highlights the factional nature of Cardiff politics was the bridge dispute of 1700. The bridge over the River Taff had fallen into a state of disrepair by the end of the seventeenth century, and by an Act of Parliament dating back to the reign of Elizabeth in 1581 the maintenance of the bridge was the responsibility of Glamorgan. By the 1690s a figure of £600 had been set by the justices of Glamorgan to pay for the renovation of the bridge, as its disrepair was starting to change the river's flow. The constable and the governor of the castle, Sir Charles Kemys, led the resistance to Cardiff's portion of the charges. It is possible that this opposition had more to do with sabotaging his gentry opponents rather than any real objection to the cost. The political rivals of the Kemys family were the Mansells of Margam, who had dominated the borough since 1689 and were preparing for the annual election at Michaelmas the following year. The dispute developed from a single issue complaint against the Mansells into a general attack on their influence. This galvanised the Mansell faction into action, and the borough was evenly divided between the two groups. The elections returned a preponderance of Mansell candidates, but Kemys, the returning officer for the borough, refused to swear them in, saying: 'I think it very unreasonable that it should be thought the election of a bailiff shall be as tumultuous as a Parliament man, and for three Justices of the County to concern themselves in the election of bailiffs seems particularly odd to me, for by the same sort of reason, all the rest of the JPs of the county that are out-burgesses may do it the same; and there will be a fine hurly burly, and must produce a great deal of good!'[55] Events indicate clearly the extent to which the gentry felt confident to intervene in the running of Cardiff politics. By the end of 1700 Sir Edward Mansell, aged 64, was trying to intimidate opposing bailiffs with physical violence. Eventually the county courts forced Kemys to swear in the new bailiffs who (as he realised) would make his campaign untenable. The election was won convincingly by the Mansells, and they maintained a monopoly on power in Cardiff for the next two decades. As for Kemys, perhaps it was the loss of the bridge dispute or the stress incurred by it that caused his death in 1702; it was widely speculated that defeat led to his unexpected demise.

Cardiff politics from the mid-seventeenth to the early to mid-eighteenth century were frequently conducted in this manner. In the same way that Elizabethan gangs had fought with one another at the behest of their gentry sponsors on the streets of Cardiff, gentry disputes continued in the town in a slightly less bloody manner.

For the majority of the century Cardiff was a country town with agriculture, fishing, brewing and other related trades being dominant. The countryside spilled over into the town, with pigs roaming the streets to the great nuisance of its inhabitants. It also seems to have had a preponderance of ale houses, perhaps because the town was an ideal stop-off point on the journey from west to east. By the 1750s there were the beginnings of industrialism. For most of the period the focus of industrial development in South Wales was Swansea, particularly with regard to the coal industry. In the Taff Valley there was an embryonic iron industry: the introduction of tin plating (using electrolysis to coat the surface of a ferrous metal with a ductile and non-corrosive metal) suddenly made iron a far more valuable commodity. This process was a home-grown South Wales industry, having been pioneered by John Hanbury and John Payne in Pontypool in 1728. The advent of war on the continent in the 1740s put the price of European iron up, and the Taff Valley had just enough wood for charcoal and water for power to make it the site of a new industry. Industrialisation occurs under a given set of circumstances: the Cardiff area had untapped potential, and was just waiting for the right set of circumstances to arise.

The first known iron forge in the Cardiff area was established at Pentyrch by Thomas Lewis. Lewis was related to other South Walian iron magnates: the know-how and finance for these early enterprises appears to have been concentrated in a few hands. In 1751 early iron entrepreneur James Howells of Pentyrch established a Cardiff forge on the site of two existing watermills, which originally ground corn into flour. This site was chosen for its pre-existing industrial base, highlighting how the foundations of one Industrial Revolution were built on the remnants of a previous one. The site is listed as being at the western gate of the town, on the banks of the River Taff, so a likely site is probably on the grounds occupied by the Wales Millennium Stadium. A small industry was established very quickly in the heart of Cardiff, with one site leased as a charcoal store and another purchased in the centre of the parish of St Mary. This forge seems to have been a catalyst for economic growth in the area. The last mention of the forge is in 1760, by which time new technology, particularly the coke-fired blast furnace, made the old charcoal furnace obsolete. That this furnace existed in Cardiff at all, even if only for a decade, must have changed the town from a sleepy agrarian community that sustained itself partly by trade, hostelry and cottage industries into something wholly new and unexpected. An industry that capitalised on new technology and markets, in a town that was starting to access European and Atlantic markets, must have created a surge in entrepreneurial thinking. Given that the eighteenth century was an era of new thinking in science, rationality and economics, the stage was set in Cardiff for

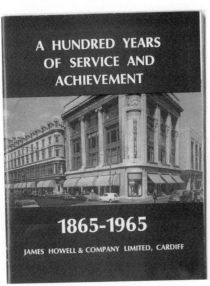

Left A hundred years of service at Howells. The department store was the creation of James Howells in 1856 and has been the longest serving and most successful retailer in Cardiff's history.

Below The Wales Millennium Centre. Initially an opera house, was planned for the site in the mid-1990s, but plans were shelved in favour of the more multipurpose Millennium Centre.

a meeting of ideas and opportunities, transforming the town into an industrial powerhouse. In addition, the agricultural depression of the second half of the century sent thousands of people from the land to towns and cities, and an influx of cheap labour is important in any industrial growth.

One of the fundamental issues that hampered industrialisation in Cardiff and indeed in the rest of South Wales was the poor transport network. There were insufficient horses to haul coal and iron ore, as they were being used in agriculture, and there were no canals or railways. Even though the decade 1750 to 1760 saw a slow start for Cardiff industrially, it was nonetheless one of the most important ten-year periods in the town's history: the basic economic structure that was to define Cardiff for the next 200 years was created in this short period. The west of Glamorgan had stolen a march on Cardiff in terms of industrialism, but coal mining reversed this trend and made the town an industrial giant.

In the eighteenth century in Britain there were often clashes between the gentry class and the new urban capitalist bourgeoisie, but in Cardiff something different happened: the two classes formed a political alliance that dominated the town. As the relative value of land fell throughout the century so did the power of the Glamorgan gentry class. Many who had relied upon the urban elites for services, and had borrowed money from them to pay for their struggling estates, began to realise that the balance of power was shifting and that a new and less socially secure future awaited them. Once it was generally established that Toryism was the political force that would dominate Cardiff for the next century, it united squabbling gentry and disaffected townsfolk. Evidence of this is the clear cooperation between the Kemys and Mansell families in keeping Whig contenders out of the borough. Charles Kemys the younger met Bussy Mansell and Edward Stradling to discuss how best to keep the Whig Thomas Matthews from taking control. Factionalism evolved into partisanship in just a generation: old scores were forgotten and hatchets were buried in order to serve a larger agenda, the control not just of Cardiff but of national politics, policy and Parliament itself. Two generations earlier many members of the gentry class had been financing radical troublemakers like William Erbury and Walter Craddock; their political and philosophical outlook could hardly have become more different.

So why was Toryism the philosophical model that the Cardiff and Glamorgan classes gravitated to? In the eighteenth century it is generally associated with the Jacobite conspiracies that dominated 1714 to 1745. The popular view of the Tory

The Wales Millennium Centre is an example of how Cardiff has become an international centre for tourism, leisure and culture in the twenty-first century as it slowly emerges from its industrial past.

party is that it was less sympathetic to urban boroughs and industrialism than the Whigs, that it was traditionally the party of country gentry and the shires, which often had contrary interests to the urban elites. Toryism and support for James II were often thought to be synonymous with one another, some Cardiff Tories going as far as espousing Jacobite ideas, often running the risk of arrest and imprisonment. For example, in 1716 Thomas Williams was taken before magistrates for saying 'that King James would come to rule and order him [someone with whom Williams had been arguing] and the rest of the shittsacks as he saw fit.'[56] The reason why so many Cardiff townsmen were willing to adopt Toryism in the eighteenth century and endorse opinions that were overtly Jacobite, a complete reversal of the radicalism that was prevalent in Cardiff in the seventeenth century, was purely commercial. As an economic satellite of Bristol, the largest slave port in the world, Cardiff benefited directly and indirectly from slavery and the colonisation of the Caribbean and the Americas, and these were the favourites of Tory foreign policy. The Tories were an Atlanticist party, and the Whigs favoured foreign policy based on expensive land wars on the continent. This was an old schism. As far back as Charles I, when war against Spain was being considered, Parliament liked the idea of cheap naval campaigns where territory and plunder were easy to come by; land campaigns on the continent were far more risky with far fewer spoils. Of course in the eighteenth century the greatest spoils of all were human: control of the slave trade made Britain as a nation, and all individuals involved, fantastically rich.

If slavery was the defining moral issue of the day, the late eighteenth century saw two political questions arise that would rival it, both of which would animate the passions of Cardiff's citizens. These were the American and French revolutions. There were many South Walians who looked upon the struggle of American patriots as their own battle. Five of the signatories of the Declaration of Independence were Welshmen, and many in Cardiff were deeply sympathetic towards the rebels. Opposition to the French Revolution inspired the Bishop of Llandaff, Dr Richard Watson, to enter into an extraordinary exchange of letters with the poet William Wordsworth[57], and two years later he locked swords with none other than Thomas Paine, whose *Declaration of the Rights of Man* had been the ideological underpinning for the American Revolution and

Welsh Assembly. Since devolution in 1997 the National Assembly for Wales has existed in Cardiff Bay as a semi-autonomous government with devolved powers. The Senedd Building was opened by Queen Elizabeth II in 2006. It is the most environmentally friendly government building in the UK and potentially worldwide as it utilises natural light and pipes groundwater that is heated by geothermal energy.

an inspiration to the French. In response to Paine's *The Age Of Reason*, which advocated secularism and the end of the indisputability of the Bible, Watson wrote *An Apology for the Bible*.[58] He later argued for the first income tax in England and Wales, to raise armies to fight the revolutionary and Napoleonic wars. The letters of Watson should not be looked at in isolation: they were a tiny part of a great blizzard of letters, papers and pamphlets that circulated in intellectual and literate eighteenth-century Welsh society. Slavery, revolution, the rights of kings, the dangers of the mob, the rights of the individual and a whole range of Enlightenment topics were common discussion subjects for the newly politicised elites in Cardiff.

One option when confronted with economic hard times was military service. The acrid diarist William Thomas, Glamorgan schoolmaster, recorded in his diary on 23 June 1762 that 'the money are gone so scarce ... that the most of men will be either soldiers or on the parishes'. In this observation he was quite correct: as the century progressed the need for standing British armies increased. In the sixteenth and seventeenth centuries standing armies were costly and at best unnecessary, at worst a danger. The eighteenth century brought the dual needs of policing and protecting a growing empire, and towards the end of the century and into the nineteenth policing a restless working poor.

seven

THE NINETEENTH CENTURY

By the end of the eighteenth century there was a crucial economic partnership between Merthyr Tydfil and Cardiff. Cardiff was 25 miles from Merthyr, and the ironworks and the collieries there required Cardiff as a conduit to the rest of the UK. Raw materials were loaded onto ships and taken down the Severn Estuary to Bristol, then on to south-east England. Cardiff relied on its position as a new metropolis with good transport links in a region that had previously been known for its inaccessibility and poor transportation. As the nineteenth century wore on matters improved. Ironmasters frequently put pressure on local MPs and central government to improve the transport infrastructure from the valleys to Cardiff. A solution that did not rely on road haulage was desperately sought: solving the problem of moving coal was the engineering challenge of the day, and would reap a rich reward for anyone who solved it. Transportation on roads was slow, expensive and led to exhausted horses and heavy wage costs. The answer lay in canals and the canal network provided Cardiff with her real wealth for the coming century.

In 1790 the Glamorgan Canal Act was passed by Parliament. In just four short years the canal was constructed to Cardiff, and in 1798 it was completed when the first sea lock was opened. The net results of these changes was a minor revolution in Cardiff's economic fortunes: the speed with which iron and coal could be transported from Merthyr Tydfil and other towns and collieries of the South Wales valleys to Cardiff was revolutionised. One barge was capable of transporting 24 tons of coal whereas a horse-drawn cart could carry 2 tons. Not surprisingly the movement of iron and coal became much quicker and much cheaper. The profitability of the whole industry and the wealth of Glamorgan and Cardiff grew to levels never previously seen. The late eighteenth and the early nineteenth centuries were a boom time.

Cardiff had an additional role to play. As towns like Merthyr grew rapidly to accommodate the new iron and coal industries, they needed to be supplied with basic consumer goods and materials. Cardiff once again became a conduit for trade as goods from the blaina of Glamorgan and the south-west of England, notably Bristol, flowed through her docks and road networks, and were transported by canal northwards to the people who work at Merthyr's factories and collieries. The late eighteenth century and the first decade and a half of the nineteenth saw an increasing demand for iron goods, especially cannon and cannon shot, because of Britain's involvement in the revolutionary wars against France and later the Napoleonic wars. The period from 1816 to 1834 was one of acute economic hardship and crisis: the wars had ended and the need for cannon and shot diminished, while tens of thousands of men returned home from the wars and Britain's export markets in Europe were devastated. A bleak poverty gripped the South Wales valleys, leading to unrest that the British Government felt threatened revolution. Cardiff, because of her metropolitan nature and because of the diversity of heavy, light and service industries, was partially insulated from

St Andrews Omnibus timetable. As modern transportation came to an increasingly industrial Cardiff, so too did the need for timetables.

this: there is, for example, far less Chartist activity in Cardiff after 1832 than there was in Merthyr. Chartism seems to have grown around traditional centres of heavy industry such as Merthyr or Birmingham, and was less pronounced in towns that were more dependent upon trade for their livelihood.

The 1832 Reform Act enfranchised a number of the new bourgeois, and a generation of wealthy Cardiffians, led by the Marquess of Bute, had every reason to support the government, but this didn't prevent magistrates from being gripped by a revolutionary terror in 1839. John Frost, the Chartist who led the attack on the Westgate Hotel in Newport, sparked a frenzy of fear in Cardiff. Magistrates ordered the reinforcement of the town against the threat of Chartist attack, although there doesn't seem to have been any credible evidence that there was a threat. The crew of an American naval vessel that had weighed anchor at Cardiff's quay disembarked to help defend the town. It is curious that an American crew so willingly assisted a counter-revolutionary action.

Throughout the 1820s and '30s, demand for iron decreased and its price fell. The only hope of an improvement in the industry was to be found in the birth of the railways. By the end of the century, Cardiff had transformed herself from a small iron producer into a major steel manufacturer. This was now the staple metal, stronger and more durable than iron, and its manufacture meant that the town maintained its position as the most active port in the region by the end of the century. By 1900 she had vastly outstripped Swansea as a port for coal, and the advent of steel meant that Cardiff became more than a port and heavy industry had to be relocated close to the docks, in order to eliminate transport costs. The price of moving materials to the South Wales valleys by the late nineteenth century had made previous steel smelting ventures financially unviable. In 1888 the most inventive solution to the problem of transportation costs came from the Dowlais works at East Moors in Cardiff, on an area of wasteland next to the docks. The designs showed an ultra-modern steelworks, ideal for making steel plate for shipbuilding. There had always been shipbuilding in Cardiff, but the means to create steamers industrially was an innovation. Cardiff had to compete with steel foundries in Tyneside, Scotland and Europe:

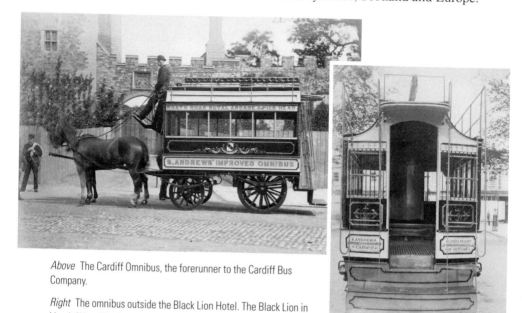

Above The Cardiff Omnibus, the forerunner to the Cardiff Bus Company.

Right The omnibus outside the Black Lion Hotel. The Black Lion in Llandaff is still a drop-off point for commuters.

the town was breaking into one of the biggest boom industries of the late nineteenth and early twentieth centuries, and competition was tough. The plant began operations in 1891 and further forges were added over the next four years.

Once again Cardiff's location had been her fortune, placing her at the nexus of economic and historical change. One of the results of this economic and industrial advance was the end of Bristol's economic hegemony.

The exploitation of South Wales coal took on a new dimension in the 1850s when the Royal Navy switched to coal-powered steam engines. The admiralty viewed the coalfields of South Wales as of vital strategic interest, thanks to Cardiff's docks. They were proved correct, as the docks were essential to the United Kingdom's survival during the two world wars. The navy made sure that there were coal reserves in coaling stations around the world, in Jamaica, Gibraltar and Malta, for example, coal was often dug in Merthyr and shipped through Cardiff.

At this point Cardiff began to grow rapidly; the historian Gwyn Alf Williams compares it with an American boomtown.[59] There were two fundamental issues: the rapid change over less than 100 years, and the relationship between Cardiff's new wealth and global imperialism, the system of trading and defence upon which the town's development relied. Cardiff became an indispensable link in the chain of empire. Its role as a way-station between east and west was transformed, as it became a vital link in the journey from north to south. The growing docks could process ever greater quantities of coal and this made the town rich. The relationship between the coalfields in South Wales and the vast market that was created by the British Empire and protected by imperial tariffs led to the kind of industrial growth the likes of which Cardiff had never previously seen or has never witnessed since. The town developed a role at the heart of the Empire's strategic and industrial firmament. An equivalent today is a strategic and financially vital hub like Singapore or Hong Kong, culturally and economically unlike its hinterland, possessed of unmatched wealth and somehow detached from the surrounding area.

Cardiff's status brought civic improvements in the 1820s that would have been unthinkable a generation before. As an example, by 1821 Cardiff was lit by gas lamps. In nineteenth-century Britain gaslight was a byword for modernity, civic pride and social reform.

By 1840 Cardiff was supplying over 162,000 tons of coal for domestic consumption in South Wales alone. In comparison the south-west of England supplied under 4,000 tons of coal to foreign destinations. A source of business that was of far greater significance than the needs of the navy was the Cornish copper smelting industry, which was smelting 6,000 tonnes in the 1720s and 50,000 tonnes by 1800.

By the end of the eighteenth century, finance had become the lifeblood of industry. It was simply not possible for industrial expansion to continue at such a rate without a new system of short term loans. Providing the loans was perhaps the most important role of banking in Cardiff. The banks also operated as clearing houses for bills of exchange between the smelters of iron, steel, tin plate and copper and other providers of raw materials, trading in industry debt. By this time the Industrial Revolution in Wales was complex and integrated. Previously Cardiff's predominantly agrarian economy had operated on payment in kind: farmers bartered and traded and used payment other than money for mutual benefit, but an

A printed notice offering a reward for information, 1821. The period immediately after the Napoleonic Wars saw increased lawlessness in South Wales.

industrialised economy required a more sophisticated system of exchange, with borrowing, lending and investment. The banks contributed to a huge increase in the quantity of currency that was available to borrow.

In banking as in other aspects of industrialisation Cardiff was something of a late starter, but the financial system made up for lost time with explosive growth. In 1770 Cardiff's first bank was opened by Lord, Evans and Como, and in 1813 James Wood, in association with Charles Evans and James Jelf, set up the bank of Wood and Co. In 1856 Wilkins and Co. (founded in Brecon in 1778) established itself in Cardiff. This was an interesting development: a bank that previously lent money to farmers and landowners to finance the purchase of land had recognised that it was industry that generated the wealth, not passive land ownership. Some early banks were directly related to the heavy industry that they financed. An example is John Guest's bank, established in 1823 and later called Guest, Lewis and Co. Guest was a prominent Cardiff ironmaster and his brother Thomas, the first mayor of Cardiff in 1836, was also a managing partner. This gives us an insight into the conjunction of local politics, industry and finance. In much the same way that the guilds had held sway over local politics for the best part of 300 years, so the industrialists and the banks that supported them declared politics in Cardiff to be their own private fiefdom. Another indication of the power and influence of Cardiff's new bankers is the resumé of John Wood. He was a landowner who was Glamorgan's treasurer, treasurer to the Cardiff Turnpike Trust and captain of the Cardiff Cavalry. From these examples, it appears more than likely that wealthy merchants, traders and industrialists became involved in the banking sector, rather than bankers being co-opted into Cardiff society's ruling strata.

In 1835 the West of England and South Wales District Bank, a new and well-funded joint stock banking company, opened its doors in Cardiff and Swansea. Originally a Bristolian venture, the bank was joined by another joint stock venture, the National Provincial Bank. The Marquess of Bute was a member of the founding commitee of the bank: he understood the need for a sound financial basis to Cardiff's economy.

Cardiff's plethora of smaller banks made them vulnerable to collapse as they were overly reliant on the heavy industries that they had been set up to finance. An example of this is the collapse of the Cardiff Bank in 1822. There was little interest in rescuing it, probably a reflection of the economic crisis facing the country. Concerns such as the Cardiff Bank were of most use to the new industries as clearing houses for large sums that came from London banks. Investors in the capital fronted huge sums of money to finance the coal and steel industry in Cardiff and Glamorgan, and Cardiff's banks administered the funds. In addition this allowed them to lend to small businesses, and hold deposits for small traders, farmers and landowners. The latter was the bank's main role for much of the time, but by the early 1820s customers were owing rather more than they deposited. Too much short-term lending, combined with long-term capital investment in factories and land, meant that the bank was unable to spread its risk enough to survive. The Cardiff Bank appears to have had a virtual monopoly in lending in the town before 1819, in which year the Towgood and Co. bank was established; within three years the Cardiff Bank had vanished. It is possible that the lending market in the town was not large enough to support two banks.

Cardiff also relied on finance from other parts of Wales and England. For the first time there was a national infrastructure of lending that saw an inflow of capital to the town. This new money had a dramatic effect on Cardiff's

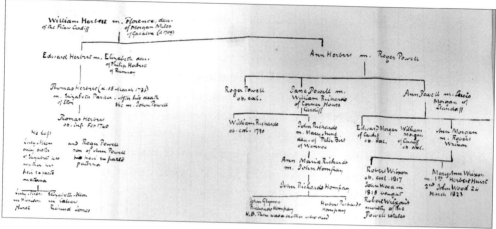

Genealogical table of Herbert, Powell and Richards' families descending from W.M. Herbert in 1600. The Lords of Cardiff were really the key Glamorgan families who dominated politics and wealth within the city for centuries.

development: the town, through its geography, was proving to be a very attractive investment.

There were abundant concerns in the lawless late eighteenth and early nineteenth centuries about the vulnerability of bullion and notes that were transported along the Irish Mail route from Cardiff to Swansea. Bank notes were often cut in half for transit to and from Cardiff, and taken in two different shipments.

After 1860 the fortunes of small independent and privately owned banks in Cardiff and across Wales dramatically declined. The large joint stock banks thrived as the Industrial Revolution entered a new and more vigorous phase.

The wealth accumulated or expedited by capital finance and the growth in joint stock banks only reveals a small part of the new economic activity in Cardiff in the nineteenth century. Working people, who had been flocking to the town from depressed rural South Wales, also needed to save their money. This new working class, attracted by the docks, steelworks and other heavy industry, was able to save and therefore be incorporated into a communal and mutual economic system that was not directly dependent on the largesse of employers, thereby determining its future character. This new working class included industrial labourers, but more commonly they were small tradesmen, shopkeepers and artisans. Cardiff established a savings bank in 1819, following the imposition of national legislation two years earlier to encourage thrift and prudent savings, probably because of the parlous state of the country's finances. By 1851 the policy had proved to be successful: in Cardiff there were 1,544 depositors in savings banks, and fifty-one separate friendly societies and charitable bodies for ordinary saving. The total sum deposited was £39,278, the majority holding balances with £50 or less. Overall the average deposit was £25 (roughly £2,300 today), which shows impressive thrift, and speaks volumes about the attitude towards money and responsibility in the middle of the nineteenth century.

After 1860 the small savings banks, or trustee savings banks, faced increasing competition from post offices, which were able to offer savings facilities for the first time. A scandal that originated in Cardiff rocked trustee savings banks across the country in 1886, damaging their reputation inestimably, and giving the Post Office an advantage it was quick to exploit. The Cardiff Savings Bank was declared bankrupt in April 1886 following the theft of £30,000 by the actuary R.E. Jones. It is clear from the size of this fraud that Cardiff's savings must have dramatically increased by this point, which is hardly surprising as her population was rocketing towards the end of the century. The impact of the fraud was heightened because of the well-established local and national media, which took the story of greed and dishonesty rapidly to all corners of the United Kingdom. The case revealed that there had been irregularities (possibly errors, possibly other thefts) in the accounting of deposits, and evidence suggests that checks and balances were insufficient. An institution such as a trustee savings bank was central to the lives of large working-class communities, and the trust placed in it was great. The long-term impact of the scandal was new legislation at national level, with the founding of a select committee to look into the affairs of savings banks. Cardiff-based savings banks died and the Swansea Savings Bank took their business.

In 1860 the Principality Building Society was created in Cardiff. The sitting MP, Lt-Col. J.F. Dudley Crichton Stuart, was one of the founders of the society, along with two future mayors of Cardiff. That the new building society was riding on the crest of a wave of industrialisation, commerce and progress for the town can be seen in its capital assets. In 1870 it held just under £18,000 in deposits, and by 1910 this was close to £500,000. By 1930, despite an economic downturn, the society held nearly £2m in deposits.

As Cardiff's role developed, it also became Glamorgan's centre of judicial enforcement, and a wide range of crimes and misdemeanours were punished. An examination of Cardiff Gaol's records from 1800 to 1830 is illuminating. The two main factors in creating crime seem to have been the grinding poverty that the rest of South Wales was suffering at the time, and the oppressive treatment of Welsh language speakers. As an example of the latter, in 1800 the labourer John Griffiths was convicted of saying, 'Damno'r Brenhin George y trydidd, myfi a wnaf well Brenhin o Bren Gwernen on'd i giltio fe a baintio fe ai hela fe ir Parlament.'[60] The Cardiff Gaol Calendar interprets:

John Griffiths, Aged 36, Committed 16 February 1800, by Richard Bevan Esq. on the Oaths of William Walter, William Lewis and John Hillard, charged with Damning King George the Third, and that he was no King, and did declare that he would make a better King out of a piece of Arl-wood being first Painted and Gilt, and did also give one Penny to William Walter, for going to Justice Bevan to make known his declaration, and did also declare to Rosser Jenkin, that he had one Thousand if not Thousands of Men of the same opinion as himself.[61]

He was imprisoned for two months.

In 1801 the Cardiff Gaol Calendar reported that John Quin, a private in the 'Iniskillen' Dragoons, 'violently robbed James Morgan, of Cardiff, labourer, at night on Cardiff Bridge, and stole from him two half-crowns and five shillings', and reported on the death of 'Rees Rees, late of Neath; murdered by lead shot from Allen Macdonald, of Bristol, the guard of the mail coach, as the said coach was being driven through the town of Neath'. Rees was running after the coach, and the guard (who appears to have been drunk) took his blunderbuss and fired at him, killing him on the spot.

In some instances corrupt practices were revealed, such as the case of William Meredith of Llandaff, the sheriff's bailiff, in 1806. He was found guilty of 'unlawfully exacting various sums of money from persons arrested by him'.[62]

With a mixture of crimes from the petty to the serious, the court rolls indicate a similar range of cases to those heard at Cardiff Magistrates' Court today. As Cardiff grew rapidly so did her social problems. The majority of cases feature South Wales's poor and dispossessed, and are probably representative of patterns of crime in new urban centres across the country. It is likely that the growth in crime and lawlessness was a direct by-product of the process of industrialisation.

The major change at this time was demographic. The nineteenth century saw an explosion in Cardiff's population and the birth of the town's suburbs. Just under 2,000 people were counted on the census of 1801 and it was nearly ten times that within half a century. At the turn of the twentieth century the process of industrialisation had brought 160,000 people to the town. Between the 1610 map of John Speed and the 1830 map of John Wood little growth had occurred, but the addition of new districts by 1830 suggests that the beginning of rapid growth and change was just commencing. By 1841 there were five times as many people living in Cardiff than in 1610. This population growth would not have been possible if it had not been for the new railways that connected the town to the rest of the country. Although maritime links with Bristol were overshadowed by the expansion of the railways, they were enhanced by the building of the West Docks by the 2nd Marquess of Bute in 1839.[63] It is he who is accredited with giving Cardiff the infrastructure that it required to become the largest and most important coal port in the world. The Bute family, descended from the Stuarts and married into the Windsors, had an impact on the industrialisation of the town that dwarfs any other.

The rural rhythms of life that had dominated Cardiff for centuries were interrupted in the first half of the nineteenth century. The town was still a principal livestock market, but gradually more and more green space was enclosed within the town walls and on the periphery workers' houses, factories, workshops, warehouses and other essential amenities were built. It is impossible to discuss this industrialisation without placing it in its regional context. As mentioned above, poverty in the South Wales valleys led to migration to the city, as economic migrants desperately sought work. This valuable human labour powered the Industrial Revolution in Cardiff.

Since the early eighteenth century the town had accommodated the poor who were unable to find work elsewhere. As enclosure and other economic changes led to an increase in people living off the parish, a forerunner of the workhouse was established in Llandaff in 1740. The Llandaff vestry, observing the Knatchbull Act, stated: 'Every person who receives relief from the parish shall be lodged in the alms house till the same is full, upon pain of having their allowances withdrawn and for their Better accommodation the overseers are to putt the said house in good repair and cause a Bog house to be built there in the most convenient place.'[64] This (deliberately) made living off alms so unpleasant that seeking work at any wage was preferable. By the late eighteenth century the situation had little improved. By 1777 the parish of St John and St Mary had workhouse places for 220 people. Considering the population at this time (probably approaching 2,000), these statistics are a stark eye-opener.

To properly prosecute the Poor Law Act of 1833, Cardiff created its own Poor Law Union in 1836. By 1839 the new parish of Canton had developed its first workhouse on Cowbridge Road. The Poor Law commissioners originally budgeted that the cost of building the large workhouse would be £5,500, but

Roath Park Lake, famed for its swans, ducks and other migrating wildfowl. The lake, now part of a long green belt strip that runs from the top of Roath to the end of Albany Road, was one of the largest and most popular municipal amenities developed by the Victorians in the late nineteenth century and continues to provide leisure and relaxation to Cardiffians today.

Cardiff indoor market on St Mary Street. Cardiff's indoor market is one of the city's links to its Victorian past. As it inches into a retail environment fit for the twenty-first-century shopper, the market is still hugely popular and also a familiar part of the city's communal life.

an 1866 Post Office Directory report concluded that the final cost was around £7,500. The building was designed roughly in the shape of a cross, with the south entrance pointing away from Cowbridge Road, and the infirmary had 164 beds. By 1880 the workhouse had been remodelled into an imposing and intimidating edifice that was consciously designed to appear forbidding and austere, and unsurprisingly it resembled a prison. Such was the criminalisation of poverty throughout the Victorian era.

In Ely in 1862 there was a new initiative, perhaps informed by the educational changes that were taking hold in Britain. Ely Industrial School educated the boys of paupers, teaching them valuable skills such as carpentry; it is most likely, given the close proximity to the workhouse, that it was for children of workhouse inmates. In 1930 the site became the Ely Lodge Public Assistance Institution. After 1948, as Ely Hospital, it accommodated the mentally ill, and was later used as a hospice. It closed in 1996.

Cardiff's later Victorian period, from the 1880s onwards, saw an explosion of modern landmarks that are instantly recognisable today. The architect William Harpur created the Civic Centre in Cathays Park, designed Roath and Victoria Parks and built (in the 1890s) Cardiff's Indoor Market. This was the heyday of Victorian public works: the vast wealth generated by the Industrial Revolution was in part spent gentrifying the town and building amenities such as the boating lake at Roath Park, creating a lasting reminder of the extraordinary achievements of the Victorian age for generations to come.

Transport

The first turnpike Act of 1764 divided Glamorgan into five separate administrative regions, Cardiff being one of them, and created a partially privatised road network for the town. The east-west route that ran through on the way to Swansea, and all the tributary roads that ran off it, were covered by the Act. Trustees were given the responsibility of maintaining the road and they controlled tolls, having the power to raise up to £5,000. Whilst Cardiff avoided the violence of the Rebecca Riots, it must have been a matter of common grievance that a 3d charge fell upon all horse-drawn carriages and that cattle drivers had to pay 10d for every drove of cattle. The dire state of Cardiff's roads, particularly those connecting outlying parishes such as Roath, Llandaff and Radyr, was a compelling reason to create toll roads, or at least to find some efficient means of financing the roads' regular upkeep. The principal beneficiaries of toll roads were farmers, as industry was not advanced enough to take advantage of them, and it was the inefficiency of horse-powered transport that created the impetus for new modes of transport.

A new Act in 1785 renewed the 1764 Act, but no significant alterations were incorporated at this stage. All the trusts, Cardiff included, borrowed money to carry out essential works almost immediately and then introduced tolls. Dominated by the men who were most likely to use the roads for commercial purposes, the trusts' purpose was to facilitate private spending on public utilities. In the long run, the Cardiff Trust, dominated by Cardiff's proto-industrialists, recouped the cost of the loan from road users and in the meantime created a usable highway for everyone, but most crucially, for themselves. Despite this, there is abundant evidence that the roads to and from Cardiff were still not adequately maintained, and by the end of the eighteenth

century the failure to create roads that were passable in all weathers led to the search for other solutions.

As we have seen, the Glamorganshire Canal Act was given royal assent in 1790, the 1790s being a decade in which Cardiff's roads could no longer support the new businesses that needed access to the town. Four canals were constructed in Glamorgan, servicing Swansea, Neath and Cardiff. They were, for the most part, separate projects but the expertise and finance needed to create them was usually sourced from a common pool. Of the four projects the Glamorganshire Canal was the biggest, and it had a revolutionary effect on Cardiff. In 1796 an Act of Parliament allowed for the canal to be extended and a sea lock to be constructed at Cardiff, transforming the town from a market with a riverside dock into a port. This was not simply semantics as it meant that mercantile operations could dramatically expand. The sea lock was opened in 1798 on the mouth of the Taff, downriver from the centre of the town and away from the existing dock, creating a separate and distinct dock area. Later Butetown would be built here. Owing to the rapid increase in canal traffic, pressure on the sea lock grew quickly, and by 1814 it had to be extended.

In 1812 the opening of the Aberdare Canal meant that iron ore could be transported south from Aberdare to the Glamorganshire Canal, then on to Cardiff. However, the inability of the main investors to get along (they fell out over rights of access) meant that plans were mooted to create a tramway along the canal to transport coal and limestone from Merthyr to Cardiff. Eventually the project would have had branch lines, to connect most of the Rhondda Valley. The matter came before Parliament in 1799, but failed to pass the Commons vote. Building went ahead on a much smaller project, which connected some of the valley's ironworks with the canal, but as this never connected directly to Cardiff it never acted as an actual replacement for the canal.

The next revolution in transport was the advent of railways. As with the canals it is almost impossible to overstate the importance of rail to the evolution of Cardiff's economy and society. By the 1840s in Glamorgan, after a century of radical change in transport, the tracks of the cattle drovers must have seemed like a distant memory. The two main players in Cardiff's incorporation into the rail network were the Great Western Railway Company and the London & North Western Railway Company. A subtle change occurred with the advent of these conglomerates. The power wielded over the roads had been held by local turnpike trusts and the power to build canals had rested in the hands of Glamorganshire ironmasters, but there was nothing local about the railways:

Bargain and Sale. For £45 William Herbert of Cardiff Castle purchased a burgage, garden and two cottages from Sir William Doddington.

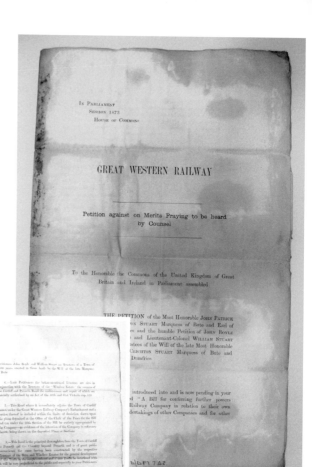

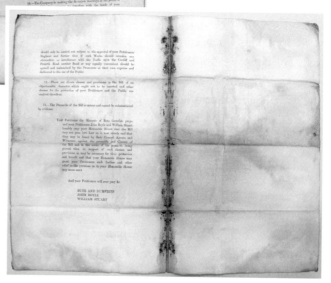

they were national networks looking to expand. The first plans for a railway network in the area were mooted by Richard Beaumont, agent to the Marquess of Bute, who was chiefly interested in connecting Cardiff to the collieries at Bute property at Llanstrisant, Llantwit and Llanwynno. By the 1830s action was needed to augment the canals because there was an enormous bottleneck of barges. There were shortages of suitable horses to pull them, and at least £100 of damage every year was done to barges colliding with another. There was also the issue of pilfering en route. Stoppages owing to drought or frost prevented 4,000 tons of coal from reaching the docks every year and led to miners being laid off, many of whom were hard to re-employ when work was resumed. It was clear that the canals had reached the limit of their usefulness. When West Bute Dock was completed in 1839 it cemented Cardiff as the destination for South Wales's new railway network: collieries, docks and railways were to take Cardiff to a new level.

An example of an early line was the Cardiff Railway, an offshoot of the Bute Docks. In 1886 a legal entity was formed by Act of Parliament in order to run the docks, and the Bute Docks Company was granted the powers to build railways. When it was completed, West Bute Dock could accommodate 300 ships, and it is this volume of maritime traffic, along with an abundance of coal, that transformed Cardiff. West Bute Dock (now Roald Dahl Plass, by the Wales Millennium Centre) was joined by a new East Bute Dock in 1855, Roath Docks in 1887 and Queen Alexandra Docks in 1907. Cardiff had to continually expand its capacity, as periods of complacency were punished by the growth of rival docks in Penarth, Barry, Neath and Port Talbot. The fact that permission for Roath Dock was granted in 1874 and it took until 1887 for it to be completed suggests that development was far from smooth. The high prices charged by port authorities to ship iron ore and coal out of Cardiff eventually dropped in the face of new and eager competition from other ports along the Bristol Channel. The rapid expansion demonstrated how quickly the West Bute Docks became congested by shipping and barges. The real explosion of trade occurred between 1858 and 1859 when a channel connecting the two docks was dug and the West Docks were joined to the Rhymney Railway. Later, in the 1860s, the East Docks were connected to the Cardiff–Caerphilly Railway, ending the monopoly of the Taff Vale Railway Company.

It was the canny David Stewart (an Edinburgh surveyor who was employed by the 2nd Marquess of Bute to map his much-neglected estate and to reform its management) who should be recognised as the strategic visionary who saw the potential in the town's location. He produced a survey in 1824, after a decade's work, and drew his employer's attention to the massive potential wealth of Glamorgan and the estate's industrial potential. In a letter to the marquess he wrote: 'The time must come when either the present Marquess or his successors will reap the benefit of the present investigation and when the enormous wealth that now lies useless will be put into full activity.' Perhaps this letter was an attempt to justify the huge costs of his survey to his notoriously parsimonious employer, but whatever the motivation its subtext was not lost on the marquess.

The marquess viewed wealth creation and economic enterprise as part of a social contract with the people. He leased land for exploitation and took a share in the profits, but also saw job creation as central to his role. This commitment to providing employment in Cardiff became a more pressing issue in the industrial age as the population swelled and unemployment became a factor for the first time since the mid-Tudor era. The Victorian sin of idleness was intolerable to the marquess: just as he was a tough and uncompromising reactionary when it came to the issue of workers' unrest, he was similarly motivated to help to provide jobs if only to prevent the need for charity.

The decision to build a dock on the Taff Estuary was taken because the marquess owned the lion's share of land along the north shore of Cardiff, and Stewart reported that, without a port, coalfields would never reach their optimum value. He also saw that there was an advantage in one man building a harbour, as there was no need to set up a corporation or trust to complete the project and raise funds, meaning there was no scope for conflict. The only likely business partners in the area were the ironmasters, who seemed incapable of agreeing between themselves about how to run the canals in a manner that was fair to all, and they shared a mutual loathing of the marquess. The failure to create a lasting partnership with the canal owners was to store up problems, however, as these men were the principal clients of Bute Docks.

It was Stewart's industrial logic that distinguished the nineteenth century in Cardiff from other eras. It was the logic of modern capitalism, of connecting raw materials to markets, that changed the town beyond recognition. Taking this into account, the marquess' treatment of Stewart was particularly shabby: Stewart made the marquess far more money than he ever cost, making it even more galling that he was dismissed because of the cost of his survey. It is entirely possible that if David Stewart had not been so persuasive the docks would never have been built, or at least not by the 2nd Marquess of Bute.

A man with the connections of the marquess had little trouble in obtaining the relevant Act of Parliament by 1830 in order to build a ship canal, and in 1834 he was able to build an entrance canal and a dock to be located at either Cogan Pill or East Moors, later the site of Cardiff's steelworks. Cogan Pill was where the Rivers Ely and Taff met, but East Moors was a more suitable location because a project to reclaim land from the sea was already underway there. By the mid-1830s the concerns held by the innately cautious and sceptical marquess were being drowned out by a chorus of voices urging him to continue with the modernisation of the port. The marquess had good reason to be nervous, however, as the dock took four years to excavate and cost £350,000 to finance, a vast increase on the original quote of £76,000. He was forced to borrow money, an act that was clearly an affront to his values, and mortgaged part of the Bute estate in order to secure extra finance. The gamble paid off, however, and without it modern Cardiff would surely be a smaller and less prosperous place, and would be unlikely to have been granted city status let alone be a capital city.

In 1839, amid much pomp and ceremony, the dock was opened and its first customer was a timber ship from Canada. Craftsmen and labourers led a procession to the castle from the dock to cheer the marquess. Although the dock took time to accumulate sufficient business, as it was initially boycotted by the ironmasters, the marquess owned much of the land they operated on so any protest was likely to be short-lived.

When the railways exploded onto the economic landscape in the 1840s, the marquess was unable to become involved because of the sums of money that he had committed to the docks. He was content to let others invest in railway infrastructure, while steering the lines towards his docks, and preventing the Taff Vale Railway Company from building its own docks.

The 54-year-old marquess died in 1848. His wife Sophia had given birth to his only child and heir just four months before his untimely death from a heart attack, and his funeral was one of the biggest public events in Cardiff in the nineteenth century. He left a mixed legacy. Having lived throughout the most important period in the town's economic and industrial development, he had single-handedly financed the building of the docks, the ticket to future prosperity. The marquess was also a divisive, authoritarian figure who opposed democratic reform in 1832 and ruled Cardiff as his private fiefdom. For the next twenty years his dynamism and drive were absent from the management of Cardiff, and trustees appointed to manage the Bute estates played little more

Newspaper cuttings regarding the Taff Vale Railway, 1891. The Taff Railway was one of the earliest and most successful lines and was eventually taken over by Great Western Railways.

than a caretaker role before the 3rd Marquess took his title in 1868. During the 1850s and '60s industrialisation continued relentlessly, despite the absence of a guiding hand. Further dock building was essential lest business be lost to Swansea or Newport, and the opening of the East Dock in 1855 allowed far bigger merchant vessels to weigh anchor. When the rival Penarth Docks were built in 1865, trade in Cardiff barely dipped.

As transport links with the Rhondda Valley improved and the mines sank ever deeper, the quality and quantity of coal reaching Cardiff improved. Hundreds of thousands of men and their families flocked from south-west England to Cardiff and the valleys to take part in the 'coal rush'.

The running of the Bute estates fell into the hands of William Thomas Lewis, a tough anti-union man who was appointed to take care of business. The 3rd Marquess, while seldom visiting Cardiff and leaving most of the business in the hands of his steward, nonetheless contributed large sums to the development of the docks and also donated large sums of money to the town. In 1882 he gave a gift of £10,000 to the council towards a university, which at the time was estimated to cost £50,000. In total the marquess spent £2 million on the docks, much of it at the suggestion of Lewis, who impressed upon him the importance of investing in new technology – particularly cranes that could lift coal wagons. The docks specialised in loading coal, and over half a century later, as the war began, this over specialisation nearly proved fatal.

One result of these changes was the birth of Cardiff shipping magnates. The docks became one of the most important shipping hubs in the world, and the remarkable character David Davies emerged as the pre-eminent shipping tycoon of his day. Davies, much like Lewis, was a self-made man, a farmer's son who had worked in a number of industries before he made his money in mining. The story of his success, perhaps apocryphal, is that he was virtually bankrupted by failed mining ventures in the upper Rhondda Valley. Just before he shut up shop and admitted defeat, his miners agreed to stay on unpaid for one more week and found the largest and richest seam of coal ever, making Davies a multi-millionaire. His surplus wealth was poured into shipping, and he founded the Ocean Coal Company. Davies used the Bute Docks for two decades and resented having to hand money over to the Bute family to export his coal, as he had mined it on land that was not dominated by them. Anxious to break the Butes' hold over mining and shipping, he proposed docks in the small coastal village of Barry in 1881. It took a titanic struggle lasting over two years to get the matter heard in Parliament, but by

Charles Vaughan Dean of Llandaff. Vaughan died at Llandaff in 1897 after serving at Harrow and was widely respected as a scholar and theologian.

1889 Davies had a fully vertically integrated mining and exporting business, because he controlled the rail links between his colliery and the deep water portal at Barry. There was a population boom, and Barry was transformed into a vital industrial town with Davies, who died in 1900, credited as its father. Once again the Bute Docks were only affected in the short run, as world trade in coal continued to grow.

The final dock-building project that occupied Cardiff and the Bute family was Queen Alexandra Dock. The marquess noted the success of Barry with concern, realising that it was now more suitable for the bigger ships of the late Victorian era than any of Cardiff's docks, and decided to compete. The Alexandra Dock was one of the biggest civil engineering projects in the world. A decade in the building, and costing over £2.5 million, it stretched over a mile and covered a vast site of over 50 acres. The 3rd Marquess never lived to see it finished, as he died in 1900 aged 52, the same age as his father. It was the 4th Marquess who saw his father's work completed.

The Bute family spent more money on the docks in three generations than they ever saw in returns. This is not to say that the Butes were not extremely wealthy and successful, just that the docks consumed vast resources and required immense capital investment. Debts began to accumulate during the construction of the Alexandra Dock and they were added to by the next venture, which was a belated foray into the railway business – the soon to be redundant Cardiff Railway. The Butes had left it far too late (some would argue half a century too late) to integrate railways into their business model, and their line only ran as far as Treforest, being partly reliant on the Taff Vale Railway Company's existing infrastructure. The 4th Marquess subsidised the Bute Docks Company, a corporate institution established to manage the docks in 1912 and 1913, as they failed to make a profit at all.

Perhaps the main failing came from the fact that the 2nd Marquess pioneered the development of the docks on his own. Corporate enterprises seem to have fared better, being more able to manage risk and loss. After the death of the 3rd Marquess the family gradually began to disengage from Cardiff, and it was the advent of the First World War and the virtual nationalisation of the docks that finally freed the Butes from their growing financial millstone.

From the 1860s onwards the sea lanes of the world were dominated by Cardiff's tramp steamers. For over half a century these iconic vessels carried coal and iron ore around the globe, taking Cardiff to the world and bringing the world back to Cardiff. Merchant seamen from Cardiff settled in Canada, Australia, South Africa, Cyprus and the Far East, and by the end of the nineteenth century there was a Cardiffian involved in shipping living in every outpost of the British Empire, normally ferried there by tramp steamer. Such was the durability of these ships that some were still in active service in 1940 and were commandeered for Operation Dynamo, the evacuation of the Dunkirk beaches.

In the heyday of the coal-exporting boom, when Cardiff was exporting 11 million tons of coal a year, owning a ship moored there was an almost guaranteed way to make money, even for the most inept of entrepreneurs. A large number of Irish migrants made the town their home, particularly in Canton, most of them finding work on the docks. Cardiff became one of the most cosmopolitan towns in Britain as thousands of merchant seamen from around the world moved there. Sailors from China, Yemen, Cape Verde and Russia all came to settle, some actively building communities in the town. The ethnic mix of Cardiff that exists today was born in the expansion of the Industrial Revolution, as are the town's different suburbs – and it is them to which we turn next.

eight

THE EXPANDING CITY

Temperance Town

One of the most remarkable attempts at social engineering in the mid-nineteenth century in Cardiff was the Temperance Town that was established by the River Taff. Cardiffians who walk from St Mary's Street to the Millennium Stadium today are probably unaware that they are walking up the last remaining thoroughfare that was part of a bid to make a new Cardiff. The official name of the district is unclear: it became known as Temperance Town because of restrictions on the consumption and sale of alcohol within its boundaries. The founder of Temperance Town, Jacob Matthews, and the land's owner, Colonel Edward Wood, after whom Wood Street is named, were both zealously teetotal, and considering the fact that Cardiff had had centuries of an active alcohol and brewing trade, their planned development was a radical departure. Methodism had grown in popularity in the town, which may explain the importance of temperance, but a more likely reason was the pressure that industrialisation was bearing on ordinary people. The middle classes in Cardiff and across Britain were growing increasingly worried about the effect of alcohol on working families, as the temptation for husbands to be feckless with their earnings was omnipresent in the minds of Victorian social reformers. The Temperance Town had a temperance hall, and three schools, run by the Wood Street Educational Board, were built. There was a church and all the amenities needed by a relatively poor working-class community. Because of the continual influx of new labour into Cardiff, there was no shortage of people to live in Temperance Town. The area was eventually demolished in the 1930s by the council: a residential district that was sandwiched between the railway station and the commercial heart of Cardiff was contrary to the council's, and the Great Western Railway's, plans.

The tragic demise of Temperance Town, a district full of families, histories, friendships and stories, represents a supreme irony. A district of housing, built by social reformers for the poor and designed to give them amenities for their own betterment, is ultimately undone because businesses needed to expand – the same businesses that had been created by the hard work of Temperance Town's inhabitants.

In examining the rest of Cardiff's suburbs, it is probably worth making a few general points. Firstly, like most large towns Cardiff was a central administrative hub that for commercial and strategic reasons stayed much the same size for most of its history. The Industrial Revolution caused almost ceaseless expansion for over a century, which resulted in many thousands of new residents and workers, and the expansion of the town to include outlying parishes and districts that at one time had a distinct life and character of their

The Senedd Building, Cardiff Bay. This was designed by Sir Richard Rogers to be the most sustainable building in Britain and won architecture's most prestigious award, the Stirling Prize.

own. One only has to visit Llandaff or Whitchurch to realise that whilst they are connected to Cardiff they aren't really Cardiff; their residents still have a sense of local identity that is based around communal values and experiences, and they are less inclined to view themselves in a city-wide context. For many of Cardiff's wards and suburbs, however, this is no longer the case. In this section we discuss the suburbs that grew as a result of the Industrial Revolution, appearing in a generation, and some that vanished equally quickly.

Canton

The story of Canton closely mirrors the experience of Cardiff in the nineteenth century. It owes its existence, in its current form, to the rapid expansion of Cardiff Docks. Like much of Cardiff, it was a manor for much of the Middle Ages, separate from the town but with its roots deep in Glamorgan's

Anglo-Norman past. The manor of Canton, called Treganna in Welsh, took lands from the diocese of Llandaff in the thirteenth century, long after *The Book of Llandaff* had been written with the express purpose of preventing any further losses of lands to knights and lords. The name originates from the sixteenth-century St Canna. Bard Iolo Morgannwg wrote a life of St Canna, claiming that she was a Breton princess who had married into Welsh Celtic royalty, only to be abandoned by her husband when he chose to become a hermit on Anglesey. Canna remarried, and her son from her second marriage was also beatified by Rome. She is most notably linked to Llangan in Pembrokeshire. Her connection with Cardiff is unclear, but it is likely that whatever settlements actually existed in Cardiff in the Dark Ages would have been an ideal way-station for pilgrims travelling to sacred sites in the west of Wales. Neighbouring Pontcanna is also linked to the saint, being Canna's Bridge. Morgannwg's chronicles of the saint link her to King Arthur, perhaps as a niece, though this is more than likely poetic licence and embellishment.

If Glamorgan, Cardiff and Cardiff's outlying manors had Anglo-Norman values imposed upon them, then there is at least some evidence to suggest that the names and language of the indigenous Welsh survived in the new Anglicised culture, and even began to influence the settlers.

Early Norman Cantonians are recorded in parish records from the thirteenth century onwards, clearly adopting the place name as their family name. A family of de Cantunes is identifiable from 1215 onwards. They appear to be landowners with a small degree of wealth, and by the mid-thirteenth century some of the de Cantunes were involved in local politics, Walter De Cantune being one of the witnesses to Cardiff's charter. It is unlikely that they were descendants of Fitzhamon's knights, as they would have held onto their Norman surnames, but probable that they were Anglo-Norman migrants who arrived in the decades after the Norman conquest of Wales. The fact that they prospered indicates that settlers treated Wales in the same way that European settlers treated the opening up of the west in America, a kind of *Terra Nullius* where opportunities abounded.

In the Middle Ages, Canton was a thriving market, the Canton cross (now the site of a pub of the same name) being a convenient place for buying and selling goods from the South Wales valleys. Merchants from Bristol and the south-west came to the market to buy and sell livestock, and then herded their animals to the dock and back across the Bristol Channel. Canton's population (there were about 200 inhabitants) remained relatively stable throughout the Middle Ages, and although it probably lost a share of its population during the Black Death there is no evidence to suggest that the manor was completely uninhabited.

Canton's real growth came in the 1840s and '50s with the beginnings of mass migration to Cardiff from Ireland – and contemporary Canton still has a distinctly Irish feel, with an Irish shop on Cowbridge Road East indicating the size of the community. The desperation of Irish migrants can be seen in the demographics of every west coast British port, from Glasgow to Liverpool, Cardiff to Bristol; hundreds of thousands of hunger-ravaged and impoverished people fled the catastrophe that had hit their homeland, the Irish potato famine. In much the same way that Irish migration and industriousness made the cities of New York, Chicago, Boston and Philadelphia, it made Cardiff too. Cardiff's identity was initially a tug of war between Welsh and English roots, but we also have to look at Cardiff's Irish soul: it was Irish labour that dug out the docks, built the roads and railways, loaded coal onto ships and lived in cramped conditions in Canton, Grangetown, Newtown and the Hayes. It can be argued that modern Cardiff was built by the Irish.

By 1875 Canton was incorporated into the city of Cardiff. Throughout the nineteenth century the last vestiges of the medieval town walls were taken down and the stage was set for nineteenth-century urban sprawl. Canton boomed in population, and its proximity to the growing docks made it an ideal place to house the new workforce. The once vibrant common, home of Canton's marketplace, was replaced by that most modern of Victorian amenities, a park. Victoria Park was built to commemorate Queen Victoria's sixtieth year on the throne in 1897, and a quintessential Victorian bandstand takes pride of place, together with a memorial to one of Cardiff's most famous inhabitants.

When I decided to write this book I wanted it to be a tribute to Cardiff's people, the story of their struggles and triumph in the face of adversity, so I planned to leave Billy the Seal out of the story. On reflection I feel that Cardiffians would never forgive such a grievous omission, so here is the story of how Billy came to be immortalised in bronze in Victoria Park. Billy was accidentally caught by fishermen on a Cardiff trawler in the Irish Sea in 1912, and was brought back to Cardiff. He was given to the small zoo in Victoria Park and seems to have charmed onlookers, who christened him. Accounts indicate that Billy was a star attraction. During floods in 1927 Billy escaped his enclosure, and swam the streets of Canton and through back gardens, even entering houses and trying to board a tram on Cowbridge Road East before being recaptured. Billy was mourned by schoolchildren across Cardiff when he died in 1939, and post-mortem examination revealed that Billy was actually female. Since her death, Billy has been immortalised in Cardiff folklore, with songs being sung about her life and antics and many stories, real and apocryphal, being passed down from generation to generation.

Cardiff's market was moved to the current site of Cantonian High School on the Canton/Fairwater border. This fixed site, with stables and a slaughterhouse, was smaller than the medieval site but administered professionally. In the late nineteenth century Canton was connected to the rest of the town by tram, and by the early twentieth century Cardiff and Canton were almost completely integrated.

Newtown

Much like Temperance Town, Newtown is a district of Cardiff that has been all but wiped from the pages of Cardiff's history; it is unlikely that many Cardiffians are aware that it existed at all. Like Grangetown and Canton, it was a purpose-built home for dockworkers, and thousands of Irish migrants flocked there. The Marquess of Bute organised the migration of impoverished Irish workers and their families to Cardiff in 1846. Already facing huge financial challenges in his construction of the docks, he was probably mindful of the need to keep down labour costs when he looked to Ireland to solve his manpower problems. During the Industrial Revolution, South Wales was not short of labour, as there had been a huge influx of working men from south-west England throughout the nineteenth century, but no doubt they were more expensive to employ and possibly more likely to be unionised or affiliated to radical movements like the Chartists. The ideal solution was desperate and malleable Irish labour. Newtown's houses were built especially for these new workers, in close proximity to Cardiff Docks.

Like Temperance Town, Newtown was a network of six streets, on a site behind the iconic Altolusso Building. This tightly knit community lasted until 1970 when it was demolished to make way for the expansion of Atlantic Wharf. Now all that marks its existence is a memorial. Community and Catholicism were the defining features of the area, and by the late nineteenth century it had built for itself Catholic schools and community associations. A strong and confident Catholic presence was established in Cardiff once more.

Newtown's most famous son was the boxer 'Peerless' Jim Driscoll, who won fifty-four of his seventy-one fights. His story is similar to that of many of the boxing greats of the twentieth century, a life of poverty and hardship, where boxing was a means of escape and a way in which self-worth could be established. Driscoll was one of five children. His mother was widowed when he was just 7 months old, when his father was killed in an accident in a neighbouring goods yard. A measure of how legendary a figure Driscoll became was the response to his own tragically premature death just forty-four years later, when an estimated 100,000 people lined the streets to pay tribute to him on the day of his funeral. No other figure in Cardiff's history has managed to achieve such a turn-out: in 1925, 100,000 people would have constituted the bulk of the city's population.

Driscoll achieved fame by being the only Cardiffian to win the Lonsdale Belt, a boxing prize introduced by Lord Samuel Wallace Lonsdale in 1909. Driscoll won the prize in 1910. At the turn of the century fairgrounds were the most common arena in which poor working-class fighters made their name, and Driscoll was no exception. In 1901, at the age of 21, he decided to turn professional, giving up his job as a print assistant at the *Western Mail*. He was clearly a gifted fighter and won twelve fights with no defeats in the first year of his career. By 1906 he had taken the British Featherweight title, and won the Commonwealth Featherweight in 1908. Driscoll travelled to the USA, where British and European boxers had toured since the nineteenth century. It was there that he won the nickname 'Peerless Jim' owing to his fluid, graceful style, which inspired generations of US boxing coaches and trainers.

The community spirit that bound Newtown together was integral to Driscoll's character, and he demonstrated this by turning down the chance to be the Featherweight Champion of the World to attend a fundraising exhibition match in aid of St Nazareth's Orphanage in Newtown, telling disappointed promoters in the USA, 'I never break a promise.'

Driscoll's career might well have continued had it not been for the First World War. He was conscripted as a physical training instructor and didn't see any of the savage fighting in France, but after the war his health deteriorated, perhaps owing to a chest infection he caught whilst in America. Eventually he succumbed to consumption, after one of the most successful professional boxing careers that Wales has ever seen. He became a hero of his community because his skill, perseverance and personal integrity echoed the values that the pioneers of Newtown tried to instil through their schools, community organisations, churches and orphanage. Driscoll was buried, his coffin draped in a Union Flag, in Cathays Cemetery. He is now immortalised with a statue, erected on the site of the boys' club where he used to train.

Butetown

It is entirely possible to argue that in the nineteenth century Butetown was one of the most cosmopolitan and integrated districts in the world. As with Newtown, houses were built along the teeming wharf for dockworkers, many of them being built by the 2nd Marquess of Bute and his son. The popular perception of Tiger Bay and Butetown that existed in the Victorian era continued until the entire district was gentrified from the late 1960s onwards. This popular perception, formed by outsiders, by Cardiff's growing suburban middle classes, by the press, the police and the courts, was one of vice and criminality, but it is possible that this was based on a less well-defined fear amongst Cardiffians of cultures that were alien to them: by the turn of the century over fifty different nationalities lived in Butetown. Perhaps the first truly globalised profession was that of the sailor. Men from Africa, Asia, Europe and the Americas all settled alongside Tiger Bay throughout the nineteenth century. The bay became synonymous with one of the first fully integrated and multicultural areas in the country. Cardiff had some non-white inhabitants, but before 1800 there were not many non-white freemen who were capable of competing for work on an equal footing with their white counterparts. The bay was a flashpoint for violence several times in the twentieth century as racial tensions boiled over into angry confrontation.

The men and women who lived and died here were hemmed into a relatively small area of waterfront, their community shaped by the global patterns of trade that transformed Cardiff in the nineteenth century. The town's ethnic diversity was clear even by 1860, when Yemeni and Adenese sailors who lived in and around Butetown established the very first mosque in Britain, in Cathays. This is still standing, now the Al-Manar Islamic & Cultural Centre. The establishment of Muslim, Caribbean, Irish and Chinese communities in Cardiff made the changes to the town's ethnic makeup permanent, and added something fundamental to Cardiff's character.

Jewish worship in Butetown predates the establishment of the Cathays Mosque. A synagogue was founded at East Terrace in 1858, but the roots of the Jewish community can be found far earlier in the nineteenth century. As far back as 1841 a Jewish burial ground was opened in Highfield, suggesting that there was an established Jewish community in the expanding Victorian town, and that the community was sufficiently prosperous to afford plots of land in the growing suburb of Roath. Bute Street was a familiar thoroughfare for Jewish businesses in the late nineteenth and early twentieth centuries, populated by many small businesses and shops, and it was this community that came to be targeted in a brief campaign of intimidation by William Joyce, the British fascist and later Nazi propagandist Lord Haw-Haw, who lived on Colum Road in Cardiff in the mid-1930s.

Another clue to Butetown's diversity of faith is Cardiff Bay's Norwegian church. Norwegians, Swedes and Danes could be found in every major port in the world by the end of the nineteenth century, and Cardiff was no exception. A Norwegian church now stands at the edge of the Cardiff Bay barrage, looking out over open water. It seems fitting that it was eventually moved here, echoing the outlook of centuries of Norwegians, who have always looked to the seas. The first great seafaring people of Europe had a home in Butetown, and their church, the *Sjømannskireken* or Sailors' Church, was built in Norway in prefabricated sections. It was erected in Butetown in 1866, the pastor of the church, Lars Oftedal, setting up the Norwegian Seamen's Mission in that year. Planning permission was granted in 1920 for a new church in Clarence Road, and £20,000 was raised to pay for it, much being donated by various Scandinavian shipping magnates, but no church or mission was built. It became important to cater for a larger congregation because by the early twentieth century there were far more seafarers coming from Scandinavia than ever before. These were the men who paid a heavy price during the Second World War on the Atlantic and Arctic convoys that sailed from Cardiff to New York or Murmansk; a lasting monument to the courage and sacrifice of merchant seamen of all nationalities is situated outside the Senydd Building.

In 1959, Tiger Bay was immortalised by a film of the same name, starring Horst Buchholz, John Mills and his daughter Hailey (in her cinematic debut). Considering the reputation the district had developed for vice and corruption, and the propensity for British post-war film noir to focus on the grim bomb-damaged face of Britain, Tiger Bay was the perfect backdrop. Much of this bleak tale of crime and retribution was filmed in Newport and Bristol, but it managed to capture real life in Tiger Bay and Butetown, showing not only its poverty (at a time when it was becoming fashionable for novelists and playwrights such as John Osborne and Alan Sillitoe to feature the realities of

Norwegian church (*above and right*).
A mission for sailors from Norway was
established in 1868 by Herman Lunde of
Oslo, and Roald Dahl – Cardiff born but of
Norwegian descent – spent the last years of
his life campaigning and fundraising for its
restoration.

The church became a great source of comfort
for Norwegian sailors in Cardiff during the
Second World War. Although it is no longer a
mission for the homesick and weary, it is still
one of the city's main cultural spaces.

working-class life) but also portraying black British people on film perhaps for the first time. This film is the most important set of images of Butetown to be captured, because *Tiger Bay* was a film made at the end of an era. The way of life that it presents was gone within a decade.

Splott

Splott is another part of the urban explosion of Cardiff from the 1840s. The medieval manor stretched along the Newport Road, occupying good arable land between the road and the marshes along the estuary. Splott, like Roath, existed for much of its life as a reasonably autonomous parish outside the town walls. Its name seems to have been derived from its farming land. Throughout the Middle Ages, Splott and Tremorfa were both divided into three main farms, Upper and Lower Splott Farms and Pengham Farm, which occupies much of today's Tremorfa. Splott, like other rural manors in the area, often changed hands: in 1740, rents for Splott were payable to Llandaff Manor, whereas earlier it was the property of Lord Tredegar. Lady Isabel Despenser owned Splott in 1440, and the Beaudripp family emerged as a political force there during the Reformation. It is entirely possible that the whole population of Splott was lost during the Black Death as close proximity to the waterfront made the illness far more virulent, because of the greater number of rats.

The real character of Splott, as with all districts close to the waterfront, was forged by the Industrial Revolution, but it was a late addition to the growing metropolis. It seems strange to think that standing at the end of Queen Street in Cardiff about 130 years ago one would have seen marsh ahead, running out to the estuary, teeming with coal ships. The birth of East Moors Steelworks changed everything for Splott. Again, a ready and available workforce was needed for a new employer, and the colonisation of the marshes began. The life of Splott probably changed more quickly and in a shorter period than most other districts. As if literally springing from the wetlands, houses, streets, shops, schools and hospitals were built. East Moors Steelworks was a titanic industrial force, crushing all competitors in its path. The new innovation of steel smelting made traditional Cardiff ironworks largely obsolete, and the Pentyrch and Whitchurch works had already gone bust. Having such a powerful industrial force established in Cardiff in 1891 gave the town greater economic stability and diversity, which saw it through the next half-century of economic crises. This steelworks was a valuable asset to Cardiff and Splott during the First World War and the subsequent Depression in the 1930s.

The southern boundary of Splott was eventually decided by the railways. A visitor to Cardiff today can look to the right on arrival from Paddington station and see row after row of former steelworkers' and dockworkers' houses backing onto the railway lines. In 1882, Splott's first school was opened by the Marquess of Bute. The size of Splottlands School gives an idea of the speed of change: it had 1,500 pupils, an enormous number by late Victorian standards.

One of the most overlooked aspects of Splott is its contribution to British aviation. Not only was its most famous son (not to overlook John Humphreys or Dame Shirley Bassey, to whom we shall turn subsequently) the aviator Ernest Willows, but Splott also had its own airport at Pengham. There does seem to be something remorselessly pragmatic in Britain when it comes to dealing with institutions or landmarks that no longer serve a purpose: Pengham airport is now covered by houses and Willows School.

The Scott monument that is situated in Cardiff Bay, outside the Norwegian church, was placed there a century after the fateful expedition to the South Pole, finally laying to rest the rivalry between Scott and the Norwegian Amundsen.

The growth of Pengham aerodrome in the 1920s and '30s was consistent with the overall picture of an emerging new economy, based on light industry, consumer goods and in no small part aviation. Before aviation proved its military usefulness in the First World War it was a hobby primarily for wealthy gentlemen entrepreneurs, and the most famous of such men to hail from Cardiff was the aviator Ernest Thomson Willows, born in Newport Road. After the site was bought from Lord Tredegar in 1910, it became a hive of activity primarily for building and testing new aircraft. The excitement that must have been generated when Willows's first 74ft-long airship was ready to fly must have been immense. Willows had originally planned to train as a dentist, but he built his first airship in 1905 at the age of 19. To place this innovation into some kind of context, it was in 1903 that the Wright Brothers had their first maiden flight, and in 1905 that they built their first fixed wing commercial aircraft. This was a revolutionary period for aviation and because of Willows' efforts Cardiff was right at the heart of it.

Willows was the first person to own an airship licence in Britain, and he piloted his first airship the Willows Number One, for a total of 85 minutes in 1905. This machine was built around a rigid but collapsible frame, the balloon was made of silk and it was piloted from a gondola slung beneath. It was powered by motorcycle engines with propellers. The Willows Number Two flew from Pengham to Town Hall in 1910, by which time the potential of airship flight was starting to be recognised by commercial and military interests. Willows' third airship was christened *City Of Cardiff* and flew in October 1910 to London, landing at White City; the following month he piloted it from Wormwood Scrubs to Paris. In December, by way of celebration, he flew around the Eiffel Tower. This airship was a third longer than its predecessors at 120ft. The penultimate incarnation of Willows's dirigible, the Willows Number Four, was purchased by the Royal Navy in 1912. The naval race with Germany had entered a critical phase, as both countries prepared for a titanic showdown that would decide supremacy on the high seas for the next century, a battle that was ultimately fought at Jutland in 1916. Britain led the field in cruisers, destroyers and dreadnoughts, but Germany was making good her lack of a surface fleet with a lethal array of U-boats, vessels that had a catastrophic effect on British shipping in the coming two world wars. The Willows airship was seen as part of a system of defence against the U-boat menace. It was the first airship that the admiralty owned, and though it was smaller than the later ones, it was ideal for training new crews. It was also able to demonstrate to sceptical service chiefs that airships could be useful in spotting U-boats and relaying their position to warships.

During the First World War, Willows continued to offer a vital service to Britain as an aeronautical engineer. He designed and made barrage balloons which, towards the end of the war, became more and more essential as Germany, in desperation, began to bomb London, and in 1918 threatened to destroy the city with a raid consisting of several hundred aircraft. Willows tragically died in 1926 at an air show in Kempston, Bedford, but he bequeathed to Cardiff and to Splott an impressive legacy, as a pivotal part of Britain's aviation industry and defences for the next three decades.

By 1931 the airport was fully operational, no longer just a workshop for airships but part of the new aviation industry that was shaping Britain. The crash of the R101 Airship in 1930 ended the Air Ministry's love affair with airships and the focus for innovation fell squarely in fixed wing aircraft. In a period that saw a gradual shift towards rearmament, especially from 1938 onwards, any town or city in Britain with its own airfield took on a new strategic significance.

Until 1932 Pengham airfield operated as more of a club than a commercial hub, as flying wasn't anything more than a sport, but the establishment of a twice daily service to Bristol, followed a year later by the patronage of HRH the Prince of Wales, saw the site's importance evolve beyond that of an aerial marina for the idle rich. By 1937 the site had been militarised and transformed into RAF Cardiff. The real explosion of rearmament began in 1938, with Neville Chamberlain's various meetings in Munich, but the fact that Cardiff had an Auxiliary RAF squadron established in 1937 suggests that air defence was a new and important priority. The previous year the world witnessed the German bombing of Guernica, the first demonstration of the terrifying potential of airports. This was surely a lesson that was not lost on British military planners, and a lesson to be repeated over Cardiff just five years later.

The war began before the squadron at Cardiff was ready. Many pilots from Cardiff were given operational training in England and their main role (fittingly) was as U-boat hunters off the west coast. By 1942 the British element of the Allied combined bomber offensive against Germany was in full swing and Cardiff's 614 Squadron took part, attacking airfields in the Low Countries, and razing cities like Cologne to the ground in the infamous Thousand Bomber Raids. The squadron, equipped with two-engined Bristol Blenheim bombers, also laid down a smokescreen for the disastrous Allied raid on Dieppe and were later deployed to North Africa. For much of the squadron's operational life it was based away from Pengham, but without the airfield there would have been no squadron to raise and no infrastructure to use.

After the war the focus of Cardiff's aviation shifted away from Pengham to Rhoose, the site of Cardiff's international airport today. RAF Rhoose was a training base for Spitfire pilots from 1941 onwards and critically it had a radar station as well, an asset that ensured its future after the war. The other key advantage that RAF Rhoose had over Pengham was that there was sufficient land for expansion.

From 1952 onwards Rhoose was the destination for Aer Lingus flights from Dublin, and in 1954 a terminus was built, all commercial flights switching to the site. Glamorgan County Council eventually inherited it, and intensive development resulted in a busy commercial European airport, visited on several occasions by Concorde. In 2007 the airport reached an all-time high, serving 2.1 million passengers in the year, a far cry from Ernest Willows's airships.

Grangetown

Within Grangetown's name is the clue to its past. The lands that were quickly dominated by Victorian housing for dockworkers in the nineteenth century had previously existed as a grange, or a farm, owned by Margham Abbey throughout the Middle Ages. Grange Farm dominated the marsh lowlands from the time of Robert Fitzhamon, and miraculously it still stands. It can be found on Clive Street and is a stunning visual testimony to the past. The whole area was rapidly developed following the establishment of Penarth Road in the 1850s and the growing importance of Penarth as a centre of trade and commerce. Gradually the rural way of life in the manor died out and the suburb of Grangetown was established and incorporated into Cardiff in 1875.

Every suburb in Cardiff seems to have had its own unique purpose during the Industrial Revolution, each bequeathing crucial improvements to the lives of the people, and Grangetown is no different. One of the suburb's biggest employers was the Cardiff Gas and Coke Company, providing hundreds of jobs for the men of Grangetown. The gas towers have made way for an Ikea superstore, signifying once more the shift from a heavy industrial past to a retail and post-industrial present.

What remains of the head offices of the Cardiff Gas and Coke Company can be found at the site of the Altolusso building. The ornate Victorian façade

Newspaper cutting from the *Daily Express* showing dancers in Roath Park.

WHIRLING INTO HAPPINESS at Roath Park, Cardiff, where the open air dancing experiment achieved a popular success.

Cardiff City Hall was built in 1897 and contains an upstairs marble hall, opened by David Lloyd George in 1916, which contains marble sculptures of great figures from Welsh history including St David, Henry VII and Owain Glyndŵr.

is all that remains of the old building, and behind it stands an ultra-modern apartment complex.

A considerable part of Grangetown was set aside for workers' houses, but there were also plenty of leafy, spacious, gentrified boulevards, which like Roath, Penylan and Cyncoed were designed to attract a generation of the well-to-do middle classes to Cardiff.

One Grangetown resident who went on to have a lasting impact was Ephraim Turner. A sculptor by trade, he established a building firm in Grangetown in 1885 and ran it until his retirement in 1896, when he handed over the company to his two sons. He was another of the handful of eminent Victorians who shaped the town, in his case by building the law courts and the town hall. It is difficult to imagine the centre of Cardiff today without the neo-Classical grandeur that he crafted.

These days Grangetown is home to Brains Brewery, which moved from its traditional home in the brewery quarter just off St Mary's Street. When Lord Ninian Edward Crichton Stuart was killed at the Hohenzollern Redoubt in Belgium in 1915, whilst attacking German trenches with the Welsh Guards, his name was immortalised in Grangetown's Ninian Park. Lord Ninian Stuart, who was son of the 3rd Marquess of Bute, had helped arrange for Cardiff City Football Club to get access to the site in 1909, and in 1910 construction had begun.

Ely

Ely stands on an ancient thoroughfare that runs from Carmarthen to Swansea, laid down by the Romans. Cowbridge Road, which runs from Canton to Ely, is the only remnant of this road and both Ely and Cardiff are products of this east-west route.

Ely was named after the river that borders it and defines its geographical boundaries. For much of its existence it has remained a sleepy village, its lands belonging to the diocese of Llandaff, and its people relying on fishing and milling for their livelihood. Industrialisation had a massive effect from the late eighteenth century onwards, as there was a steady growth in population and commercial activity, and a turnpike trust was established to maintain the road that connected West Wales to Glamorgan and England. The growth in trade and commerce in Britain made any main thoroughfare a more valuable asset than before, and this in turn provided jobs and wealth. The real growth, however, came in the nineteenth century when heavy industry arrived in Cardiff.

In 1849, Cardiff was ravaged by an outbreak of cholera. This was not a unique problem. Cholera was largely unknown in Britain before 1831, but from that date until 1850 there was an epidemic of the disease, largely the product of cramped and unsanitary living conditions due to the rapid expansion of towns and cities. As doctors began to turn their thinking away from the miasmatic theory of communicability of disease (that it was something to do with 'foul airs' and pollution) and realised that there was a connection with water, they started to look to places like Ely for a solution. The outbreak in Cardiff was exacerbated by poor sewerage and communal taps. Whilst there had been some improvement in sanitation in 1774, the efforts of the town's authorities could not keep up with the constant growth in population. The epidemic cost the lives of some 350 Cardiffians, and only the conversion of the old corn mill on the River Ely into a pumping station, which began to supply the town with fresh water, saved it from spreading. Cardiff was lucky with the timing of the outbreak. The first main wave of deaths across England had been in

1832; Liverpool, Ormskirk and Warrington had been hit hard, along with many other new industrial centres of the North. By the time Cardiff was struck, some seventeen years later, lessons had been learned and some understanding of the relationship between cholera and poor sanitation existed.

Brewing was a vital part of Ely's life during the mid-nineteenth century. With arable land for barley and hops, the Ely Brewery and Croswell Brewers established themselves there. During the cholera outbreak drinking beer, a natural antiseptic, was considered a safer option than drinking water. The Croswell Brewery Company, renamed the Rhymney Brewery, based in Dowlais, competed with Ely Brewers until 1960 when they bought out their rival. The Ely Brewery Company was a feature of life in the suburb for a century, an employer, a landmark and an important part of the community's pride and identity. Similarly the business empire created by Samuel Chivers, a malt vinegar brewer, whose business grew in conjunction with the beer brewing trade in Ely, was a main employer for the district. Chivers, who created popular pickles, preserves and jam and sold them under his own name, eventually passed the company to his two sons, who later rebranded the jams and preserves as Golden Grove. Both the brewery and the pickling factory were bought out and eventually shut in the 1960s and '70s. The Rhymney Brewery was purchased four years after they had bought the Ely Brewery Company by Whitbread, which closed both the Ely factories shortly afterwards, depriving the community of jobs and destroying one of the industrial and social features of the suburb that had provided immense community cohesion.

Another example of how Ely was both enriched by and then failed by industrialism is the example of Ely's paperworks. This huge site, established in the heyday of Victorian newspaper journalism and pamphleteering, was the biggest supplier of newspaper print in Britain, and therefore one of the biggest in the world. There can be few countries that rivalled the British in the mid- to late nineteenth century in their appetite for newspapers, and it was Ely and her paperworks that sustained much of that demand. All the more remarkable was the fact that at this time Ely was still a village: these vast new industrial sites weren't accompanied by vast urban estates until after the First World War. The Ely paperworks was situated next to the new railway, and when it was opened by Thomas Owen in 1865 most of the machines were steam operated, which meant a steady supply of both coal and water was necessary. Cardiff's booming port meant that paper could be shipped all over the British Empire, and one report on the company's progress indicated that much of the newsprint of the colonies was manufactured in Ely. The great chimney at the paperworks could be seen as far away as Canton and Llandaff, and became one of the new features of the industrial skyline of Cardiff.

Thomas Owen was a rare example of a genuine Victorian entrepreneur who came from exceedingly modest circumstances. He was the son of a yeoman farmer from near Machynlleth, and seems to have built up the company with little more than effort and innate ability. After the Second World War the factory modernised, but this was not enough to prevent the company from progressively losing market share throughout the post-war era, and eventually it was bought by Anglo-French paper giant Wiggins Teape. Production was shifted away from newsprint to printer paper, but the factory eventually closed, unable to compete with increased global competition. The factory was finally demolished in 2006.

Ely was finally incorporated into Cardiff in 1922, by which time an ambitious house-building project was underway. David Lloyd George had announced at the end of the First World War that there must be 'homes fit for heroes', and that a massive housebuilding project was required. Ely was the ideal choice for houses in the South Glamorgan area, with its wide open spaces, good transport links and close proximity to Cardiff. Lloyd George was doing more than simply answering his conscience. The whole economy had been put on a wartime production footing for several years, involving most of the adult population, and peace threatened mass unemployment. What better way to counter this and prevent a post-war slump, the likes of which had been experienced a century before after the Napoleonic wars, than to galvanise industry to build badly needed houses. Taking a walk through Ely today, it is easy to spot these Edwardian homes, but it is less easy to understand their importance. Ely and countless other suburbs across Britain exist partly for the needs of demobbed men, but mainly to prevent the country from collapsing into a deep depression. This, however, was not completely avoided, just postponed for a decade.

nine

THE BUTE FAMILY

The story of the Bute family is significant because their influence has shaped nearly 300 years of the life of Cardiff. So how did a family of ancient Scottish heritage come to dominate the town's political and economic life?

On the death of the 7th Earl of Pembroke in 1683 his Welsh estates including Cardiff passed to his daughter, Charlotte Herbert. Her first husband, John Jeffries, died in 1702 and she married Thomas, Viscount Windsor, who had fought bravely at the Battle of Blenheim under the Duke of Marlborough. Through this marriage he inherited the Lordship of Cardiff, and the Windsor family retained it until in 1766 another Charlotte was married into an aristocratic family and the title once more changed dynastic hands. Charlotte Windsor, granddaughter to the original Charlotte Herbert, married John, Lord Mountstuart, the eldest son of the prime minister, Lord Bute. The Bute family drew their title from the Scottish island, and had originally been closely allied to the Stuarts of Scotland.

The 1st Marquess of Bute (1744–1814)

The 1st Marquess, Lord John Stuart was elevated to the position of Lord Cardiff in 1776 and served as a Member of Parliament for Bossiney. He had a variety of official and honorary roles, including a place on the privy council and the job of special envoy to Turin. It seems highly likely that he was something of an absentee landlord, taking highly paid and prestigious roles in London and further afield, and doing very little for Cardiff itself. This was not unusual at the time, with countless gentlemen having titles that related to places they seldom visited.

In the marquess we see the archetypal late Georgian dandy – handsome, feckless, dissolute and fond of gambling. The estates that he inherited suffered immensely because of his spendthrift ways. When his first wife Charlotte passed away in 1800 the marquess quickly remarried, his new wife being Fanny Coutts, daughter of a banking family, hoping to use her wealth to dig himself out of his financial mess. An aristocrat marrying a fortune based on commerce was unseemly and only financial desperation would have motivated such a move.

To ensure continued political and economic control of the vast swathes of South Wales dominated by the Butes, Cardiff had developed some degree of strategic importance to the marquess, and he wanted to see his son (who predeceased him) elected as MP for the borough. Cardiff, in his eyes a dreary market town with little to recommend it, was a strategic launch pad for his son's new career.

Upon his death in 1814, and despite his best efforts, there was still a large estate. It was only thanks to effective management by his agents that parts of the parishes of Roath, Cathays and Leckwith were purchased and added to the Bute estates. When he died no monument was raised to his memory, which is telling. One of his achievements which has been overlooked (and for this alone perhaps a plaque is in order, if not a statue) is the creation of Cathays Park, a great example of the Georgian art of landscaping and horticulture that flourished in the eighteenth century. This is perhaps the most lasting legacy of his stewardship. Lord John left almost all his personal estate to his second wife, with the remainder to his son Douglas, who bought back the estates from his stepmother for the enormous sum of £32,000.

The 2nd Marquess of Bute (1793–1848)

John Crichton Mountstuart was a man of the industrial age who lived the role of the nineteenth-century industrialist every bit as much as his grandfather was the epitome of his own times. Unlike his father he was no absentee landlord. The job that he faced was daunting, to reorganise and finance the vast and neglected estates that his grandfather had bequeathed him. He was just 20 when he inherited much of Cardiff, but already the values of the age were firmly embedded in him. The marquess was zealous in his commitment to hard work, and he believed that the greatest of all virtues were financial prudence and the thorough exploitation of material resources for the purposes of accumulating wealth. He was an exemplar of the age that was dawning, a real

Left The South African War Memorial at Cathays Park. Soldiers from the South Wales Borderers and other units saw action during the conflict particularly during the relief of Kimberley.

Below The dragon bust at Cathays Park.

man of the nineteenth century. The marquess realised that part of the problem of his grandfather's Welsh estates was geographical: they were scattered across South Wales. It was recommended by the Bute family's principal agent, David Stewart, a man of great acumen, that he try to consolidate the estate, which he did by purchasing land in Llandaff, Rhydypenau, Llanishen and Penylan, and in the valleys where prospecting for coal and iron was taking place. Thanks to Stewart's advice the Butes became possibly the wealthiest family in the country. As a result of this, the marquess had a position of power, political, economic and social, in Cardiff, and paid the town regular if brief visits. His patronage for a particular tradesman or business could mean an enormous boost to financial fortunes.

The marquess had a thorough grip on all aspects of his business empire. He frequently delegated to administrators, such as his reliable steward E.P. Richards, who served the Butes for four decades, but he intervened directly when it suited him. Richards, mindful of this, told the marquess that he 'would not spend a shilling' without the direction and approval of his master.

Such was the impact of the marquess on Cardiff that his visits were akin to a state event. By the 1830s he was undisputedly the most famous and influential of its citizens. Records show that Bute had become a *de facto* ruler and during his visits ordinary Cardiffians lined the route of his journey to pay their respects. This is all the more significant because this decade was a time of unprecedented class strife in Britain, and the campaign against the poor laws, the struggle for a repeal of the Corn Laws, the campaign for parliamentary reform, and the Chartist movement made acts of deference very rare events, particularly in South Wales, scene of both the Merthyr and Newport Risings.

The lack of parliamentary reform aided Bute's control over the town. Cardiff was important because it was a parliamentary seat, a valuable commodity if much of the land in the borough was yours. The marquess controlled local and national electoral politics in the town through incentives and veiled threats. As a man he was known for his arrogance, temper and political ruthlessness, but he was not without scruples and funded many different charitable organisations although this largesse could be easily withdrawn if he was displeased.

It was to be the crisis surrounding the 1832 Reform Act that exposed the marquess's political colours. The Whig reformers were attempting to end the corrupt patronage that saw a borough MP becoming the lord of the manor's 'man' in Parliament, but it was precisely this kind of arrangement that suited the marquess best. In the winter of 1832 the sitting MP happened to be his brother James.

Lord Patrick James Herbert Crichton Stewart was the absolute political contradiction to his brother. Convinced that parliamentary reform was necessary and allied to the Whig party, James, who had held Cardiff since 1826, was defeated by John Nicholl, who held the seat for twenty years after the monumental reform election of 1832. He had been financed by the marquess, who had few ties of familial loyalty when it came to winning political advantage. The era of such naked political gerrymandering was drawing to a close, however, and even if the Chartists failed to achieve their People's Charter and gain secret ballots, the day when they were introduced was not far off. The growth in literacy, prosperity and organisation amongst the working class of Cardiff meant that corrupt practices could not continue for much longer. The population increase in the 1840s also made it less possible for the marquess and his descendants to fix elections.

The Scott Memorial at Roath Park Lake, erected in 1915. Robert Falcon Scott sailed from Cardiff in 1911 in an ill-fated race to reach the South Pole before Roald Amundsen. He never returned but has been honoured by the city ever since.

Urban life improved in Cardiff because of the civic work done by the Bute family, but again, as with all the marquess's actions, hard financial logic accompanied this. The Bute arable land had steadily begun to fall in value, and the end of the Corn Laws meant that land ownership was no longer a licence to print money at the urban workers' and middle-classes' expense. New streams of revenue had to be found in order for families like the Butes to stay solvent, and one easy way to do that was to capitalise on urban holdings. Originally the 1st Marquess's scattergun approach to acquisitions left him holding unprofitable urban estates in Cardiff, but as the docks, canals, railways and ironworks grew up a steady flow of new workers poured into Cardiff, and with them a newly educated and proficient middle class. In order to entice them to stay and to add to rents, the gentrification of the town had to be undertaken. Cardiff was bidding for industrial and mercantile talent, and the Butes were aware that a pleasing ambience would pay off.

The marquess was the epitome of the Victorian philanthropist, but there is another side to him, one which shines a light on many of the conflicts and tensions of the industrial age. That he was a generous patron of charity is well established, but what is more intriguing is the extent to which he challenged the actions of ironmasters established on Bute land. In the first explosion of raw and unregulated capitalism, workers featured simply as factors of production, rarely as human beings. The same marquess who had opposed the 1832 Reform Act acted against the ironmasters' corrupt practices, probably out of a sense of paternalistic Christian duty as opposed to any feelings of social justice. Ironmasters often controlled the communities that had grown around their forges politically as well as economically, and the marquess prevented them from gaining judicial power as well: he was lord lieutenant for the whole county and had power of appointment over magistrates. In an age of intense industrial tension, where strikes were illegal and union membership unrecognised and sometimes even treated as sedition, an industrialist with the power to prosecute and imprison was a very dangerous thing indeed. To break the power of the ironmasters the marquess replaced their militias of private policemen and prisons with an official, supposedly unbiased, Glamorgan Constabulary.

Before we take an overly sentimental view of the marquess, we should examine his role in the Merthyr Rising and the execution of its leader Richard Lewis, aka Dic Penderyn, who was hanged at Cardiff Gaol in 1831. The marquess commanded the Glamorgan Militia to put down the rising, sparing no force against the workers who had demanded better conditions for themselves and their families. Despite a nationwide campaign to get a reprieve for Penderyn, the marquess was unmoved and refused to back the campaign. The crowd of 500 Cardiff and Merthyr workers who surrounded the prison as the sentence was carried out were a silent but visible reminder that the question of workers' rights was not about to go away. Penderyn, although a Merthyr rebel, is remembered as a workers' martyr in Cardiff today.

ten

THE EARLY TWENTIETH CENTURY

K ing Edward VII granted Cardiff city status on 28 October 1905. The mayor became a lord mayor and the city acquired a Roman Catholic cathedral in 1916. This growth in civic importance was matched by industrial progress and in 1913 the docks reached their zenith with 107 million tons of coal exported through them.

The tensions that industrialisation built up in Cardiff in the nineteenth century, coupled with the stresses on working people that the city's introduction to the global economy and labour market had brought about, exploded into violence in the period of the 'Great Unrest' between 1908 and 1914, when there was industrial strife across the country and a working-class militancy that has never been seen since. A century of rapid industrial growth and the formation of an educated and politicised working class was hardly likely to be without consequence. In Cardiff the result was racial violence against and intimidation of the Chinese community in 1911, when sailors and dockworkers went on strike in support of the Liverpool Seamen and Dockers, who had been part of a general transport strike in Merseyside. In a bid to keep the docks open and coal moving to ports across the world, Chinese sailors and dockworkers were employed, triggering a frenzy of attacks against the strike-breakers and against the Chinese community that had lived in Canton for much of the nineteenth century. This was exceedingly rare in Cardiff's history. There was ethnic violence triggered by economic desperation and communities pitted against one another by shipping magnates desperate to end the dispute. The level of violence and disorder that summer was sufficient to urge Home Secretary Winston Churchill to deploy 500 soldiers to the city to ensure the return of law and order. This was not the last time that racial violence born of economic struggle would grip the city. Following the First World War there was another outburst, again focused on the docks but this time attacking the black community.

The Welsh National War Memorial is
situated in Cathays Park, Cardiff. Built in
1928, it was designed by Sir Ninian Comper.

It might well be that the level of success enjoyed by Chinese small businessmen provoked a deep-seated resentment. By 1910 there were twenty-two Chinese laundries employing fifty-five Chinese, seven ordinary houses occupied by Chinese, and four Chinese licensed boarding houses accommodating ninety-eight seamen. Only 2 per cent of seamen signing on were Chinese, although union officials constantly called for support against the threat of job losses, and there was an unspoken racism that stemmed from an ignorance about Chinese culture. There was a fear that the industrious and hard-working Chinese would drive down wages or be used as scab labour. This competition between ethnic and social groups is now established practice in our post-industrial world, as jobs are routinely outsourced to the Third World.

The material concerns of the strikers were clouded with imaginary fears and suspicions about the Chinese. For example there were raids on Chinese lodging houses, where it was alleged that white girls were being held against their will. The obsession that chaste white women were being corrupted by crafty foreigners is hardly unique in the annals of bigotry but it gives us an insight into the unspoken fears and anxieties of workers who felt their status threatened.[65]

The attack on the Chinese in 1911 shows how ethnically diverse Cardiff had become, and how far as a community the city had to go before it was able to resolve the ethnic tensions and differences that were thrown up by the new global economy it had joined.

The Temple of Peace

In Cathays Park stand two physical embodiments of the unexpected catastrophe that engulfed Europe, Britain and every city, town, village and hamlet in the British Isles. One is the War Memorial, unveiled in 1928, and the other is the Temple of Peace, created by the League of Nations during the 1930s, which was dedicated to preventing a repeat of the bloodshed of the First World War. The Welsh National Temple of Peace and Health was opened in 1938 when the last desperate attempts at establishing 'peace in our time' were failing. It was opened twenty years and a fortnight after the guns fell silent on the Western Front and still stands today, a beautiful but sombre fusion of neo-Classical and modernist architecture. The creator of the temple, Baron David Davies, intended it to be a lasting tribute to the enormous sacrifice of men

The Falklands War Memorial, dedicated to the Welsh Guards killed at Bluff Cove during the conflict on 8 June 1982.

around the world who had fought and died in the First World War. The Liberal peer and pacifist was part of a generation of activists who worked during the 1930s to further the cause of the League of Nations. He was interested in the possibility of using psychoanalysis to deal with mankind's inherently aggressive and destructive nature, though when the projected timescale for this turned out to be a couple of centuries (known as 'the Morbid Age'), Davies devoted his energies to other more practical issues.

The building initially housed the Welsh National Council for the League of Nations Union and the King Edward VII National Memorial Association, dedicated to alleviating tuberculosis. Lord Davies continued to campaign throughout the Second World War for an end to war and the establishment of a supreme international body that would eliminate the need for it and make it illegal. He died in 1944, just ten days after D-Day, his dreams of a peaceful world in tatters, with only the temple standing as a lasting testament to his works. It is tempting to look upon the notion of outlawing war as naïve, but we should remember that Lord Davies represented an enormous mass movement against war and in favour of the League of Nations throughout the 1930s, which only began to lose support after the Czech crisis, when war with Hitler appeared to be inevitable.

The Temple of Peace also houses the Welsh National War Memorial, which dates from 1928. It was first proposed by the *Western Mail* in 1919, and the newspaper started a fund to establish it. It has been suggested that the location of the memorial in Cardiff was controversial, perhaps because the city was seen as unrepresentative of Wales as a whole. In May 1919 the *Cardiff Times* wrote that Councillor H.M. Thompson had misgivings about establishing a national memorial in Cardiff: 'He did not think it would be possible to secure agreement with North Wales for a National Memorial at Cardiff, as most likely they would prefer memorials to their fallen in their own localities. What was wanted was a great memorial for Cardiff itself and not for the whole of Wales.'[66]

Contemporary accounts suggest that the response from across Wales was distinctly lukewarm: of those local authorities contacted, only sixty-three responded and of those only twenty-one responded favourably. Cardiff was felt to be too far away – in 1919 visiting it would have been beyond the means of many people in Wales, and most rural communities established their own small civic memorials. Those authorities which sympathised, such as Pembroke, did not have the finances to contribute to the project. Hostility towards Cardiff as a predominantly English-speaking city was a motivating factor in some instances, especially in North Wales. A particularly sour editorial in the *North Wales Chronicle* sheds light on how the city was viewed:

We offer our condolences to Cardiff. The cosmopolitan self-appointed 'metropolis' of Wales has experienced yet another and very serious rebuff. Public authorities in Wales have actually had the temerity to refuse to pander to Cardiff's ambitions, and declined to fund the funds for erecting an imposing National War Memorial in Cardiff, intended partly for the commemoration of Welsh heroes in the war and largely for the glorification of Cardiff in Wales. Some 200 public bodies in Wales were circularised by the Lord Mayor of Cardiff and invited to assist Cardiff in erecting a National Memorial in a town which prides itself ten times more on its cosmopolitan than upon its national character. Only one authority out of every ten so circularised even expressed willingness to send representatives to another Cardiff 'national' conference to discuss the proposal. In a huff, the Cardiff City Council now declares it can do without Wales, and will forthwith erect its own Peace Memorial.[67]

The Welsh National War Memorial. The memorial was inspired by Roman architecture in North Africa dating back to the reign of Emperor Hadrian and is a Grade II listed structure.

The Inner frieze (*below*) reads: 'Remember here is peace those who in tumult of war, by sea, on land, in air, for us and for victory endureth unto death.'

The Inscription reads: 'FEIBION CYMRU A RODDES EU BYWYDDROS EI GWLAD YN RHYFEL MCMXVIII': TO THE SONS OF WALES WHO GAVE THEIR LIVES FOR THEIR COUNTRY IN THE WAR 1918.

There was considerable controversy when it was built as North Walian communities who had lost men to the war felt that Cardiff was not representative of Wales and therefore not the place for a national memorial.

Glamorgan Home Guard annual parade at Cardiff Castle. During the war, Cardiff's men who were too young or old to fight overseas joined the Home Guard.

The requisite funds were raised, with the majority of the money being raised in Cardiff and even a few donations from overseas. When it was unveiled the Peace Memorial was the largest memorial in Wales. The recriminations and bitterness as the memorial was commissioned and built identifies the disconnect between rural and North Wales and Cardiff (it had sprung up as a metropolis in a generation and lacked legitimacy in the eyes of many Welshmen) and the unspoken national trauma that would hang over Wales for the next two decades. All this was a far cry from the scenes of jubilation and enthusiasm that greeted the announcement of war in Cardiff in 1914.

The First World War

David Lloyd George, whose career went from strength to strength during the war, leaping from armaments minister in 1914 to prime minister in 1916, oversaw the creation of the 38th Welsh Division, a body of men that raised several battalions from Cardiff. Welsh nonconformism, nationalism and socialism all had a strongly pacifist sentiment, which meant that many battalions were staffed by Welsh officers with the rank and file from England. However, 1,000 men were recruited in the winter of 1914 for the 16th Cardiff

City Battalion, even though initial euphoria had been replaced by a more sombre and solemn attitude to volunteering. Some travelled from other parts of South Wales, but for the most part these men were Cardiffians. Recruiting drives at football matches, rugby games, places of work and music halls were all used, and open-air concerts by military bands saw men joining up. In all it took eight weeks to get the full quota.

An indication of the success of recruiting at sporting events was the number of Welsh international rugby players in the 16th, including Capt. John L. Williams, Lt H. Bert Winfield and Lt J.M. Clem Lewis. Club vice-captain Maj. Fred Smith was second-in-command of the battalion and became its commanding officer when Lt-Col. Gaskell was killed in 1916.

The battalion trained in Britain for a year, and finally arrived in northern France in December 1915 and saw their first action in the Givenchy-Festubert-Laventie area (where Lt-Col. Gaskell was killed). Their losses for May 1916 were comparatively light at only fifty men. In contrast, Cardiff paid an extremely high price on the Somme, with at least half the 16th Battalion being killed or wounded at the Battle of Mametz Wood. On the site of the battle today a memorial to the 38th Division stands, a red dragon grasping barbed wire. It is a small reminder of the unimaginable slaughter that the Welsh Division and its Cardiff contingent faced over the five days between 7 and 12 July.

One of the other Cardiff battalions was the 8th Pioneers, who took part in the Dardanelles Campaign. They landed as part of Winston Churchill's disastrous strategic blunder on 5 August 1915 and spent four murderous months under a hail of Turkish gunfire, contending with artillery, disease and lack of supplies before being evacuated in December. The men had been ill-equipped, had not been trained for the kind of fighting they were faced with and orders were vague. Along with the rest of the 53rd Welsh Division, they were used by the same generals who had wasted the lives of the Australian and New Zealand troops who had come before them. Following their evacuation from Gallipoli to Egypt, the battalion took part in the 1916 invasion of Mesopotamia (now Iraq) and the capture of Baghdad.

Cardiffians served in every branch of the armed forces, and the city's maritime importance led to many young men enrolling in the Royal Navy. The fact that over 1,000 black Cardiffians from Butetown and Cardiff's Docks fought and died in Jellicoe's navy has been shamefully under-reported in official histories.

Of the 1,356 Victoria Crosses issued, the Welsh have featured extensively, and Cardiffians in particular have a strong presence in the list of those

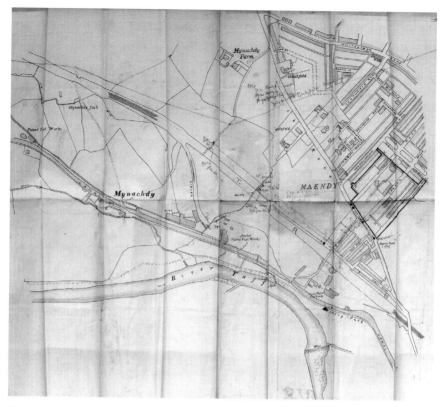

Plans and sections of streets in Maindy, an architect's design of the streets of the district. Maindy was redeveloped in the late nineteenth century from land provided by the Marquis of Bute.

decorated. Here are just two of the soldiers from Cardiff who were honoured with the Victoria Cross:

Frederick Barter of Daniel Street, Cathays, and later Harold Street, Roath, was born in January 1891, one of four children. He was educated at Crwys Road Board School before working for the GWR as a porter. Barter went on to become one of the most highly decorated soldiers in the First World War, all the more amazing as he was turned down for regular service before the war because his chest measurement did not meet minimum requirements. Forced to give up on his ambition to join the regular army with his brother John, Barter joined the militia battalion of the Royal Welsh Fusiliers, enrolling at Maindy Barracks on Whitchurch Road in 1908. He was quickly promoted from private to lance-corporal in 1909, corporal in 1910 and sergeant in 1911. Military reforms pushed through in 1908 in response to the sabre-rattling of Kaiser Wilhelm II disbanded the militia battalions, and Barter was incorporated into the special reserves of the Royal Welsh Fusiliers. At the outbreak of war he was sent from Cardiff to Wrexham, where he was promoted to the rank of company sergeant major. By this time the 1st Battalion of the Fusiliers had already seen their first action in France, and one of those reported missing was Private John Barter.

The Special Reserve Battalion was quickly sent to Belgium to relieve the mauled 1st Battalion, and spent a long winter defending the frontline against further German attack and conducting raids into German trenches. In the spring the 7th Division, of which the Royal Welsh Fusiliers were part, moved south, Barter and his men being positioned for a spring offensive. This started with the bloody and unsuccessful battle of Neuve Chappelle, but it wasn't until four days later on the 16 May, that Barter really saw action, at Festubert. Here, in an attack that cost approximately ten lives for every yard of territory captured, 16,000 British and Commonwealth troops perished. The Special Reserve Battalion quickly lost its commanding officers during their first advance, a night attack, where even the company commanders were killed. Barter led the men in an assault on German trenches, and when he called for men to volunteer to take part in a hand grenade attack eight men stepped forward. The tiny platoon quickly cleared 500yds of trenches and took 105 men prisoner, including three officers. By the end of the battle on 24 May the whole division had captured 4,000yds of trench, an eighth of which had been captured by Barter and a handful of men.

Barter was awarded the Victoria Cross on 29 June and was treated to a hero's welcome when he returned to Cardiff. He was honoured with war bonds by the Cardiff Coal Exchange, and welcomed back to Crwys Road School, surely their most famous alumni. His exploits did not end there, however. By the end of the war he had been honoured with the Military Cross, the 1914–1915 Star, the British War Medal, the Allied Victory Medal and the Order of George 3rd Class. This last award was made by Czar Nicholas II of Russia. Before returning to France, Barter was gazetted second lieutenant and became that rarest of things in the British Army, an officer from the ranks. Barter's career would likely have been cut short in 1916 had he experienced the Somme, but fortunately he was involved in training at the time of the battle.

By 1918, after a sojourn in India, Barter was in Palestine, transferred to the Queen Alexandra's Own Gurkha Rifles. On 12 March at Benat Burry Ridge, under the command of General Allenby, he led an attack on a Turkish and German machine gun position that almost wiped out the company. He had to feign death for five hours until he was rescued by a Gurkha, Rifleman Karanbahadur, who was also awarded the Victoria Cross for his bravery. By the end of the war Barter was a captain, and he eventually left the army in 1922. He spent the next three decades in the south of England but returned to Cardiff three years before his death in 1950, living out his final years in Dogfield Street in Roath.

If the story of Fred Barter shows us how an ordinary soldier from a working-class background could rise through the ranks (largely because of the slaughter of the officer corps) and be recognised for his bravery, the story of Richard Wain allows us to examine the battlefield innovations that were devised to break the deadlock. Richard Wain was one of the pioneers of tank warfare.

Born in Penarth, Wain grew up in Llanishen, a new and growing suburb of Cardiff at the turn of the century. His father, a solicitor, sent his son to the Cathedral School in Llandaff, and thence to a boarding school in Cumbria to complete his education. At the outbreak of war, Wain enlisted in the 7th Reserve Battalion of the Welsh Regiment, but quickly transferred to the Middlesex Regiment when it became clear that the 7th Battalion would not be leaving Britain. After the decimation of the BEF in 1914, Lord Kitchener raised his 'New Army', consisting of Pals battalions. Wain was assigned to a public schools battalion, and quickly gained temporary lieutenant status, rising from private. Even though he had not experienced battle, he was promoted for largely the same reasons that Barter was: the wholesale massacre of officers in the first year of the war. A public schools battalion was an ideal training ground for junior officers, and by 3 July 1915 Wain was posted to the Manchester Regiment.

Wounded at the Battle of Montauban in 1915, having sustained a bullet wound to the leg, Wain was evacuated back to Britain, where he spent his time recuperating in hospital and in Cardiff. He was back in action in January 1917, and transferred to the Heavy Branch of the Machine Gun Corps, leaving his comrades at the Manchesters. The Heavy Branch was the embryonic Royal Tank Corps, whose innovations had produced mixed results during the Somme six months earlier. Wain was once again sought after as a junior officer, the corps needing enthusiastic and able men to fill its growing ranks. Now a full lieutenant, Wain was trained on tanks and captained his own A company, made up of twelve vehicles in all. As part of the 33rd Brigade, he and his company fought at the Battle of Messines in June 1917. From his own account of the battle, one of the main problems Wain faced was confusion and chaos.

The record of the offensive begins at 8.50 a.m. and by 3 p.m. the first activity he reported was fire from British guns on his tank, wounding one of his men. For the rest of the day there was no contact with German soldiers at all.

On 11 November Wain began to make preparations for the first great tank offensive in history, the Battle of Cambrai. As part of the crew on the tank *Abou-Ben-Adam II*, Wain, now a captain and commanding a section, was in the first wave of the attack at 6.10 a.m. on 19 November. The tanks, supported by a huge British artillery barrage, took the first German line in just over an hour. The second objective, the next line of German trenches, was attacked at 8.50 a.m., but shortly before the *Abou-Ben-Adam II* could reach the line it was diverted to help a group of British infantry soldiers who were pinned down by German gun fire and did not have a tank to support them. The tank was hit by five trench mortar shells in succession, killing the driver, two other crew members and wounding Wain. Detaching a Lewis gun from its mounting, Wain charged the enemy machine gun nest, despite being 200 yards ahead of the rest of the infantry. He appears to have killed the German machine-gunners and mortar men, but was hit in the head by rifle fire and killed instantly. He was 20 years old. Records kept by other British soldiers record that surviving German soldiers surrendered, and in the end the company took 130 prisoners.

Wain was awarded a posthumous Victoria Cross and was buried on the battlefield, somewhere near the wreck of the *Abou-Ben-Adam II*. His name is recorded on the Cambrai memorial.

The 1920s and '30s

Four years of exhausting war ended in November 1918 and ushered in two decades of radical social change in Cardiff, but also two decades of uncertainty and anxiety about the state of the world and the pace of social change. The 1920s and '30s were to become in Cardiff, as in other parts of Britain, a battleground for competing ideas and ideologies in a time of rapid modernisation, and an almost unbearable sense of grief and guilt over the war.

In the interwar years, Cardiff saw divisions created by the 1926 General Strike, by the presence of sympathisers with Oswald Mosley's Fascist Blackshirts and by attitudes towards the Spanish Civil War.

The first major change to affect British public life after the war was the extension of the franchise to women. A striking statistic is that (outside London)

Cardiff University is a relatively late addition to Cardiff's cityscape, established in 1883.

Cardiff had the largest suffragist movement in Britain by 1912. In 1908 the Cardiff and District Women's Suffrage Society (CDWSS) had reformed after a period of inaction. Mrs Henry Thomas of Tongwynlais, a Conservative Party member, stood as the president and challenged the view that conservatives were universally opposed to the introduction of the vote for women. The society's vice-president, Millicent McKenzie, stood for Parliament in 1918. She was married to a professor of philosophy at Cardiff University. It is interesting to note that the Liberal MP for Cardiff, Ivor Guest, was cousin to Mildred Mansell, an active member of Emmeline Pankhurst's WSPU. However, the CDWSS was affiliated to the National Union of Women's Suffrage Societies (NUWSS), the more moderate union of suffragists that was led by Millicent Fawcett.[68] The society held forty-six public meetings and by 1914 had 1,200 members, having established an office in Queen Street. In July 1913, 200 women from the society led a march through the city, although many members had misgivings, feeling the march was not in keeping with the values of the movement.

The NUWSS held sixty-seven public meetings in Cardiff in the year 1913–14. While the WSPU also had a Cardiff branch it attracted proportionately fewer women, though the impact of their activities was often far more dramatic. The only act of direct protest that occurred in Cardiff was in 1912, when a suffragette leapt out in front of the home secretary and North Monmouthshire MP Reginald McKenna, who was on a visit with the king and queen to Llandaff Cathedral.

The Women's Freedom League was the third force in the campaign for female suffrage that had branches in Cardiff. During the war the WSPU and the NUWSS swung behind the war effort. The focus of their publications shifted towards how Cardiff women could be useful to the war effort and thrifty in the home. The long-term strategy was to demonstrate that women could be trusted with the vote because of their dedicated war service.

The journey for suffrage in Wales from the mid-nineteenth century was perhaps more challenging than in most other parts of the UK. As elsewhere there was a notion that there were separate spheres of life for men and women, and this had been strengthened by the city's rapid industrialisation. There were jobs for men in heavy industry and on the docks, which engendered a degree of chauvinism within Victorian and Edwardian Cardiff.

The political education for some of Cardiff's working-class women was born of hardship. Slumps and strikes could devastate working-class families, and it

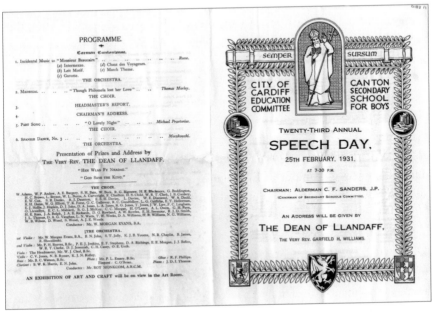

Programme of the International Peace Congress official service held at Llandaff Cathedral on 16 June 1919–39. The experience of the First World War and the tradition of non-conformist pacifism in Wales made Llandaff a prime location for a peace conference.

was very often the woman's place to go without. Working-class housing in Roath, Grangetown, Cathays and Butetown was frequently cramped, cold, damp and dirty, and it was not until the 1930s that Cardiff saw radical modernisation of its housing stock. There was an attempt to improve conditions for working-class girls from the 1870s onwards, during the golden age of educational reform. By 1911 there were nine specialist cookery schools and three laundry schools. The former recouped the cost of ingredients by making cakes and biscuits to sell in the city. They taught the girls a lot about baking cakes, but probably not much else. For the most part working-class girls were effectively excluded from education due to financial barriers. The rationale behind teaching them how to cook, sew and clean was in order to provide a large and skilled labour force for domestic service – giving a clear insight into attitudes towards the value of working-class women. In the first three decades of the twentieth century this was the largest employer of young women in the country, giving them a life that was often of boredom, spirit-crushing drudgery and loneliness. An anonymous letter to the *South Wales Daily News* is a good example of a contemporary woman's opinion: 'I consider I am treated more like a slave than a human being … driven from 6.00 a.m. until eleven and twelve at night, eating my own meals while running about waiting on others.'[69] Most girls in service had extremely long days and perhaps one Sunday a month to themselves, whilst surviving on meagre wages from which a uniform had to be purchased. The growth of department stores offered new avenues for women. David Morgan and Howells in Cardiff were employers who offered an alternative to domestic drudgery, but even so the work was hard, and only in 1900 were proprietors legally obliged to provide shop assistants with chairs. Before this the fainting female shop assistant was not an uncommon sight.

At the other end of the scale at the turn of the century were women dockworkers. The unloading of coal was strictly the preserve of men, this being rigorously enforced by dockworkers unions, but there were several hundred women who unloaded foodstuffs at Cardiff Docks. Many of them were Irish immigrants, open to exploitation thanks to the level of anti-Irish sentiment in Victorian Britain. In a whole raft of light industries women were cheap sweated labour, such as in manufacturing and packing preserves, cloth and tobacco. As has already been seen, the experience of industrialisation in Cardiff took a politically dormant male working class and galvanised it into a powerful political force by the beginning of the twentieth century. Women also experienced politicisation, and the attempts to confine them in the sphere of domesticity failed because of the impact of major social and economic changes.

New Theatre. Part of the city's cultural life through two world wars, the theatre, built in 1906, has seen acts as diverse as Shirley Bassey and Laurel and Hardy perform there.

Paranoid thinking about venereal disease, mixed with no small amount of casual racism, led to the Contagious Diseases Act being imposed on Cardiff. This Act was designed to incarcerate prostitutes who presented a threat to the sexual health of barracks towns, but presented no sanction for their clients. Spurious research fixed the blame for venereal disease on the predominantly black district of Butetown, and the unsubstantiated link between the docks, black Cardiffian and foreign mariners and the prostitutes whom they frequented. The survey represented an aspect of British imperial hypocrisy and anxiety, and gave voice to a general feeling that the empire was great as long as it stayed overseas. Cardiff's women were incensed at the possible imposition of the act, perhaps out of solidarity with their fallen sisters but more likely out of a fear that the trade might be legalised and licensed. This type of activism was linked closely to the Temperance movement.

The same kind of attitudes seem to have been prevalent in Cardiff's middle classes as well. Those who had been made wealthy from coal, shipping, manufacturing and other heavy industries had wives who were either content to be divorced from such activities as bookkeeping, or were alternatively feeling a sense of boredom, alienation and frustration at having no stake in an increasingly dynamic society and economy. Studies of the composition of Cardiff's suffragists from 1890 to 1914 show that the vast majority of activists were middle class. These were women with education and time to commit to the cause. There were some working-class activists affiliated to the Labour Party, but for the most part, as with the rest of Britain, universal suffrage was a middle-class struggle.

By 1894 women were allowed to vote in and stand for local parish and district elections, but there was a qualification in that they had to be rate-payers. The extension of the franchise in 1884 meant that there were millions of new potential voters, and because the Corrupt Practices Act of the same year forbade professional canvassers a small army of new volunteers was needed by both political parties. Women were for the first time actively sought to canvas for the parties, but both Liberals and Conservatives refused to put votes for women in their manifesto pledges. The Liberal Party, however, established an office of the Welsh Union of Women's Liberal Associations in Cardiff in the 1890s. There were many suffrage campaigners within the union and one can only imagine their anger and dismay at Herbert Asquith's steadfast refusal to grant women the vote in 1906. This, combined with the fact that for the past half-century Liberalism had been something akin to a political religion, made the disappointment all the greater, and when the Labour Party endorsed votes for women in 1912 it became the beneficiary of a groundswell of female support, formerly reserved for the Liberals. The war put an abrupt end to the struggle for the vote, but it also presented Cardiff's women with new opportunities to work towards suffrage by supporting the war effort.

The war caused considerable suffering for Cardiff women. The loss of husbands and sons was felt acutely, and in South Wales there were fears that there would be a famine by 1917, owing to the successes of German U-boats in the Atlantic. In Cardiff, despite these pressures, women on the Home Front gave shelter to refugees from Belgium, who had fled the fighting. The CDWSS helped the dependants of fighting men and provided assistance. They helped the Belgian aid and assistance societies, acted as translators and raised £4,000 for a Welsh hospital in Serbia.

There is some evidence of a growing, if minority, anti-war movement among Cardiff's women in the mid- to late war years. The Women's International League for Peace and Freedom appears to have had as many as fifty members at its Cardiff branch between 1915 and 1917, perhaps as a result of a letter written by Gwenda Gruffydd of Rhiwbina to the *Welsh Outlook* in 1915:

> I feel sure that there are thousands of my countrywomen ready to do all they can in this great cause, since it is we women who are so keenly alive to the damage to the race resulting from the war, and the grief, the pain, and the misery it entails. I feel inclined to suggest that the names of sympathizers should be placed on record, and when we have a long list, who should decide what steps to take, whether we should affiliate ourselves to an English Society or form ourselves into a separate Welsh one.[70]

By 1916, following the Somme and with the war going disastrously for Britain, there were large-scale anti-war public meetings in Cardiff, one in the autumn numbering some 2,000 people. The peace movement that combined with Welsh nonconformism in the 1920s and '30s can perhaps be seen to have its origins in such public protests. With the outbreak of war, working-class women, the most economically vulnerable social group, suffered disproportionately from the immediate downturn in the economy as spending on all the industries women were chiefly involved in, retail, domestic service and light industry making consumer goods, dwindled. A new age of austerity was planned for, and there was an upsurge in female unemployment in Cardiff that would not abate until the country was shifted to a total war footing under Lloyd George. The *Western Mail* reported in September 1914 that over a dozen large firms in the city had put their female staff on part-time hours. In an echo of the domestic schools that were introduced in the previous decades, the Cardiff Central Relief Committee set up a scheme to teach women toymaking in order to provide them with an income following the loss of their jobs.

By 1916, however, the situation was different. There was a variety of new job opportunities for women following the introduction of conscription: women staffed the telephone exchange and drove taxis and trams, even though men initially refused to work with the women who were taken on as conductresses. They delivered post and worked in all aspects of heavy industry. Cardiff's female population was also involved in essential war work, following Lloyd George's reorganisation of military production. In Cardiff, women made artillery shells and created the component parts for barrage balloons. The increased job opportunities, particularly in the realm of public transport, communications and infrastructure brought to young, single, working-class women a level of prosperity that they had previously never experienced, even if their wages and bonuses were on average about half those received by men. The biggest draw for women was in the munitions industry, which had been privately owned before the war, but when Britain realised the scope of the struggle ahead, national coordination left the companies privately run but subject to government control, under the auspices of the Ministry of Munitions. These national shell factories were sited all over Wales, and there was one at Barry.

Nursing took Cardiff's young women across the European and Middle Eastern fronts, from France to Salonika to Egypt and Serbia. One particularly high-profile example of this was the pre-war posting to Belgium of Cardiff nurse Elizabeth Wilkins, who, along with the martyred Edith Cavell, helped stranded British and Allied soldiers to escape. Elizabeth Wilkins was Edith Cavell's chief sister and the only nurse to stay with her when the hostilities broke out, the rest of the staff of the hospital, Dutch and German nurses, being sent home. Wilkins and Cavell were well aware that the Germans had told the Belgians that anyone helping Allied soldiers would be shot, but they had both heard stories of the Germans shooting captured British soldiers. A combination of patriotism and Christian devotion to the sick and wounded (the two women nursed many German soldiers in the Red Cross hospital they staffed) motivated them, though they were very much amateurs in underground work and were easily uncovered. Edith Cavell was tried and executed in 1915, to the horror of world opinion. Elizabeth Wilkins was released: her silence had kept her safe and the court martial had no evidence to convict her with. Edith Cavell believed German interrogators when they told her that other members of the underground had betrayed her and she gave a full confession, sealing her fate.

Cardiff's NUWSS contributed funds to set up hospitals in Serbia. Scottish Red Cross nurse Elsie Inglis addressed the society in 1915, and as a result 200 beds were made available for Allied troops, and staffed with nurses from all over Wales, including Cardiff.

A huge expansion in policing was required in wartime Britain to manage the radical social changes that were happening as a result of the strains of total war. In Cardiff, women were enlisted into the police under the Defence of the Realm Act. Their primary responsibilities seem to have been discouraging prostitution and the spread of venereal disease to the troops, shepherding refugees (especially female ones) and policing the wave of hedonism and infidelity that the war had engendered. The patrols were made up of Cardiff

NUWSS members. They had no official powers and seemed to have had a moral emphasis, creating public virtues by denying private vices.

Another essential part of war work was the Women's Land Army. With millions of men taken out of the agricultural economy, women had to participate in the hard work of heavy agricultural labour. Training centres for agricultural workers were established all over the country, with Cardiff's centre being opened at St Fagans.

An indication of how desperate Britain had become for uniformed service personnel was the creation of the Women's Auxiliary Services. On 17 July 1917, at a huge public meeting in Cardiff, women were encouraged to join the Women's Auxiliary Army Corps, established in 1917. Parents seemed to have feared that immorality in the ranks might prevail. The roles assigned to young women were in administrative and support positions

Picture of Dorothy Frances Curtis of Cardiff employed in war work, 1918. Female munitions workers in Cardiff played an essential role in helping to secure victory.

initially, and even before the meeting had taken place, a contingent of fifty Welsh girls set sail from Cardiff to France the previous month, to take up roles in everything from driving to telephony to working as mechanics.

During the war civil liberties were curtailed, something that is quite commonplace in twentieth-century societies fighting total war. One incident tells us a great deal about prevailing attitudes towards women. The obsessive fear that the fighting man might be incapacitated by venereal disease seems to have motivated a curfew, which was imposed by Colonel East, Commander of the Severn Defences, on women whom he considered to be unsuitable or women 'of a certain character'. A handful of women were banned from public houses between the hours of 7 p.m. and 6 a.m., and were curfewed to their own homes overnight. Five women who broke the curfew were sentenced to two months in jail after being arrested in Bute Street. The case provoked a storm of controversy across the country.

In Cardiff a prevailing attitude was evident that the wives of fighting soldiers were to some extent public property and their behaviour could be collectively commented upon, disapproved of and managed. The amount of alcohol consumed by women, particularly those with a separation allowance, was commented upon by a Cardiff vicar, who claimed that in a half-hour vigil a staggering 115 women had bought alcohol from an off-licence while he watched.

The Representation of the People Act in 1918 saw all married women over the age of 30 given the vote, and whilst Millicent McKenzie failed to be elected to office, the wartime experiences of Cardiff's women left the city changed forever. The city would see a generation of women emboldened by new voting rights, and by the knowledge that they had been essential during the war.

Dennis Morgan, the pre-eminent chronicler of Cardiff's past, wrote in *The Cardiff Story* that traders in the city who waited for a return to some semblance of economic normality were sadly disappointed. Shipowners in Cardiff, having lost countless vessels at sea, were compensated for their losses and enjoyed a short-lived boom. Speculative capital was invested in shipping and during the early 1920s there was 122 shipping companies in Cardiff, outstripping any other port in the world. It made clear commercial sense as Britain relied on imports more than ever, as did the rest of ravaged Europe, and the Atlantic was the new highway for America's massive food surplus. Now the U-boat menace had gone it was assumed that good money could be made on the transatlantic routes to Cardiff. These routes would once again become part of Britain's fight for survival in the next war, and Cardiff would be integral to that journey. However, over-confidence in the size of the world shipping market and a lack of judgement led to a collapse in shipping prices. Whilst America enjoyed a post-war economic boom, the truth was that much international trade was sluggish and there was far less need for shipping than originally thought. By the end of 1921 Cardiff's fleet had lost 80 per cent of its value in twelve months. By 1932, at the height of the Great Depression, 60 per cent of ships were laid up. The crash must have seemed a double disaster for Cardiff shipping magnate Sven Hansen of Hansen Shipping in 1921, a year that was also blighted by the mysterious disappearance at sea of the ship *Stevenstone* which was travelling from Northumberland to Denmark. Six Cardiff men were lost with this ship. Hansen was the son of an entrepreneurial Norwegian migrant who started out in business during the coal boom in South Wales of the 1860s importing pit props, and he later branched out into exporting coal.

Cardiff buildings damaged by air raids during the Second World War (*above and below*). De Burgh Street in Riverside was the most heavily bombed, with fifty Cardiffians in that street alone losing their lives. Grangetown, Canton and Riverside were heavily damaged due to their proximity to the docks.

Sven Hansen was savvy enough when setting up on his own to buy ships and collieries, and despite the heavy losses he accumulated through lost shipping during the war and through the slump afterwards, he was still rewarded with a baronetcy for his wartime services.

Throughout the 1920s and '30s the coal industry of South Wales was in decline: a combination of factors gave the industry seemingly insurmountable threats. Low investment in new technologies and a lack of foresight into possible economic revivals throughout the world created harsh conditions in Wales. When the coal industry in the valleys suffered, Cardiff's docks suffered too. The city's role as an export hub for coal was the ticket to its prosperity, but would also be the cause of its economic decline. Once Cardiff was part of the global economy it was largely dependent on commodity prices decided at an international level, and was very much at the mercy of world conditions.

The beginning of the crisis in Cardiff's docks was the Tiger Bay race riots of 1919. The shortage of employment was the main cause of simmering trouble, and Tiger Bay, a community born of Cardiff's connections with the Atlantic world, was not only the site of racial violence, but of copycat racial violence – attacks on black people in dockside communities seemed to be happening all across the Western world in 1919, much of it linked to the desperation of returning soldiers and the slowdown in global trade. Butetown's black population had increased during the war because of the million or so colonial subjects who were recruited by the British to help with labour shortages and to work in the Merchant Navy. Inevitably some of these men stayed and gravitated to the already established ethnic minority communities in places like Cardiff. One possible reason for racial hatred against black men in Cardiff at the end of the war was that so many of them had been involved in the maritime war. Black workers in labour battalions from across the empire were strictly curfewed, and while black men were welcome to come and work for Britain they were not welcome to socialise with her people, especially her women. Butetown's black sailors, however, were exempt from this ruling. In 1917 the chief constable of Cardiff objected to the sexual allure that black men gained from playing cricket in flannels rather than their workaday corduroy, and protested against white girls being allowed 'to admire such beasts'.[71]

The outburst of violence hit most of Britain's major ports: Glasgow, Liverpool, South Shields and Cardiff were all rocked with violence, but in Cardiff it was by far the worst. A boat carrying black families was pelted with stones, the murder of a demobbed white soldier was blamed on a black man, an Arab man was killed by a rioter (though it was also speculated that he was killed by a policeman) and another white rioter was shot through the heart. Butetown was cordoned off by the police to protect residents after homes and businesses were destroyed, but other areas where black people lived were left undefended. Even when the violence ended an air of mutual suspicion and hostility hung over the community for several decades to come.

The pre-war working-class militancy that continued into the 1920s reached its zenith in 1925 and 1926. Cardiff had long been a battlefront in the struggle between unions and bosses, and the highly politicised nature of this struggle can be seen in the 1925 trial of the Ammanford anthracite miners. Because there were 167 accused they could not all be tried in Carmarthen, so for reasons of logistics as well as political expediency half of them were sent to Cardiff. The charge was that they 'on 29 July 1925 in the county of Carmarthen unlawfully and riotously assembled to disturb the peace, and then did make great riot and disturbance to the terror of His Majesty's subjects'.

The following year the government decided to have a showdown with the workers, and the country was rocked by the General Strike. The fate of Welsh miners and Cardiff dockworkers was interdependent, so the city's strike action should be seen in that context.[72] The strike was organised by the Cardiff Trades and Labour Council (CTLC), which had close relations with the South Wales Miners Federation. In South Wales the government faced resistance from a broad coalition of miners, railwaymen, dockers and engineers. On 3 May, when negotiations with the government finally broke down, Cardiff unions passed on directives from national union leaders that a strike would begin at midnight. The following day all heavy industry and transport stopped. The following day there was a report from union organisers in Cardiff to the TUC: 'Reports from all over Cardiff show the spirit of the men to be fine, every place solid. Dowlais works completely solid. All railwaymen standing firm. Transport workers solid.' The only workers who did not join in the strike locally were seamen. This was only a minor problem for the strikers because almost all the business of the ports was coal, so the seamen had precious little to transport. The trade union movement in Cardiff had a long memory, however, and the strike-breaking sailors were remembered during the miners' strike fifty-eight years later.

Cardiff was not unanimous in its support for the strike. Cardiff's business community and middle-class supported the government, but it would be planning and organisation that won the strike, and this was something the unions in Cardiff lacked. There was also far more disunity in the labour movement in Cardiff than most accounts reveal, as the CTLC disaffiliated the south ward of the Labour Party for having elected a communist, indicating that the organisation was fairly centre-left compared with other labour organisations. A letter in the *Workers Weekly*, written on 23 April 1926 (a fortnight before the strike), speaks volumes. This frank and revealing account of disunity claimed that organisation in Splott, Adamsdown and Cardiff Central had been thorough and united and the Communists and left-wingers should be praised. However, the anonymous writer claimed that the CTLC had been disorganised and complacent, and responsible for a 'bad feeling' that ran through the labour movement in the city.

As the strike began a Cardiff Central Strike Committee (CCSC) was set up, with delegates from all industries and unions that were involved, Labour Party members, councillors and parliamentary candidates. The makeup of the committee was in keeping with the moderate line taken by the CTLC, and veered away from radical or revolutionary talk. Because of a lack of communication between the TUC and local branches and strike committees across the country, the CCSC took on the role of chief organising body in Cardiff, making itself responsible for picketing, communications, permits and propaganda. The centre of operations was at 51 Charles Street, or Strike Street as it was more popularly known during and for some time after the strike. The Joint Railway Union Strike Committee, which was running a separate but parallel strike, was next door in no. 49.

Other organising grounds for strike action were the Ward Labour Halls. Records have been found for the strike committee of Llandaff North and Whitchurch, indicating it used the Llandaff North Cooperative Room. The CCSC, having little direct supervision or assistance from the TUC, had to create systems for managing the strike as it went along, and this problem wasn't made any easier when it was given responsibility for Blaina Gwent, Merthyr and Bridgend. Strike committees across South Wales looked to Cardiff for leadership and information.

Given the slightly ad hoc, improvised and disorganised nature of the strike, the Conservative government had an ideal opportunity to deal the labour movement a major defeat. The government had been planning a response to the strike in South Wales and especially in Cardiff, as the regional and administrative centre for the south-east was a prime location for staging a fightback. The Earl of Clarendon was dispatched to be the civil commissioner for the city, and was accompanied by a battalion of soldiers of the Cheshire

Regiment. The government had promised that no armed service personnel would be used in strike-breaking activities, so the motivation for drafting in troops at such short notice can only have been in order to intimidate. On the day of the strike a navy submarine docked at Cardiff, and on the 5th a navy cruiser arrived at the docks, with naval ratings later being used to protect strike-breakers. Quite what use a submarine was is unclear, other than a large and visible military presence that spoke volumes to onlookers.

In a clear indication of where loyalties lay, 688 special constables were recruited in Cardiff mainly from white collar clerical workers and university students. The *Western Mail*, clearly on the government's side, reported that many of the students at St Michael's College were spoiling for a fight with the strikers. Again, this suggests that the people joining the government's side were far from impartial bystanders. The specials were split into four groups and sent to protect key installations such as the Roath power station, petrol stations, railway bridges and gas works. The Earl of Clarendon put out a call for volunteers from his offices in the Dominion Building and seems to have had a very vigorous response from the middle classes, with doctors, lawyers and other professionals doubling up as transport workers. A total of 6,630 people from across the city came to the government's aid, about half the working population. There was only a small degree of success in offloading ships at the dock, but volunteers managed to get two tugs and a grain elevator to work and unloaded food, which was a key priority of the government. A large grain ship from Canada was not unloaded, as workers at the Spillers Flour Mill threatened to go on strike if it was. The GWR employed 209 volunteers to work as drivers and firemen on the locomotives, even though strikers cut the signal wires at Grangetown and Penarth.

One figure who stands out in the dispute is the lord mayor, Alderman W.B. Francis, and he seems to have made one of the greatest contributions towards winning the strike. Francis was a successful lawyer and head of the local Conservative Association. In order to undermine the strike amongst the transport workers, on 5 May he ordered twelve buses, manned by volunteers, to be run from Llandaff bus depot. Striking tramway men were told to return to work or face dismissal, and they were replaced with volunteers. A measure of their effectiveness and the comprehensive nature of their deployment was the nickname they were given by striking tramworkers: LMOs, the Lord Mayor's Own.

The breaking of this aspect of the strike threw the TUC into an unexpected quandary. Workers at Roath power station threatened to walk out unless the trams stopped. The TUC had never intended the strike to affect power workers, and their walking-out was not sanctioned. Managerial and technical specialists stepped in to keep the power station open and running. *Western Mail* reports of the next few days indicate that the issue of buses in Cardiff was deeply inflammatory and a flash point for trouble. Crowds of angry strikers and their supporters surrounded buses, and over the next three days trams and volunteers were stopped and attacked. This led to special constables being carried on buses for protection. One spot that seems to have been particularly hazardous for tram volunteers was Queen Street and St John Square. On 6 May crowds gathered in Queen Street between 3 p.m. and 5 p.m., and the police dispersed the mob after a stone was thrown at a tram driver. A report sent to the Home Office indicated that the use of mounted police had been successful in clearing the streets and restoring order. The area around St John Square was seen as a danger zone and a centre for future trouble. Three-quarters of Cardiff's police were deployed there, some 250 men in 16-hour shifts. This indicates how tense those days must have been. The police presence in a small area of central Cardiff was overwhelming, and it appears the authorities were preparing for insurrection. Soon the numbers of patrolling police in Cardiff rose to over 600.

Equally, the union movement demonstrated an impressive show of numbers. The CCSC held a weekend demonstration in Cathays Park, perhaps one of the largest ever to have assembled in Cardiff. Some 20,000 people were in attendance, with speakers from the London TUC and the CCSC. At the rally the resolve of workers to carry on with the dispute and to stay out on strike was reaffirmed. However, strike leaders were slightly perturbed by the lessening of control of their members: a symptom of this was the attacks on trams and buses. Whilst they were determined to win the strike, violence and intimidation were not tactics that the leaders were willing to employ or condone. The CCSC sent out a circular stating that 'violence and disorder must everywhere be avoided, no matter what the incitement'. The circular recommended that trade union members should spend time with their families, go out of the city for the day or tend their gardens rather than become involved in violent picketing. There does not appear to have been a similar repeat of the disturbances on Queen Street following this intervention.

At the start of the new week some of the tramway workers began to return to work, aware that the lord mayor would be replacing them if they did not – the advertising of their jobs was a hint that was not lost on them. The real concern was the presence of un-unionised men who were happy to break the strike and take strikers' jobs at the end of the dispute. The vast majority of the rest of the strikers held firm in the second week. If anything the strike became more organised and powerful in the city, largely because a second wave of industries nationally joined the strike, and Cardiff's shipwrights and boilermakers downed tools in solidarity with their fellow workers.

It came as an unexpected blow when the TUC called off the strike. Cardiff union organiser Allen Pope said, 'Then the blow fell. In the heat of the battle we had almost forgot that our General Staff did not believe in the war.' Jimmy Thomas, the Railway Unions leader (formerly of Splott and later the lord privy seal in Ramsay MacDonald's 1929 Labour government) began the climb-down, fearful of the forces that had been unleashed during the strike. Possibly the disorder in Cardiff and other cities indicated that the rank and file union membership was starting to ignore directives from above. Charles Street became the temporary scene of jubilation as confused strikers assumed that they had won, and when they discovered the truth the mood of the crowd quickly changed. Pope wrote:

In common with the rest of the country, we first heard the hateful news from the enemy camp – the BBC [at the time Lord Reith of the BBC was firmly against the strikers and had colluded directly with Stanley Baldwin against the strike]. The demoralisation that followed the calling-off of the Strike extended to the Cardiff Central Strike Committee, and after an hour or so of vainly phoning the TUC for information the local strike headquarters were closed down! It may be urged in extenuation of the failure of the Committee at this juncture that its members were overwhelmed by the demands of their particular organisations; but the fact remains that valuable opportunities for salvage from the disaster were lost.

There are memories of that historic 12 May that still burn. One was accused at every step for information as to the terms of the settlement; how could one explain to those fine comrades the conviction that there were no terms? There are memories of events at the Labour Hall. Reports of incredibly degrading terms offered to those who had presented themselves for work; insulted and resentful deputations returning from phone calls from all over the district, some asking for information, others expressing a determination to fight on for the miners TUC or no TUC.

A second huge demonstration took place in Cathays Park that night. Despite the level of anger, resentment and sense of betrayal directed at the TUC leadership, most local leaders still endorsed them, believing that they were essential to securing the best deal for returning strikers, and that the TUC could ensure guarantees that no one suffered. At the demonstration, however, strikers were directed towards hustings particular to their industries – leading them to fear that a sectional strategy was being imposed, making it far easier to dismiss them when the humiliating climb-down eventually arrived. Forty of the tramway men faced losing their jobs. Some of them were veterans of the First World War and less productive. This sparked further strike threats as the dockers, railwaymen and other unions threatened to stay out until the issue was resolved.

Employers threatened returning workers with savage reprisals, partly because of a desire to treat their rebellious workforce as punitively as possible, but largely to break the union movement forever and crush the threatening solidarity that had been close to altering the social make-up of the country. On the railways only half the staff were rehired, and those on day-to-day contracts: with permanent job insecurity further unrest could be prevented. The same treatment was meted out to Cardiff printworkers. When the employers' measures were revealed the CCSC called on the TUC to resume the strike, and demanded that the Labour Party take up the issue of local victimisation. The collapse was total, however, and most local union branches were left to fend for themselves.

The Cardiff railwaymen were still ready to fight, demanding that the punitive terms were lifted, and the chief constable for Cardiff feared that the demeaning terms being heaped upon striking workers could lead to further unrest. He ordered that another 150 police constables be deployed. The Royal Navy remained moored in Cardiff.

A third demonstration took place on 15 May and this time the CCSC decided it was going to overrule the TUC: they told workers to stay out until told to do otherwise. Solidarity disappeared over the next few days as desperate men in different industrial sectors fought to hang onto their jobs, and to agree on working conditions that did not leave them feeling vulnerable. The forty tramway men were successful in keeping their jobs, while dockworkers returned on pre-strike terms on 17 May – but owing to the slump in coal production (because of the initial miners' strike) only a quarter of them were retained. On the 18th dry-dockworkers returned, as did the fuel workers, while printers went back the following day on day-to-day contracts. At Dowlais the first 200 men to go back retained their jobs, and a week later tug-boat men at Cardiff docks returned to work.

Enemies of the strike celebrated the defeat of the unions. The volunteers were treated in Cardiff as if they were war heroes, having a reception by the lord mayor and the *Western Mail*. They were rewarded by railway companies and other employers who had used them as strike-breaking labour during the dispute, and many were offered jobs. In November 1926 Stanley Baldwin was made a freeman of the city.

Cardiff was a crucial battleground during the General Strike, as the country's pre-eminent coal port, a major centre of heavy industry and an important transport hub. Its close association with the South Wales coalfields made the nature and the intensity of the struggle all the more important. Following the strike the punishments meted out to the eight people who had been arrested for various offences in the city came not just from the employers but also from the state. William Welsh, 46, was jailed for four months for offences relating to interfering with public transport. Williams Stratton, 29, was given two months; Charles Ward one month; Charles Mann, 31, twenty-one days' hard labour; George Clarke fourteen days' hard labour; and Eden O'Brien, 49, one month – all for an attack on a tram in Ely.

One of the main causes of failure of the strike at national level, and to some extent locally, was the reluctance of the leadership to directly confront the state and a willingness to back down when they thought the rank and file membership was getting out of hand.

The only people in Cardiff who were prepared to be more confrontational were the Communists, but their influence on the CCSC was minimal. The cause of Communism in the city in the 1920s and '30s remained a minority calling, but involvement in the local branch of the Communist Party of Great Britain led a small number of Cardiff Communists all the way to Moscow and to the heart of Stalin's war in Spain.

In 1930, Len Jeffries, a full-time Communist Party of Great Britain organiser in Cardiff, went to Moscow to study at the secretive International Lenin School.[73] Jeffries had been a miner in Gwent before the First World War and had served on the Western Front as a gunner. He joined the Labour Party in 1917 and on his return to Britain in 1918 he became a branch secretary in Cardiff. He took the entire branch over to the Communist Party in 1923, following the involvement of the British in the Russian Civil War, which convinced him that there was an attempt by the British state to destroy the new workers' government in Russia. Jeffries was seen by the Soviet authorities as a model student, and he was educated in strict party discipline and the arts of propaganda. Like many gullible Western onlookers, he was shown the 'successes' of the Five Year Plans and became ever more convinced that Communism was the only economic model that could drag the world out of economic crisis. Some of the students at the Lenin School were educated in subversion and guerrilla warfare, but it is not known if Jeffries was among their number. He certainly travelled the length of Russia and met workers and farmers during his year in the USSR.

Two years later Jeffries was arrested and tried on a charge of incitement to mutiny after distributing a newspaper called the *Soldier's Voice* to the soldiers at Maindy Barracks. He was jailed for three years. Jeffries stayed loyal to the Communist Party long after the horrors of the Soviet Union he had loved were revealed, and was a member until his death in 1979.

A far more colourful example of the allure of the International Lenin School was Will Paynter. Paynter, born in Whitchurch and formerly a checkweighman at Cymmer Colliery, conducted clandestine visits to the heart of Nazi Germany and fought in the Spanish Civil War. He made no bones about the fact that the General Strike had been a radicalising experience for him, and he was a convinced Communist before he joined the party in 1929. He went to the International Lenin School, and following training in concealing documents he was used as a courier to Scandinavia and Germany. In his biography *My Generation* he wrote:

I was in Moscow when Hitler came to power, having arrived there in December 1932. A little time previously I had attended a Communist Party school in Abbey Wood, Kent, which lasted for several weeks. It was at this school that I first came to know John Gollan, now the British national secretary of the Communist Party. He had arrived at the school straight from serving a prison sentence for distributing allegedly seditious literature to soldiers. After leaving the school he became the leader of the Young Communist League, and I was given the opportunity to continue my studies of political economy and social history in Moscow.

I left London on a Soviet ship in the company of a number of other students and we spent four or five days on a very interesting trip going through the Kiel Canal and up the Baltic Sea to Leningrad. It was especially interesting and exciting for me because it was my first sea voyage (unless one counts day trips on a paddle steamer from Cardiff to Weston-super-Mare as a sea voyage) and I was going to a socialist country ...[74]

On one of his periodic returns to Wales, Paynter was elected in Cardiff to lead the first of the hunger marches. He led three major hunger marches, in 1931, 1932 and 1936. On the 1932 march he was treasurer of the South Wales contingent and in 1936 he was one of the leaders of the South Wales contingent, who had been democratically elected at Cardiff by the marchers. These marches were protests against the government's limitation of unemployment relief to the poor at the height of the Depression.

By 1937, Paynter had been selected by the South Wales Miners Federation to look after its members in the International Brigades of the Spanish Civil War. The major task was to sort out problems in the British battalion's leadership and to make recommendations for its reorganisation. There had been reports of disobedience and desertion amongst the British volunteers. Paynter acted as a brigade commissar, and more than likely saved many British volunteers from the firing squad. In his autobiography he wrote: 'The penalty for desertion is harsh in any army, especially in wartime. Together with representatives of the American battalions, whose problems were similar to ours, we pressed the Brigade command to set up a centre where those whose morale had fallen could be rehabilitated. We emphasized, too, that military weakness in supporting organisations had contributed to the problem. Eventually the command agreed and a camp was created where men in the same plight were brought together from the various battalions in an effort to rehabilitate them.'[75] The camp returned the majority of its men to active service on the frontline with morale fully restored.

After the destruction of the Republican cause in 1938 at the Battle of Ebro, Paynter returned to Britain. He spoke at the Trade Union Congress at Blackpool in September: 'It must be clear to every delegate in this Congress that the issue in Spain is one of which the outcome will not only determine the destinies of the people of Spain; it must be clear to everyone that the outcome of the conflict in Spain will involve the destinies of the people of all countries ... The conquest of Spain can well mean the commencement of further attacks upon other European democracies.' His observations were astute and in keeping with the changing feeling in Britain at the time, in the run-up to the Munich Agreement that November.

Paynter was not the only Cardiffian to go to Spain. Frank Thomas, from Rhiwbina, also volunteered to fight in Spain but on the nationalist side: he was a volunteer for Franco. It is probable that there was a large constituency of opinion in Cardiff that passively supported the nationalist cause, and a lot of the letters written to periodicals like the *Western Mail* had a distinctly pro-Franco flavour. Frank Thomas seems to have had conflicting personal beliefs, and to label him a Fascist is misleading and inaccurate as his motivations were far more complex. He had no love for Italian Fascism, and was an ardent supporter of the royal family, but he seems to have been attracted to the nationalist cause because of his opposition to the enforced secularism that a socialist government might impose on Spain. In his writings Thomas seems to have been a libertarian when it came to religion, and the rights of people, whether Christian, Jewish and Muslim, to worship how they saw fit. After the rising in Spain he wrote to the *South Wales Echo*: 'Liberty is the corner stone of democracy and if priests (or mullahs or rabbis for that matter) are not permitted to carry out their holy offices and are murdered simply because of their calling then liberty, and therefore democracy, does not exist.'[76]

Thomas fought as a rifleman in the Spanish Foreign Legion and only by chance did he avoid fighting other British volunteers on the Republican side. He was shot through the jaw and neck during a Republican offensive in the Gredos mountains in which most of his comrades were killed. Thomas decided to desert while he convalesced, not a decision taken lightly by this veteran warrior, who had been promoted twice during his active duty and had seen 90 per cent of his original comrades slain – but had also been treated with suspicion and disdain by his Spanish officers. Happy that he had helped to save Spain from Communism, Thomas wrote to the Finnish Embassy in 1940 when the USSR invaded Finland. Answering their appeal for help, he cited his Spanish experience and pointed out that he disliked both Communism and Fascism.

Assistance for Spain wasn't limited to fighting volunteers, and on some level the whole city was affected by the conflict. It was a decade after the General Strike but the unions and the workforce in Cardiff were still deeply politicised, and a strong sense of common cause with Spain was prevalent. The community was far from indifferent: one of the first acts of compassion was to rescue Spanish children from the conflict by offering them shelter as refugees. In a combined effort with Newport, the Cardiff Aid Spain Committee found homes across South Wales for Basque children. Among the organisers and station greeters was the eminent Cardiff University-based Marxist historian Christopher Hill.

Help came not only from leftist quarters but also from those with business connections with Spain, who were equally moved by the plight of the conquered peoples of the Basque region. Frederick Jones, a Conservative councillor and a shipping magnate who owned the Abbey Line, and Lord Glanley of Tatem and Co. were both moved to act through humanitarian rather than ideological impulses. Perhaps it is to their credit that they didn't act purely from business motives: they may have made handsome profits from shipping to the Republican side when the war seemed to favour them, but they continued to supply them when things were not going as smoothly.

Llandaff Cathedral. After two centuries of religious upheaval and change, the early eighteenth century saw Llandaff Cathedral's renaissance. Much of what we see today is the result of a restoration project that began in 1734 and lasted until 1869.

As the hopes of peace in Europe began to fade, the growing cruelties of the Third Reich was more present. During the tense negotiations and shuttle diplomacy of the Munich Conference, when Neville Chamberlain hurried back and forth to make an accommodation with Hitler, an extraordinary sight greeted Cardiffians: a Nazi flag, replete with swastika, draped over the front of the town hall. It was requested by Lord Mayor O.C. Purnell in an appalling misreading of public sentiment. He described it as a 'gesture of jubilation', mistaking an outpouring of relief that war was averted for approval of Nazi policy (and for that matter British policy). Belatedly realising how ill-advised this was, the mayor quickly took it down. By 1939 few could be in any doubt that war was coming, and for 3-year-old Susie and Lotte Biechoffer it had already arrived. The twins were part of the Jewish Kindertransport and found their new home with the Mann family in Cardiff. The Manns were devout Baptists who felt a duty to help those less fortunate than themselves. They adopted the two girls and changed their names to Eunice and Grace, often denying after the war that the children were adopted at all. Their real mother was murdered at Auschwitz in 1943.

For Lisbeth Davies, a pupil at Howells School, war began in Llandaff Cathedral on Sunday, 2 September 1939 and eventually took her as far as Colombo with the Women's Royal Naval Reserve in 1945. In her memories of the war she wrote: 'On Sunday September 2nd 1939, Dean Jones brought a wireless set into Llandaff Cathedral at the 11 o'clock service and we all heard Neville Chamberlain declare, sorrowfully enough, that Britain was at war with Germany.'

As a young boy Ron Burden listened with a mixture of trepidation and excitement:

> I was 14 and I remember sitting around the wireless set. It was sobering. It had been gathering momentum for 12 months so we weren't surprised. We'd thought war would happen a year before. There were four of us around the wireless – me, my brother Alan, who was seven then, and my parents, Harry and Ada. It was broadcast at 11am which was church time but I don't think we went to church that day. It wasn't frightening. For young fellas, it was exciting. We thought 'we'll get rid of this mob'.
>
> We lived in Pentrebane Street in Grangetown. Everyone was listening to the radio. There were still a large number of people about who remembered World War One and after the broadcast we went to talk to neighbours. There was quite a sombre atmosphere in the street.[77]

So began an ordeal for the country and for the city. War at first seemed distant and uncertain, but by 1941 it was engulfing Cardiff in heavy bombing raids as she became an unlikely frontline.

Cardiff buildings damaged by air raids during the Second World War. Cardiff was damaged by heavy raids in 1941 and 1943.

The city's experience of the Second World War is a story based upon a series of strategic assumptions that turned out to be wrong, or at the very least based on the previous war. From 1936 onwards the British Government was extremely conscious that the main threat to Britain would come from city bombing: the destruction of Guernica in Spain was a practical example of what the rest of Europe could face if another war broke out.

Cardiff was vitally important. Ports along the North Sea and the Channel were considered to be far too dangerous following the declaration of war in September 1939. Just as the navy had blockaded Germany in the First World War, so it was thought the Germans would blockade the ports nearest to her. This left the Atlantic ports of the Severn Estuary: Cardiff, Swansea, Bristol and Pembroke Dock. In 1939, Cardiff was out of the range of German bombers, but the fall of France the following summer changed the city's fortunes dramatically.

The key to the victory of the Western Allies in the Second World War was maintaining a vastly superior rate of production of arms and munitions, and ensuring that precious food, munitions and fuel were deployed effectively. After the failure of the Battle of Britain and the abandonment of Operation Sealion, the planned invasion of the British Isles, Hitler's strategy was one of attempted starvation, hoping that the British Government would be brought to its knees. The principal strategy was to target Atlantic convoys sailing to Britain's western coast and to destroy coastal ports. Cardiff lost 357 of its citizens in the bid to destroy the city's docks and the rail network between Wales and England. By 1941 the docks were struggling to keep up with the vast quantities of material being offloaded, but had they been destroyed, or had the rail link been severed, it is possible that Britain would have been starved out of the war. The stakes for city and country were extraordinarily high.

In the late 1930s, as tensions on the continent grew, the government undertook a strategic review of British ports along the Severn Estuary, mindful that the German U-boat campaign in the First World War had come close to succeeding. Concerns were raised as early as 1937 that Cardiff would not be able to deal with the scale of the challenge that might face her. Millions of tons of goods would have to be diverted from other ports to Cardiff's docks, a facility chiefly designed to load and offload coal, and a railway network that was designed to serve the South Wales coalfields was not geared up to moving a variety of goods. The port lacked proper warehouses for the storage of commodities such as food, military equipment and oil. The cargo container

One of the many ships that still use Cardiff Bay as a dock.

was yet to come, being an innovation of the 1960s, and before its invention the offloading of different commodities involved a range of skills, most of which were in short supply in Cardiff. To British strategic planners it looked that the docks could become a gigantic bottleneck, and to make matters worse every significant port on the west coast (Bristol, Swansea, Liverpool and Glasgow) had similar problems. There were no alternative destinations to relieve the pressure.

As Cardiff's strategic role in the war became clearer, railway companies (now effectively nationalised under the control of the Minister For War Transportation) had to work to update their lines. From July 1940 to January 1941, £117,000 was spent on additional sidings for the east–west mainline route and £257,000 was spent improving the line between Newport and Severn Tunnel Junction.

Cardiff had an additional role to play in the Battle of the Atlantic. As ships limped into port damaged after U-boat attacks, many were carrying cargoes they had never been designed to hold on rough seas, leaving them with damaged holds. A queue of ships waited to be repaired at Cardiff, and as attacks on merchant shipping increased, Britain and America could not afford to let them sit idle. The Luftwaffe recognised the vulnerability of these vessels, and targeted the ship repair yards. As soon as France fell and Britain's west coast ports came into range, German air force chiefs became convinced that bombing them was the key to Britain's downfall. British planners had always believed that the Severn Estuary and South Wales would never be vulnerable. Aerial reconnaissance over Cardiff was routine by October 1940, as Germany's strategy switched away from destroying the RAF to attacking Britain's cities. The Luftwaffe's bombers were not designed for strategic city bombing, whereas Allied bombers of 1942 onwards were specifically created for this task. German aircraft were created as terror weapons from the air but in support of blitzkrieg: they were light bombers designed to create havoc that advancing troops could capitalise upon. Equally, German military planners were not trained in waging economic warfare and their analysts were not trained in decrypting aerial reconnaissance photos and identifying potential targets.

Cardiff was subject to a number of minor raids, most of which focused on Butetown Docks. One of the first, on 20 June 1940, saw a direct hit on the SS *Stess*, a merchant ship. There were two heavy raids of particular significance.

Glamorgan Home Guard annual parade at Cardiff Castle. The city became progressively more militarised during the war with a large Home Guard presence and with various other regular army and foreign (US, Polish, Belgian) troops stationed in the city.

The first began at 6.30 p.m. on 2 January 1941 and Grangetown, Riverside, Llandaff Cathedral, Cardiff Arms Park and Cathays Park were all hit, suggesting perhaps that German bombing was less than effective in hitting important military and economic targets. That night an unknown Air Raid Precaution Officer wrote: 'After signing on at the post we went out in patrols in pairs. The whole arena was lit up with the artificial light of magnesium flares that had been dropped by the enemy ... The searchlights were busy and the anti-aircraft guns of the ground forces burst into life ... During this time I happened to walk down Westbourne Crescent towards The Parade, where at that lookout point I could survey what was going on in Cardiff. When I got there the glare from the scattered fires in the city was clear and substantial damage could be surmised.' The ARPs did invaluable work throughout the war in a city that was repeatedly targeted by the Luftwaffe. There were ninety-four posts manned twenty-four hours a day and seven days a week from 1939 to 1944, with a total of 4,000 voluntary and part-time workers.

Another eyewitness to the 2 January raid was the teenage Violet Williams, who saw the city lit up from Whitchurch:

In 1941 I was living with my parents in Cardiff together with my older sister Maud whose husband was in the RAF. Because Maud had no children at the time she was required to undertake essential war work and in 1941 she started as a munitions worker at Patton's factory in Taffs Well. Although I was only 15, my sister applied for me to join her at the factory and I became the youngest one there. On a cold and heavily frosted night as our shift ended on 2nd Jan. 1941 the massive German air raid on Cardiff began. The bombing became so bad that the management of the factory gave the workers the option of remaining in the shelter for the duration of the raid or for local people to return to their homes. My sister and I and another Cardiff girl called Maureen decided to go back home. We saw flares and searchlights crossing the sky and heard the explosions and ack-ack fire in the distance, but we girls did not realise the danger. Later as we reached Whitchurch Common we could see the vast panorama of the city on fire and the stricken Cathedral at Llandaff.[78]

A prime target for the Luftwaffe was the Royal Ordnance Factory at Llanishen. Cardiff's Royal Ordnance Factory No. 17 opened in 1940 for the construction of field guns and other weaponry, and over 20,000 people worked there. (In 1960 it became part of the Atomic Weapons Establishment and, as AWE Cardiff, switched production to the manufacture of components for the nuclear weapons programme.) During the war, munitions workers often thought their contribution to victory was overlooked, referring to themselves as a 'forgotten army'. The testimony of Edna Goshov, an 18-year-old munitions worker, indicates the professionalism and dedication of these workers, but also the comparatively favourable conditions that they worked in:

I was an engineer at the Royal Ordinance Factory at Llanishen, I was trained and I was good. We worked 11 hour shifts, day or night. I was a blue girl, wearing blue overalls, a hairnet and goggles. I worked in P-Shop making breach blocks for 85 mm naval guns. I worked on a Cincinatti lathe as big as a house, and overhead women worked on cranes. The crane women lifted the guns and the breach blocks off our machines. We had to produce eight breach blocks per shift. If we reached our targets, providing our breach blocks were perfect we got a bonus. We made sure the breach blocks were perfect and if the machines broke down we repaired them. The blocks and guns had to be absolutely spot on for our boys in the Navy. The wages were good in the Royal Ordnance Factory and they looked after us. We were privileged because of our training. Doctors examined us regularly. If our husbands came on leave we got a few days off, but we were warned 'try not to get pregnant'. You see it took time to train an engineer. Welsh women engineers had no medals but bloody well deserved them. We gave our all to the war effort. We kept our boys supplied. We had to, there was no one else. We are the forgotten army, we are the mams and grandmothers who did our bit for king and country.[79]

Despite the bombing creating havoc for terrified civilians and destroying their homes, remarkably few of Cardiff's strategic war industries were damaged. The Luftwaffe could ill afford such ineffective raids, as each one ate into dwindling reserves of aircraft and pilots. By 1941, after 18 months of fighting across Europe, Hitler was more concerned about amassing all of the Reich's resources for conquest in the East. But this did not stop the Luftwaffe exacting a heavy human cost across the city: on 26 and 27 February 1941 there were fifty-one people killed, and just one Heinkel bomber lost. A further raid on 4 and 5 March saw nearly 50 tons of high explosive dropped on the city. To put this figure in context, a year later the RAF dropped just over 4,000 tons on Cologne, and an equivalent amount on Hamburg a year after that.

On 18 May 1943 the most notorious raid of the war began. Of the 376 people who died in Cardiff during the war, a total of forty-three were killed that night. In one particular incident a barrage balloon site on Colchester Avenue was struck

Cardiff buildings damaged by air raids during the Second World War. In total some 355 people were killed by bombing during the war.

The city was in bad need of redevelopment after the war as bomb damage had devastated districts that had stood for over a century.

Although the Luftwaffe were more interested in damaging Cardiff's docks than her housing, the bombs fell all over the city.

directly, killing Women's Auxiliary Air Force servicewomen Betty McAskel, Paddy Brand, Betty Stanford and Betty Reynolds, and seriously injuring Terry David, Marjorie Oats and Lillian Ellis. Lillian Ellis was later awarded the BEM for Gallantry. An American Army base in the woods at Heath Park is believed to have been one of the reasons for this raid. The Battle of the Atlantic had effectively been lost, and there was little or no point in the Germans continuing to attack the docks. Arthur Mark, then a schoolboy, recounted his memories of that night to the *South Wales Echo* in 1993: 'A landmine landed on the ground between Mrs Bond's shop and Wedal Road, blowing out a vast number of the windows in the street and causing a crack in the shop that remained there until its demolition many years later. The next morning we descended on the crater and many a piece of shrapnel found its way to school to be bartered for blood alleys or the odd Dinky toy.' For one survivor of the Luftwaffe onslaught, Freda Schiller, the bombs had a special significance. She was Jewish, originally of German origin, and discovered after the war that many in her extended family had perished in Auschwitz. Mrs Schiller lived in York Street in Canton, and may have been saved by her sofa which she pulled in front of the entrance to her cellar, so that it absorbed the blast. The bombs, aimed at the railway line that runs through Canton, killed her neighbours at No. 37 York Street, but Mrs Schiller's efforts saved their daughter, Grace. She dug through the rubble to find the girl and took her in after the raid: 'I accompanied her to hospital but didn't have the heart to tell her that her parents had been killed.'

One theory, put forward by Cardiff historian John O'Sullivan, is that Hans Henri Kühnemann, managing director of the German-owned Flotmann Drill Factory in Allensbank Road from 1935 until September 1939, directed Luftwaffe planes to attack the city with such a devastating effect on that particular night. Kühnemann had returned to Germany. Many local historians have claimed that he was a Nazi spy, though the allegation that he had a large picture of Adolf Hitler in his office suggests that his skills as an undercover agent needed some work.

In 1945 the peacemakers had to create a post-war world that recognised the new realities of the Cold War. It was a deeply compromised settlement, with many injustices overlooked and brutal war crimes in many instances unpunished. One such involved Royal Artillery men from Cardiff and Japanese naval officers. The very same anti-aircraft gunners who had defended Cardiff during the raids of 1941, the 77th Anti-Aircraft Battalion, were shipped to Java in 1942 to help the Dutch and Americans effect a defence of the vast

Glamorgan Home Guard annual parade at Cardiff Castle. The Glamorgan Home Guard took part in civil defence and were active in catching German prisoners of war who escaped from their camp at Bridgend.

and oil-rich colonies of Java and Sumatra (today Indonesia). They joined an American, British, Dutch and Australian force to defend the island, part of the 3,500 British troops, the majority of whom were anti-aircraft units and troops intended to defend the island's airstrips. They were considered to be vital, because the Japanese had demonstrated their air superiority months earlier at Pearl Harbor. The men were taken prisoner almost as soon as they had arrived, as Java fell to the Japanese on 12 March. For a while the Welshmen were imprisoned on the island, but in 1943 they were sent to Changi Gaol, in Singapore. Some remained there, while others worked on the Siam to Burma Railway. It is now clear from military records that other Cardiff prisoners of war were taken to Japan.[80] In November 1943 the prisoners taken to Japan to work as slave labourers discovered that they were soon to be shipped back to Java to carry out essential war work for the Japanese. They were loaded into the hold of the 4,645-ton *Suez Maru*, a Japanese freighter; in total there were some 422 British servicemen and 127 Dutch prisoners of war. The *Suez Maru* was escorted by a minesweeper. It was standard practice for the Japanese navy to paint International Red Cross insignia on military shipping so as to discourage enemy submarines and aircraft from sinking vital capital ships, so the escort was painted with false International Red Cross insignia. The *Suez Maru* was not given any such protection, and was subsequently torpedoed by an American submarine, the USS *Bonefish*, 200 miles east of Java. Many of the prisoners of war drowned in the hold, but for those who escaped there was no mercy. As many as 250 men were able to cling to flotsam, but after the minesweeper had picked up Japanese survivors, on the orders of Captain Kawano, they were shot. The Japanese Government informed London that all the men had died when the ship had sunk, and it was not until 1949, when a Japanese officer who had witnessed the atrocity came forward, that the truth came out. Possibly tormented with guilt about what had happened, Lt Yoshio Masaji wrote to Supreme Allied Commander General Douglas MacArthur, at that time the de-facto ruler of Japan, explaining that as they had cried out for help the prisoners of war were gunned down in the water. He wrote: 'Some of them waved their hands. The bursts of machine-gun fire did not cease for some time.' Some men were reported to have stood on debris so the Japanese could shoot them more easily: so helpless was their situation that they must simply have hoped for a quick end.

The fate of these men was sealed by an order by Emperor Hirohito in 1942, saying that irrespective of the outcome of the war no Allied prisoners should be left alive or returned to Allied hands. Quite why this order was made is unclear, but one can only suspect that it was principally an attempt to cover up Japan's various war crimes and atrocities. The deaths of the Cardiff men, including Gunners Raymond Cowell, Robert Robertson and Leonard John, were never prosecuted, not even after a full confession from the ship's Captain Kawano and other officers admitting that they had falsified the ship's records to cover up the murders. MacArthur knew that the final blame rested with the emperor himself, still head of state long after the war. Without his cooperation Japan would have been impossible to govern, so the atrocity had to be brushed under the carpet. It was this kind of cynical logic that allowed the murderers of Cardiff's anti-aircraft crews to go unpunished.

The *South Wales Echo*'s Victor Lewis reported extensively about the courage and tenacity of the men who survived in the Far East. He told how they kept secret notes written on rice paper, despite the fact that any soldier found in possession of such contraband would more than likely have faced a death sentence.

A programme of the concert given by the Polish Army in 1944. The Poles, exiled from their own country due to Nazi and Soviet occupation, were grateful to their Cardiffian hosts and fought alongside the British Army in North Africa, Italy and Holland.

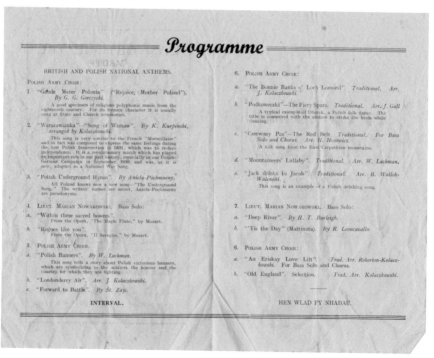

Programme

BRITISH AND POLISH NATIONAL ANTHEMS.

POLISH ARMY CHOIR:

1. "Gaude Mater Polonia" ("Rejoice, Mother Poland"). By G. G. Gorczycki.
   A good specimen of religious polyphonic music from the eighteenth century. For its hymnic character it is usually sung at State and Church ceremonies.

2. "Warszawianka"—"Song of Warsaw". By K. Kurpinski, arranged by Kolaczkowski.
   This song is very similar to the French "Marseillaise" and in fact was composed to express the same feelings during the first Polish Insurrection in 1831, which was to restore independence. It is a revolutionary march which has played an important role in our past history, especially in our Polish-German Campaign in September, 1939, and was, as it is now, adopted as a National War Song.

3. "Polish Underground Hymn". By Aniela Pochmurny.
   All Poland knows now a new song—"The Underground Song." The writers' names are secret, Aniela Pochmurny are pseudonyms.

4. LIEUT. MARIAN NOWAKOWSKI. Bass Solo:
   a. "Within these sacred bowers".
      From the Opera, "The Magic Flute," by Mozart.
   b. "Rogues like you".
      From the Opera, "Il Seraglio," by Mozart.

5. POLISH ARMY CHOIR.
   a. "Polish Banners". By W. Lachman.
      This song tells a story about Polish victorious banners, which are symbolising to the soldiers the honour and the country for which they are fighting.
   b. "Londonderry Air". Arr. J. Kolaczkowski.
   c. "Forward to Battle". By St. Zajc.

INTERVAL.

6. POLISH ARMY CHOIR:
   a. "The Bonnie Banks o' Loch Lomond". Traditional. Arr. J. Kolaczkowski.
   b. "Podkowecki"—The Fiery Spurs. Traditional. Arr. J. Gall.
      A typical example of Oberek, a Polish folk dance. The title is connected with the custom to strike the heels while dancing.
   c. "Czerwony Pas"—The Red Belt. Traditional. For Bass Solo and Chorus. Arr. H. Hosowicz.
      A folk song from the East Carpathian mountains.
   d. "Mountaineers' Lullaby". Traditional. Arr. W. Lachman.
   e. "Jack drinks to Jacob". Traditional. Arr. B. Wallek-Walewski.
      This song is an example of a Polish drinking song.

7. LIEUT. MARIAN NOWAKOWSKI. Bass Solo:
   a. "Deep River". By H. T. Burleigh.
   b. "'Tis the Day" (Mattinata). By R. Leoncavallo.

8. POLISH ARMY CHOIR:
   a. "An Eriskay Love Lilt". Trad. Arr. Roberton-Kolaczkowski. For Bass Solo and Chorus.
   b. "Old England". Selection. Trad. Arr. Kolaczkowski.

HEN WLAD FY NHADAU.

One Cardiff gunner sent to Japan was Les Spence, once a Cardiff forward weighing in at 14 stone, but reduced to 6 stone after two years' slave labour in a Japanese coal mine. On 9 August he witnessed the second of the atomic bombs dropped on Nagasaki, describing a 'blinding flash'. Years later as secretary of the Welsh Rugby Union, in a spirit of reconciliation he met the manager of the Japanese touring rugby team Shigi Kono. He told Mr Kono that the bomb had saved his life, and Mr Kono replied that it had also saved his, as he was training as a kamikaze pilot at the time.

Only 20 per cent of the 77th made it home to Cardiff. Most of the men had been raised from Cardiff's sporting and athletic associations; the regiment was similar to the pals regiments in 1914. Many of the returning prisoners of war had damaged health and never played sports again.

Throughout the war Cardiff was home to a number of foreign military and civilian personnel, members of the many countries allied against the Axis powers. There were organisations to offer support and solace to exiled Frenchmen, Belgians and Poles, for the most part set up by existing emigrés who suddenly had hundreds of their countrymen in barracks nearby. An Anglo-Belgian club was opened in James Street, an Anglo-Polish Club opened in Windsor Place, and Polish bandsmen from the Free Polish Army performed concerts in the Reardon Smith Lecture Theatre. The Friends of Free France were at No. 36 Park Place.

As Cardiff was a port it is hardly surprising that she saw a large number of American service personnel from 1942 onwards. American troops arrived in South Wales from spring 1942 onwards, and Cardiff saw her first liberty ship, *Artemis Ward*, in August 1942. The incredible speed at which liberty ships were produced and the subsequent improvements in Cardiff's docking facilities and transport network meant that the city eventually became a busy thoroughfare for men and materials. After the Battle of the Atlantic had been won and Admiral Doenitz's U-boat wolf packs were on the retreat, it became safe to transport the bulk of the D-Day invasion force from America and Canada to Britain – and Cardiff was one of the main disembarkation points for GIs and other servicemen. US bases were established in the grounds of Heath Hospital and on Whitchurch Common, and American soldiers became a familiar sight across the city. A plaque on Whitchurch Common commemorates the American army's presence and the tidy-up job done by their 2nd Evacuation Unit. The trees that grace the common today were planted in 1945 by American soldiers as a thank you for Whitchurch's kindness and hospitality.

Cardiff, like most other places in the UK with large numbers of GIs, also had to accommodate the reactionary racial politics of the New World. Cardiff had been a multi-racial community for at least 200 years at this point, perhaps even longer, as had most British ports since at least the Elizabethan era. Whilst racial tensions had always existed in Cardiff's Butetown, they were relatively insignificant when compared with equivalent struggles on the other side of the Atlantic. Cardiff, and indeed British, attitudes towards ethnic minorities seem often to have been a surprise to white American soldiers. An incident in Duke Street during the war is an illustration of this. A white American officer ordered the proprietor of a café called the Silver Lounge to throw out his black GI customers. The owner refused, and seems to have given the officer a short lecture on the café's policy of equality. It is hardly surprising that in an industrial city that owed much of its wealth to trade with the rest of the world, was enriched by its links with empire and had seen the development of Afro-Caribbean, Yemeni and Chinese communities, would have developed broadly tolerant and accepting attitudes.

The American authorities were careful not to let their soldiers upset and offend the local population, and in most militarised areas they kept a contingent

The *Iberian Coast*, the last ship to be repaired in Bute Dry Dock. The departure of the *Iberian Coast* signified the end of an era for Cardiff.

of military police. The American white-helmeted military police, or 'Snowdrops' as they were nicknamed, often dealt with unruly soldiers with swift and brutal justice. Eyewitnesses report them breaking up a drunken fracas on Queen Street, beating brawling American troops with truncheons 'like hammers'.

Maindy Barracks became home to some 700 black GIs who were part of the Quartermaster Corps. These soldiers, still segregated from the rest of the American army, were known as the 'Jim Crow' army, a reference to the segregation laws in the Southern states. They were shipped to Cardiff from Liverpool, and were the subject of prurient curtain-twitching by the locals. Lurid tales of debauched housewives having sexual liaisons with black GIs were common, although there are few accounts that seem more concrete than gossip.

During the war, Cardiff's docks and Penarth effectively became American territory. Penarth Dock was converted into a dry dock for repairing landing craft in 1943, and was thereby at the heart of a deep rift in Allied military planning. At the Casablanca Conference that year Churchill had persuaded the Americans to concentrate on an invasion of Italy, the 'soft underbelly' of Hitler's Europe, and to abandon a cross-Channel offensive for another year. Crucial to both strategies were landing craft. Churchill got his way, and a long and bloody Italian campaign began with the invasion of Sicily in July. By spring 1944 a deadlock in Italy at Monte Cassino and Anzio led Churchill to demand further landings north of Rome, but a shortage of landing craft prevented this. All available vehicles were earmarked for Normandy, and with the American occupation of Penarth and other sites like it across Britain, it was unlikely that any would be released for the prime minister's pet projects. The Americans decamped from Penarth just weeks after the landings, having no more need for the port.

By mid-1944 nearly 80 per cent of all supplies for American forces were arriving at Pembroke Dock, Cardiff or Swansea. A massive amount of materiel was stockpiled at Cardiff, and an American port commander was appointed. He had far-reaching powers in the docks area and the entire area was tightly patrolled. American soldiers, both black and white, pitched in with Cardiff dockers to get the millions of tons of tanks and ammunition disembarked. A vast wasteland by the Queen Alexandra Dock was christened the Prairie: it was dotted with tents for US soldiers, and fields of tanks, lorries, jeeps, DUKWs, artillery pieces and more. Cardiff's docks, having survived the bombing of the Luftwaffe in the early stages of the war, were going to be part of a process that would land 150,000 Allied soldiers in German-occupied Normandy.

Llandaff Cathedral.

Right The battle colours of the various Welsh regiments hang in the cathedral, charting campaigns in Europe and the British Empire.

Below The building has always had a deep and symbolic relationship with the Welsh regiments and divisions since their incorporation into the British Army from the eighteenth century onwards. The Welsh Regiment Memorial Chapel was built after the Second World War.

In the first week of June, Barry Island was closed to the public. Unbeknownst to the rest of Britain, an intense debate gripped those closest to Supreme Commander of the Allied Expeditionary Force Dwight D. Eisenhower. The cross-Channel weather caused delays in the date of the assault, and there were two cancellations in late May and early June. On 2 June the first ships began to sail down the Bristol Channel, but their progress was halted by a last-minute recall. The ships from Cardiff carried all the tanks, field guns, lorries and jeeps that the troops would need to break out from the beach-heads and take the towns of Caen and St-Lô. The operation was synchronised so that the heavy equipment was disembarked on D-Day, shortly after the beaches had been taken. The ships that sailed from Cardiff set out earlier than the main invasion fleet owing to the 30-hour journey.

Cardiff also became a treatment station for British and Allied soldiers wounded in France. Ron Burden, a teenager at the time, told the *South Wales Echo*: 'When the second front started, casualties from France were loaded on trains and some were shipped here. As scouts we helped unload the casualties from trains arriving in Coryton and took them to hospitals. There were serious casualties. In the Home Guard we trained with rifles and it was all a game to some extent but we soon realised the serious side of things.'

eleven

THE POST-WAR CITY

One man who almost immediately reaped the benefits of the new post war Cardiff was its first post-war MP James Callaghan, elected to Parliament to serve Cardiff in 1945 in the Labour landslide victory. Originally from Portsmouth, he defeated the existing Tory incumbent Sir Arthur Evans, running on a campaign of quick demobilisation of men from the forces, and a new era of modern housebuilding. Cardiff's rejection of the Tory Party was dramatic, with Labour gaining all three Cardiff seats with sizeable majorities. Cardiffians rejected the Conservatives for many of the same reasons that the rest of the country did. No one was in any doubt that Churchill had successfully led the country to victory, but the sacrifices of wartime and more importantly the harm that Stanley Baldwin's Conservatives appeared to have inflicted on the country during the Great Depression would not easily be forgotten.

A belief in the efficacy of state planning and organisation, a principle put into good effect throughout the war, was very popular when peace returned, and it was generally thought that a new central push for housing and health care would help Britain progress into the 1950s. Cardiffians had paid a high price for peace, both on the battlefields of Europe, Africa and Asia and also in their own communities, where bombing and rationing had been constants of life for nearly half a decade.

Callaghan defended various parliamentary seats in Cardiff for the rest of his career, even when he was prime minister from 1976 onwards. His modest beginnings as a back-bench MP for the soon-to-be capital of Wales resulted in him being at the heart of government under Harold Wilson, struggling with Britain's ailing finances at the end of the 1960s, the beginning of the troubles in Northern Ireland, and the Wilson government's failed attempts to tackle the trade unions.

On Callaghan's death in 2005, Labour MP Alun Michael wrote in the *Western Mail*:

> Jim Callaghan personified the link between national leadership and the people. Coming from a poor family, he never forgot his background. He was a trade unionist before he was an MP. And above all his personal roots and loyalty to the people who first elected him in 1945 never wavered – even long after he stood down after 42 years as the MP for Cardiff South & Penarth. At the heart of our constitution is the relationship between the MP and the constituency – talk of Ministers being 'out of touch' ignores the fact that each Minister is also an MP, returning each weekend to family, friends and the people who send us to Parliament. As the only person ever to hold the four great Offices of State, who better to set the tone for Parliamentary democracy than Jim?[81]

Callaghan was Cardiff's longest serving MP and his career is a very useful measure of change. During his four decades of service to the city, he probably saw more social and economic change in Cardiff than at any other point in its history. It is easy for those who examine the past to look at Tudor or Norman times and see dramatic change; events like the Reformation are very much 'larger than life' historical happenings. We sometimes ignore the fact that we live in no less important or dramatic times ourselves, it is just that historical change is happening for the most part gradually and all around us. The Cardiff we know now, as one of the hubs of the post-industrial world with its shops, bars, museums and marinas, sprawling estates, social exclusion, sporting triumph and devolved government was born in this era. This was part of a trend that affected not just Wales and Britain but eventually the rest of the Western world, as the focus of industrialism moved elsewhere. Cardiff's change, once again, was symptomatic of greater global and historical trends.

The post-war period saw Cardiff's heritage become a public asset. The 5th Marquess of Bute bequeathed Cardiff Castle to the Corporation of the City of Cardiff in 1947, and in 1946 St Fagans Castle had been given to Cardiff by the Earl of Plymouth. In many ways the marquess' decision to divest himself of Cardiff Castle was a landmark moment in the history of the Bute family and the history of Cardiff: the dynasty that had developed Cardiff as a hub of world trade, yet never quite seen a return on its original investment, was ending its relationship with the city. An unbroken history of lordship over Cardiff was at an end, one that had lasted since Norman times. It was perhaps fitting that a city that had voted overwhelmingly for a 'people's' government in 1945 should be spared the anachronism of a Lord of Cardiff Castle.

Despite Britain encountering several profound economic crises in the immediate aftermath of the war, and one of the coldest winters on record in 1947, there was a flurry of expansion, rebuilding and progress in the city over the next decade. The High Street was transformed with the replacement of trams by trolley-buses, steel wire rod production began at GKN in Tremorfa, in Ely Trelai Park was opened, and in 1955 Colchester Avenue industrial estate was completed.

One economic fact that could not be ignored, however, was the catastrophic slump in the coal trade, with just 1m tons of coal being exported in 1946, compared with 107m tons in 1913. The Second World War had in many ways been the first oil war; there was a struggle to control oil reserves particularly in the Middle East, and then a race to convert the British and American economies and military forces so that they were predominantly oil-powered. Much of this process, particularly with warships, had begun towards the end of the First World War, but the shift towards oil-powered heating in domestic and industrial contexts took a hefty toll on the coal industry, and on a coal port like Cardiff. The waves of pit closures from the 1960s onwards, carried out by the National Coal Board, were an unwelcome sign to South Wales that the tides of globalisation that had raised Cardiff from a sleepy backwater to a pivotal element of the global economy were now flowing in the other direction. As the empire also began to fragment, and decolonisation began, guaranteed markets for Welsh coal were no longer such safe bets. The last ever shipment of coal left Cardiff's docks in 1950.

By the late 1940s the well-established and relatively harmonious multi-ethnic community on Butetown was finally recognised by social observer Kenneth Little. Little's groundbreaking book *Negroes in Britain* (1948) told a story that Butetown residents already knew; that there had been a black African and Caribbean presence in Britain since the sixteenth century at least, and that Tiger Bay had been one of the most important centres of black community life in Britain for the previous two centuries. However, with the beginning of mass immigration into Britain at the end of the 1940s, previously harmonious race relations were tested. One Somali sailor and resident of Butetown in 1950 told the *Picture Post*: 'If I go up into town, say to the pictures, why man everybody looks at me as if I left some buttons undone.' The reporter Bert Lloyd told his readers that Butetown often resembled a ghetto (a word, so shortly after the horrors of the war had been

Cardiff buildings damaged by air raids during the Second World War. Cardiff's resolve in the face of the air raids was essential to keeping Britain supplied during the war.

If the German Luftwaffe had managed to destroy Cardiff Docks, it would have caused a huge crisis in Britain as the docks were one of the few lifelines of food into the country.

One of the heaviest raids was in May 1943, thought to be a retaliation for the successful 'Dam Busters Raid' on the Ruhr Dams.

revealed, that was laden with meaning), and he described the process by which black Cardiffians were often overlooked: 'Locals applying for jobs outside the dockland area are familiar with the routine treatment: the employer fears his hands will refuse to work alongside a coloured man.'

By the mid-1950s the dismantling of Cardiff's industrial heritage had begun, with the filling in of the Glamorganshire Canal, and the most important new public sites were principally based around the need for Cardiffians to enjoy a greater degree of leisure and affluence than the city had ever experienced. The world economy had begun to revive in the 1950s, and whilst Cardiff's main export had vanished at the start of the decade, the city's economy reached such a degree of diversity and integration with the rest of the country that it was capable of ongoing affluence, even without coal. The decline in coal exports left many dockworkers and the communities that had grown up along the waterfront facing profoundly uncertain times, and communities like Butetown stagnated, presenting town planners with the opportunity they needed to redevelop the district, sweeping away the last vestiges of Victorian Britain along the dock front.

From the Beveridge report in 1944 to Harold Wilson's 'modernising' government in 1964, the winds of change that were blowing through British society and affecting Cardiff were focused on planning and scientific modernisation. The city gradually abandoned heavy industry, adopting light manufacturing industries and a growth in retail, as it benefited from a nationwide boom in consumerism when the austerity years gradually came to an end. Throughout the 1950s the city centre continued to evolve, with the establishment of the bus station in 1954, another real sign of the times, considering Cardiff had previously been so orientated around the railways. Successive post-war governments had put their faith in the car and in road-building, and Cardiff's road and motorway infrastructure developed progressively, taking a huge step forward with the building of the M4 motorway in the 1970s.

A lasting legacy of the wartime bombing was the pre-fab aluminium bungalow. Gabalfa in Cardiff was particularly renowned for these ubiquitous homes, which were intended to be quick and cheap mass housing after the war, and a short term solution. They started to be built in 1948, and were still in existence decades after they had been first commissioned. The Gabalfa pre-fabs were churned out from aircraft factory production lines at the rate of one every 12 minutes, and were made up of four sections that could quickly be

Cardiff buildings damaged by air raids during the Second World War. Winston Churchill visited Cardiff in 1941 to inspect the civil defences and the anti-aircraft defences of the city.

transported to their destination, assembled, sealed and connected to power and water. It began fashionable to belittle pre-fabs in the decades after the war, but for many who lived in them a genuine affection existed, which is why there were headaches for local authorities who tried to demolish them later. Families moving from bombed-out, cramped conditions near the docks were pleasantly surprised by the spacious modern new homes, with room for storage and a fitted kitchen. They were far from unpleasant places to live.

In 1998 the case of Mahmoud Mattan, a Somali sailor, was reviewed at the Court of Appeal, and his conviction for murder in Cardiff in 1952 was judged to be unsound. Mattan had been the last man hanged for murder in Cardiff prison, accused of killing Lily Volpert, a shopkeeper who owned a shop in Butetown. A key witness had placed Mattan at the scene. Simply reading extracts from the trial gives a sense of how the procedure might have been compromised. Witnesses for the prosecution with poor or weak testimonies were called, witnesses for the defence were ignored and the judge failed to direct the jury adequately. The murder was committed with a razor blade and the star witness, Harold Cover, who placed Mattan at the scene, tried to murder his own daughter with a razor blade in 1967.

Mattan had settled in Cardiff in the 1940s and married a local girl. Though mixed race marriages were not uncommon in Butetown, it is clear that the

Cardiff buildings damaged by air raids during the Second World War. Cardiffians pulled together throughout the heaviest periods of the bombings. Winston Churchill eventually revisited Cardiff but not until 1948 when he had left office. Churchill was given the freedom of the city of Cardiff.

couple had to endure no small amount of racial prejudice. The description of the 'Somali' that Cover gave to the police matched that of another Somali man in the area at the time, Taher Gass, who was later convicted of murder and sent to Broadmoor. Cover received a £200 reward for his efforts, but the idea that he might have been incentivised by this was not raised at the trial. In 1970 leave for appeal was declined by the home secretary, but the Court of Appeal began proceedings in 1997.

The granting of capital city status in 1955 was given to Cardiff by Gwilym Lloyd George, home secretary under Anthony Eden and son of the great Liberal leader. Throughout the post-war period the Parliament for Wales Campaign had been gathering strength, and it was Gwilym Lloyd George's sister Megan who presented him with a petition for a Welsh Parliament in 1956. Gwilym had been appointed by Winston Churchill as home secretary and had also been given the job of Minister for Welsh Affairs, giving him a great deal of say over such issues as granting capital status. Churchill had been a huge admirer of Lloyd George, and the two had been close political allies, but the decision to grant capital status to Cardiff initiated a slow process of devolution that eventually culminated, four decades later, in the kind of political future for Wales and the rest of the United Kingdom that Churchill would have been appalled by. The struggle for devolution was, of course, something that predated Cardiff's city status, and reached a climax of radicalism in the 1970s with the brief emergence of a Free Wales Army. Much of the nexus of that struggle was in West and North Wales, and many more radical nationalist voices throughout the post-war period have taken a dim view of Cardiff in general. Other communities argue that Cardiff is barely Welsh at all, that it is an Anglicised colony imposed upon Wales. For much of Cardiff's history this has been true, but it has become increasingly difficult to describe the city as Anglicised when there are cultures from every corner of the world

Gwilym Williams of Miskin was one of the most important advocates of the Welsh language in nineteenth-century Wales, ensuring that bilingual judges were appointed.

living there side by side. Cardiff, like London, Leeds, Glasgow or Bristol, has a cosmopolitan identity of its own that makes simple binary distinctions between Welsh and English very difficult to sustain.

The arrival of the Commonwealth and Empire Games in Cardiff in 1958 was perhaps a perfect prism through which to view this debate on identity. The current and former empire that Cardiff had been supplying with coal for over a century had come to the capital city of Wales to compete. Over thirty-five nations and 1,335 athletes took part. Even though Cardiff is now a city renowned for having international sporting venues, the Commonwealth Games must still have been one of the largest sporting events that Cardiff has ever hosted.

In 1968, Merthyr boxer Howard Winstone won a gold medal for Wales fighting in the bantamweight category. Winstone's achievements, recently immortalised in film, were all the more remarkable considering he lost the tips of three fingers on his right hand in a factory accident when he was an amateur boxer.

New Library and John Lewis. The massive redevelopment of the Hayes has created retail, study and leisure spaces that have brought Cardiff into the twenty-first century.

The 1960s saw the scourge of hideous concrete buildings, one of the worst culprits being the city's first multi-storey car park, built in Greyfriars Road, soon to be followed by another multi-storey in Westgate Street. Across Cardiff, from the docks to Llanedyrn to Llanishen, concrete flats and office blocks started to emerge. The central library, officially opened in 1988, was still heavily influenced by the design principles of the 1960s: its glass and concrete design was meant to be airy and inviting, but (as with much of the architecture of the time) it fundamentally failed to achieve this.

In 1964, West Bute Dock finally closed after a century and a half of exporting coal; Cardiff's future would now have to be found in other industries. The setting up of a Rover factory in Tremorfa signalled that the city could find its way in manufacturing, but Cardiff's post-industrial future was a confusing time. It is arguable that this struggle for an identity has only really been successful with devolution for Wales and the reinforcement of Cardiff's capital status with a degree of political autonomy.

Throughout the 1960s Cardiff incorporated more and more territory. Llandaff, Whitchurch, Rhwbina and Llanedyrn were all incorporated into the city, and Cardiff came to resemble many other post-war British towns and cities, incorporating large tracts of urban sprawl. Communities like Whitchurch and Llandaff have managed to retain a sense of individuality and independence, but large sections of the greater Cardiff area were incorporated into major housing projects. Much of this had begun before the Second World War, but the pace of development increased markedly. By 1960 Cardiff had just over a quarter of a million inhabitants, partly because of international immigration, but largely due to local and regional migration, the decline of the coal industry in the valleys, the isolated nature of many valley communities and the allure of the city. Cardiff was once more an irresistible magnet, drawing people from across the region in search of work and better standards of living.

In 1963 a tragedy on the other side of the world united a congregation of Cardiff churchgoers, demonstrating the very best qualities of compassion and humanity. These frequently go unreported when looking at the life of a city, but are telling if one is attempting to understand what holds a community together. At the height of the struggle for civil rights in the former slave-owning states of the confederacy, the 16th Street Baptist church in Birmingham, Alabama was targeted by white racists who detonated a bomb in the church, killing four

Brochure for ladies' fashions, showing how Cardiff became a centre for retail, leisure and consumerism from the 1960s onwards.

girls and sparking outrage across America and around the world. In Cardiff, Carmarthenshire artist and glass worker John Petts decided, with *Western Mail* editor David Cole, to respond to this atrocity. He said in an interview in 1987: 'Naturally, as a father, I was horrified by the death of the children. As a craftsman in a meticulous craft, I was horrified by the smashing of all those windows. And I thought to myself, my word, what can we do about this?'[82] The *Western Mail*, to its great credit, ran a campaign to raise money to replace the church windows, asking for no more than half a crown. This ensured that ordinary people would contribute and that wealthy donors would be unable to buy up the campaign. The result was a fundraising effort that galvanised the whole community, and the *Western Mail* was able to publish images of interracial solidarity and harmony across Cardiff, as black and white children in Butetown handed over pocket money for the campaign. Petts toured the Deep South before the windows were installed. 'They had never heard of Wales,' he said. 'They had no idea where it was, but they were very quickly told something of the little country Wales was, and how it put great value on independence and freedom, to bandy with the great big words.' He eventually designed an image of a black Christ suffering on the cross, in bold defiance of the Southern white racists. The story of the Wales Window, as it became known, and Cardiff's pivotal role in raising the money indicates that people in the city had a wider perspective on the world, thanks to Cardiff's history as a port, and certainly they tended to be more receptive to events happening overseas. The city's mixed ethnicity and the experiences of many Butetowners left them with a commitment to racial tolerance and a feeling of solidarity and concern for people in far-away places.

When Cardiff itself was the focus of terrorist activity in 1967, and a bomb was detonated at the Temple of Peace in Cathays Park, the reaction to the attack was different. The bomb was planted as part of a campaign of attacks across Wales to protest against the investiture of Prince Charles as Prince of Wales (he had been created Prince of Wales in 1958 but was only invested with the office in 1969). The bomb went off probably earlier than planned. 'The entrance hall at the Temple of Peace, Cardiff, was wrecked by a saboteur's bomb early today – only hours before the opening of an all-Wales conference at which 450 civic leaders, Lord Snowdon and the Secretary of State for Wales, Mr Cledwyn Hughes, were to plan celebrations for the investiture of the Prince of Wales,' reported the *Western Mail*. In comparison with the troubles in Northern Ireland, the damage caused by Welsh nationalists was comparatively minor. It was suspected that the group Muddiad Amddyyfin Cymru was responsible, but no

The Glamorgan County Hall in 1958. The town hall was spared any wartime damage and today is still a symbol of civic pride in the city.

one ever claimed responsibility. The same group later conspired to assassinate Prince Charles, but failed and several of their members were killed preparing explosives in Abergele. Had a major loss of life occurred at the Temple of Peace, there would have been a huge change in the history of Cardiff and of the rest of Wales. Westminster's reactions to the troubles in Northern Ireland were draconian, with both the Wilson and Heath governments missing opportunities for peace and inflaming the situation unnecessarily. Could a similar situation have arisen in Wales? Perhaps not on such a scale, but certainly inept bomb-making skills saved Wales from an enormous post-war crisis, and a possible ongoing campaign of terror.

As the 1960s drew to a close, a decade of relative affluence and liberalism also came to an end. In the 1970s, Cardiff, like many cities, began to feel the force of trade union unrest, inflation and discontent. The immense size of trade union membership in the 1970s, coupled with a new consumerism and ever-rising expectations of living standards while a growing inflation ate away at those hopes, led to an explosion of militancy in Cardiff that had not been seen since the General Strike of 1926. Once again it took volunteers to hold public services together. One example is the walk out at the pumping station in Penarth Road in October and November 1970, when council workers were on strike. The new Heath government was clumsily trying to draw a line in the sand with the unions on the matter of pay increases: asking for restraint hadn't worked and the unions had memories of the previous two years, when the Wilson government had tried anti-union legislation. The council workers' walk out over pay claims hit the country hard, but for Cardiff it could have been catastrophic. If volunteers hadn't worked 18-hour days to keep the plant running, the streets would have been flooded with raw sewage.[83]

Despite the onset of troubled economic and industrial times in Cardiff, change continued at a relentless pace. There was the symbolic destruction of the last vestiges of docklands culture and history with the demolition of the last remaining aspects of Newtown. This district had been in terminal decay since the decline of the docks. Much as valley towns experienced a decade or so later with the wholesale closure of the pits, once the economic lifeblood of a community is cut off the community starts to stagnate and die. A compulsory purchase order was placed on much of Newtown by the Welsh Office and it was earmarked for the wrecker's ball by 1966. It stood in the way of a new motorway flyover, and it was believed that the families in Newtown would be happier in more modern housing in Ely, Fairwater and Llanedyrn. The destruction was complete in 1970 when St Paul's church was knocked down along with the nearby school. It is no coincidence that it was also in 1970 that Bute East Dock was closed. All that now remains are fourteen houses, and no real indication that a community once stood there.

The early 1970s saw one of Cardiff's most important amenities and landmarks open. The Heath Hospital combined much of the city's health services, many of which had evolved over the previous century in an unplanned manner. The Gabalfa flyover was purpose-built to enable access to the hospital, recognising that traffic in Cardiff, along with car ownership in general, had been creeping up for the previous decade and new transport infrastructure was essential. Decades later, in 1999, the Heath took on the role of Cardiff's primary emergency hospital as Cardiff Royal Infirmary was closed, much to the anger and indignation of most Cardiffians.

The 1970s saw the closure of East Moors Steelworks, and in the story of this particular piece of post-industrial decline is a means to understand Cardiff today. The East Moors site was a vast sprawling giant by the late 1970s. It could be seen beyond Splott, dominating the skyline in the same manner as the Llanwern or Port Talbot steelworks. The sheer size of the site made it a

Church Street in 1970. A peaceful Church Street at
the start of a decade of division, protest and crisis.

The High Street Arcade in 1970, leading to
Cardiff's huge Victorian indoor market.

St Mary Street in 1970. Traditionally Cardiff's busiest
shopping street, in 1970 it was a far cry from the
centre of nightlife that it is today.

fundamental part of the city, and its closure had a massive impact. The East Moors site was taken over by the newly founded Welsh Development Agency in 1980, and the lengthy process of site clearance began. The land was eventually put to use as part of the new bay development. Many of the 3,000 workers who lost their jobs when the site closed never worked again.

This failure was part of a pattern of British decline that had begun before the Second World War, and was largely preventable. Other competitor countries, Germany and Japan for example, made investment in industry compulsory, but Britain squandered the advantages that previous generations had given them. The industrial might of Cardiff was stripped away, asset by asset, from the 1950s onwards. There was no empire to cushion the blow of tough international competition, and also a lack of new equipment. It was more convenient for investors to put their money into the City of London, where they were guaranteed a good return and high interest rates, instead of making long-term investments in industry and those who worked in it. Cardiff's post-industrial landscape is a direct result of these failings, although the official story about the selling-off and shutting-down of industry is one of inevitability, of embracing change, of modernisation. Cardiff now has more museums and monuments to its industrial past than it has industry.

In 1979 the people of Cardiff rejected the idea of devolution in a national referendum. The vote, held on St David's Day, saw just 12 per cent of the voting population say yes to the idea of a devolved parliament in Cardiff Bay. In 1979 the plans for housing the government of Wales were far more modest than the award-winning Sennydd building that currently exists: politicians would have sat in the Cardiff Coal Exchange. It would be unfair to say that Cardiff rejected the idea of devolved government because it was on some level more closely allied to Great Britain, as there seems to have been a national rejection of the policy (a ratio of four votes to one against the policy was pretty consistent across the country). Welsh nationalists might have rejected the entire process rather than allow themselves to be ruled from Cardiff. Many of the generation of people who were polled probably had no love for Westminster, but having lived and served in a world war (most Second World War veterans would not have been at retirement age by 1979), a sense of loyalty to the country for which so much had been sacrificed would have been prevalent. The other probable reason is that Wales was yet to experience Thatcherism, an ideology that, when viewed from the jobless streets of Grangetown or the former mining towns in the valleys, appeared to be set up to benefit the south-east of England.

The last remaining docks, Cardiff Bay. Cardiff's docks are still used commercially, though they are a shadow of their former selves.

Former dockland. The task of redeveloping Cardiff Bay is still ongoing.

It seemed to do this, in the eyes of many Cardiffians in the 1980s, at the expense of the south-east of Wales.

The face of old Cardiff underwent radical changes in the 1980s. In much the same way that docklands in London and Liverpool were regenerated throughout the decade, and the focus of economic activity shifted from heavy industries to property, leisure, retail and entertainment, so Cardiff was about to experience a similar transformation. It took most of the decade to negotiate and plan the future of the bay area, but by 1987 the Cardiff Bay Development Corporation was established by the British Government to transform the derelict former industrial heartlands. The secretary of state for Wales, Nicholas Edwards, said the mission of the corporation must be 'to put Cardiff on the international map as a superlative maritime city which will stand comparison with any such city in the world, thereby enhancing the image and economic well-being of Cardiff and Wales as a whole'. One of the key objectives was badly needed, 'to re-unite the City of Cardiff with its waterfront'. Much of the land that existed between Splott and the coastline bore little resemblance to the rest of the city, and there was a serious imbalance between the lives of Cardiffians on either side of Newport Road. Two Cardiffs existed: the winners and the losers of the fall-out from the end of heavy industry.

What ensued was perhaps the largest engineering project that Cardiff had ever seen, with the construction of a barrage across Cardiff Bay to create a huge man-made fresh-water lake. As part of the Bristol Channel, Cardiff Bay drained twice daily, leaving miles of open mudflats, unappealing to investors and prospective house buyers. This was important because the 1980s was a decade of property speculation that had few parallels, and the 1990s was similarly obsessed. The sale of council housing by the Thatcher government had created a boom: as it became unlawful for local authorities to pour the proceeds back into house building they had to spend it on reducing the rates. In one fell swoop property owning became cheaper, and therefore more desirable, and the number of available properties declined. This created an incentive to own property, and it was inevitable that developers turned their attention to the bay. However, despite this redevelopment there were still deep divisions between rich and poor in the bay area, with the communities of Butetown, Grangetown and Splott being areas with high levels of deprivation.

There was fierce criticism of the plans to build the barrage. Even the future first minister, Rhodri Morgan, was critical, claiming that the expense of building the barrage would be unsustainable and that money could be better

Old warehouses, Cardiff Bay. The warehouses are a reminder of Cardiff's past as a huge coal port.

Old warehouses, Cardiff Bay. During the Second World War these warehouses became essential to the task of bringing supplies into Britain from Canada and America.

Cranes at Cardiff Bay. Whilst most of the bay area has been turned over to leisure, much of the site is still being developed.

spent elsewhere. Environmentalists also feared that valuable nesting and feeding grounds for birds would be lost. But by 1993 the Cardiff Bay Barrage Act had been signed into law. This provided for the creation of wetlands for birds along the Bristol Channel and a submerged channel that would allow fish, particularly salmon from the River Taff, to make their way to breeding grounds in the estuary. Work was completed in 1999, and with it the bay was transformed. The barrage, which runs from the old Alexandra Dock to Penarth Head, incorporates a cycle track, an arts installation and permanent exhibition, and pedestrians can walk across to Penarth. This kind of redevelopment was repeated in almost every major industrial city in Britain, and was a defining feature of the 1990s.

When Tony Blair swept to power in 1997 the cosmetic changes seen in Cardiff and elsewhere were precisely the kind of modernisation he preached, and if they left behind forever a working-class culture that involved heavy industry and strong trade unions, so much the better. Under the Blair government Cardiff was transformed again, as devolution brought national government to the city.

Devolution for Wales has a long history, far too long for this book to do it justice, but it is impossible to write a history of modern Cardiff without examining it on some level. In 1964 the Wilson government created the Welsh Office, and this established an important principle: Wales was a separate administrative constituency that had its own needs that were not adequately catered for by other Whitehall departments, and it needed additional structures of governance. Many in Wales would have wondered if it would have been more useful to have a properly devolved government.

Wilson, perhaps in the wake of worrying developments like the Temple of Peace bomb, set up the Kilbrandon Commission in 1969 to investigate the possibilities of devolved government in Wales and Scotland. It was Edward Heath's government that received the final report, in 1973. This suggested an elected chamber with some limited legislative powers, fewer than those that might be offered to the Scots, an elected premier, a reduction in Welsh Westminster MPs and the abolition of the Welsh Office. As we have seen, the first referendum of devolution was rejected wholeheartedly, and it was another eighteen years before the issue was back on the agenda.

In November 1997 the second referendum gained a yes vote by the slenderest of majorities: just 50.3 per cent voted yes. Whilst this is a huge

Cardiff Bay and the Pierhead building. The Pierhead building still reminds Cardiffians of the city's past as a coal port.

increase on earlier votes, that tiny 0.3 per cent should indicate something about Wales's overall enthusiasm for devolution.

The National Assembly for Wales was established following the passing of the Government of Wales Act 1998, and its first home was in Crickhowell House, opened in 1993 for the Welsh Office. There was considerable resentment in other parts of Wales that Cardiff was being favoured with an assembly, even though other communities had arguably stronger claims on Wales's democratic past. Machynlleth, once the seat of Owain Glyndŵr's Parliament, in the eyes of Welsh nationalists the last legitimate Welsh government, contested the choice of Cardiff. It was to no avail, however, as Ron Davies, the Welsh Secretary, made his thinking

The Pierhead building, first built in 1897, was the central administrative building for the docks, managing the import and export of millions of tonnes of goods weekly. It is still the most iconic building in the bay.

clear: Cardiff was 'too compelling to resist … We are a small country and must build upon our achievements to date. Cardiff is established now not only as the capital of Wales, but as a leading administrative and financial centre.' Liberal Democrats and Plaid Cymru wanted the Assembly to be established in Cardiff City Hall, but the Welsh Office announced that it would be housed at the Waterfront and that Crickhowell House would be temporary accommodation. Initially, after consultation, the Welsh Office also favoured Cardiff City Hall, but according to Audit Commission reports it needed a purchase price of £5m or less in order to make the project feasible. Leader of Cardiff City Council Russell Goodway presented Ron Davies with a bill for £14m for the building – and alternative arrangements were subsequently made.

There was an international competition to create a new home for the Assembly with the winning design picked by a panel chaired by none other than former prime minister and adopted Cardiffian, Lord Callaghan. The result is one of the most iconic and innovative buildings in Britain. The Senedd Building, designed by Sir Richard Rogers, was opened in 2006 at a total

Above The coat of arms at City Hall. The coat of arms was granted to Cardiff initially in 1906 and shows the Tudor Rose and the three white ostrich feathers of the Prince of Wales.

Right The red dragon bust at City Hall. The red dragon symbolises Cardiff's role as the capital of Wales

The Water Tower at the Roald Dahl Plass, Cardiff Bay. Both the Water Tower and Roald Dahl Plass feature in the BBC TV programme *Torchwood*.

cost of £70 million. Its design, with huge glass walls on all sides, expresses the idea that government is, or should be, transparent. Visitors are able to freely enter the upper levels of the building while the debates take place in the chamber below. The building was designed to be as environmentally friendly as possible and to have a design life of at least a century. It is probably the only government building in the world that uses geothermal energy: boreholes have been drilled 300ft below the ground and during the winter water is pumped through the pipes so the natural heat of the earth warms it. It is then pumped around the building, providing zero carbon heating. Over 1,000 tons of Welsh slate was used in the building. Part of the design brief was that as much locally sourced material as possible had to be used. This made it more difficult for the Assembly's detractors to argue that Cardiff Bay was remote from or was ignoring the rest of Wales. Building ground to a halt in 2000, and First Minister Rhodri Morgan insisted that a review of the entire process be undertaken. The following year the contract with Richard Rogers Partnership was terminated, the Assembly claiming that excessive costs that had not been factored into the original job were mounting. Following a bitter legal dispute, RRP was granted over £400,000 in compensation, and the Assembly was not awarded costs. New project managers and subcontractors were introduced to finish the job, and the building opened with much fanfare, rather ignoring the fact that the project had been a magnet for criticism from all political parties since it had been announced, being described by both Labour and Tory AMs as a waste of public money. Few could argue that the finished product was a very impressive piece of architecture, even a work of public art.

It would be all too easy to stand in Cardiff Bay, looking at the Senedd building and the now equally magnificent Wales Millennium Centre, and think that the struggles and conflicts of the past have been resolved, that Cardiffians now live in the kind of post-industrial and post-ideological Britain that New Labour hoped could be created. If one story punctures that myth, it is the story of Allied Steel and Wire.

As the world market for steel became a progressively more competitive environment in the 1980s and '90s, ASW, based squarely between Tremorfa and Cardiff Bay, found it more and more difficult to compete. In 2002 the company collapsed and went into receivership, with the loss of most of the jobs at the massive plant, once part of GKN, also owners of East Moors Steelworks. A skeleton staff was kept on to help wind up production, and everyone else received redundancy. This was bad news, but there was worse to come: rumours abounded about the state of the steelworkers' pension funds, and a week after the closure of the site, on 18 July 2002, it was announced that the pension fund was also being wound up. Suddenly hundreds of ASW workers' plans for their retirements were thrown into crisis.

Ivor Novello, born Ivor Davies in Canton, was arguably the world's first pop star after he became famous for writing popular songs. During the First World War the sentimental 'Keep The Home Fires Burning' reminded families of loved ones fighting in France and beyond.

There appeared to be enough money to pay a full pension to existing retirees, but men who were a long way off retirement, but had paid into the scheme for years, seemed to be facing a future where only 40 per cent of the pension they were entitled to was likely to be received. In 1995, government legislation had introduced the minimum funding requirement, by which employer funding for pension contributions was set. The legislation was clearly flawed: even though ASW had set aside the required amount, they had allocated far too little to cover their commitments. Pensions campaigner Dr Ros Altmann took up the issue of what she called 'pension theft', and in 2004 the government was forced to act to protect future pensions – but very little could be done to compensate the ASW workers. In 2007, Welsh Secretary Peter Hain agreed a package of £2.9bn in compensation for all victims of failed pension schemes, giving 1,000 ASW workers access to 90 per cent of the monies lost.

Cardiff's industrial past lingers even now. Although only light and high tech industries might exist, complemented by a service sector and retail, the way of life that forged the city's identity and created its soul, still lives on, if only in public monuments and private memories.

epilogue

THE VIEW FROM
ST PETER'S STREET

S t Peter's Street in Roath is a convenient place to end this story of a city. Once, in the seventeenth century, the fires of religious radicalism burned brightly here but now, as with much of Cardiff, it is as religiously pluralistic a suburb as you could find. Next to St Peter's church is Cardiff's Buddhist Centre, and half a mile up the road in Cathays is the Shah Jalal Mosque and Islamic Cultural Centre. Still further into North Cardiff, on the edge of Cyncoed and Penylan, is the United Synagogue. On the other side of Newport Road, in Pearl Street in Splott, is the Sikh Gurdwara. At the end of St Peter's Street in City Road there are numerous Lebanese, Moroccan and other Middle Eastern restaurants and takeaways, and further up the road there are Japanese and Chinese eateries. Shops selling African and Caribbean produce, Polish food and Indian saris sit side by side with fish and chip shops and haberdashers. If you take a walk up Crwys Road it presents an interesting snapshot of contemporary Cardiff: smart cafés and coffee shops, where 20- and 30-somethings spend their Saturday mornings, sit next to a growing number of charity shops, where the same 20- and 30-somethings offload the clothes, books and CDs they no longer want, driving many smaller retailers, already competing with supermarkets, into liquidation.

The streets surrounding St Peter's Street for a square mile or so are top heavy with students from around the world because of the close proximity of Cardiff University, a product of late Victorian Cardiff, established by a Royal Charter in 1883. The university is counted amongst the top destinations for sixth form leavers in Britain, and attracts the lucrative overseas student market. Taking pride of place in the new exhibition about Cardiff's past in the Old Library building, in a display cabinet of artefacts that tell the story of contemporary Cardiff, is a student's T-shirt listing the pubs visited and alcohol consumed in one night.

Whilst this might be topical and captures the zeitgeist in an irreverent and post-modern way, it underlies another fundamental truth about Cardiff in the

Above, left Roath Park Lake. The lake was originally dug to provide leisure pursuits to the new wealthy middle classes of the late Victorian era.

Above, right John Batchelor, a great Victorian entrepreneur and merchant, was also involved in Liberal politics and earned the enmity of the Tory Bute family. He put much of his energy into campaigning against slavery.

twenty-first century. A rather toxic mix of 24-hour licensing, cheap alcohol promotions, a large student population, a weekend influx from towns that are often lacking in excitement, and legislation that encourages more and more pubs, has made the city centre a no-go area for non-drinkers on Saturday nights. The pedestrianisation of St Mary's Street was completed in part to make the thoroughfare safer for Saturday night revellers. Lonely Planet, the world-famous travel guide, describes Cardiff as 'A prodigiously boozed town'. In 2009, Cardiff's reputation went global when *Wall Street Journal* reporter Jeanne Whalen wrote an article for the prestigious American paper after a visit to St Mary's Street. 'Such raucous partying routinely turns the weekend streetscape here in the capital of Wales into a scene from *Night of the Living Dead*. Drunken young men and women stumble through streets fouled with trash and broken glass, while the police labor to maintain order and tend to those needing help.'[84]

This rise in public alcoholism, benignly rebranded as binge drinking, has been a nationwide phenomenon, and it has been accepted in Cardiff as a normal facet of twenty-first-century life. It must not be ignored, however, because of the extent to which it has transformed life in Cardiff. Other social issues, such as drug use and homelessness, comprise a hidden Cardiff, one that exists parallel to the city centre that most see every day. Take a walk down Charles Street at about 6 p.m. and you might glimpse it. Charles Street, where a cluster of gay-friendly bars and clubs are full of revellers during the weekend, is also where Cardiff's street sleepers receive warm soup, sandwiches and pies from charity volunteers at dusk on weeknights. The doorway next to Waterstones bookshop on the Hayes is rarely without signs that rough sleepers have used it as a temporary shelter, and the Hayes has become a perfect spot for shoplifters and bag snatchers to congregate.

> **Special Announcement**
> # THE
> # DAVID EVANS
> # STORE
> ## FASHION DEPARTMENTS
> *HAVE BEEN*
> ## TRANSFERRED
> *TO*
> ## 207 & 208 HIGH ST.
> ### (OPPOSITE MACKWORTH HOTEL)
> **DAVID EVANS & CO. (Swansea) Ltd**

Announcement in the *South Wales Evening Post* of the movement of the David Evans fashion department to temporary premises as a result of bombing in January 1943.

Cardiff city centre manages to accommodate a darker side whilst still being home to some of the most expensive and prestigious brands. Many of the new shops in the huge new shopping centre St David's 2 would not look out of place on Oxford Street. That shops selling expensive watches, fountain pens and perfume have stayed in business during the longest recession since the 1930s speaks volumes about Cardiff's relative affluence, and about the kind of economic crisis that this country is experiencing. At least in Cardiff people have not stopped spending money on high-end goods, even though almost everyone has seen their income decrease.

Along with drinking and shopping, Cardiff's other main obsession is sport. When Wembley Stadium was closed for refurbishment from 2003 to 2007, Cardiff's Millennium Stadium was the venue for dozens of national and international football matches, bringing huge revenues to hoteliers and retailers in the city, and tens of thousands of fans from across the country and around the world.

Cardiff's love affair with rugby has become something of a secular faith. Match days in Cardiff result in an almost spaghetti-western silence in city centre streets as fans tensely watch the events unfolding on widescreen televisions in pubs and bars. Shops selling rugby shirts and all manner of Welsh paraphernalia still seem to thrive, irrespective of the financial climate.

Even though so much of Cardiff's past has been swept away, Cardiffians still cling onto their memories with a fierce pride. The number of books and magazines about local history and collective memories is immense. As in all communities, the past means something so deeply profound that it cannot be easily articulated; it is more a feeling. It is a sense of belonging, of shared roots, of struggles borne together and of triumphs achieved. It is because of this shared past, born in the cramped houses of Butetown,

Royal Arcade. The Victorian arcades house some of Cardiff's smallest niche shops, including Spiller's Records, the oldest record shop in the world.

in the munitions factories in Llanishen, in the medieval fairs at Market Cross or on tramp steamers crossing the oceans of the world, that Cardiff's uniquely unpretentious, down to earth and ultimately welcoming attitude exists.

NOTES

Chapter One

1 Andrew Hayes, *Archaeology of the British Isles: With a Gazetteer of Sites in England, Wales, Scotland and Ireland* (Palgrave Macmillan, 1993) p.194

2 Graham Webster, *Rome Against Caratacus: The Roman Campaigns in Britain AD 48–58 (Roman Conquest of Britain)* (Routledge, 2003) p. 34

Chapter Two

3 Graham Webster, *Rome Against Caratacus: The Roman Campaigns in Britain AD 48–58 (Roman Conquest of Britain)* (Routledge, 2003) p. 57

Chapter Three

4 Stewart Williams, *Glamorgan Historian Vol. 1*, first edition (Aberystwyth: Stewart Williams, 1963) p. 191

5 *Ibid.*

6 Royal Commission on the Ancient and Historical Monuments in Wales, *An Inventory of the Ancient Monuments in Glamorgan: The Later Castles from 1217 to the Present vol. 3, Pt. 1b: Medieval Secular Monuments (vol. 3)*, 2nd edition (Royal Commission on the Ancient & Historical Monuments of Wales, 2000) pp. 3–16

7 *Ibid.*

8 *Ibid.*

9 William Henry Hart (ed.) *Historia et cartularium Monasterii Sancti Petri Gloucestriae* (Cambridge Library Collection – Rolls, vol. 1), 1st ed. (Cambridge University Press, 2012) p. 81

10 *Ibid.*

11 Wendy Davies, *The Llandaff Charters*, second edition (National Library of Wales, 1979)

12 Anne Rutherford, *I, Giraldus: The Autobiography of Giraldus Cambrensis* (1145–1223) 2001

13 Wendy R. Childs, *Vita Edwardi Secundi: The Life of Edward the Second* (Oxford Medieval Texts), revised edition (USA: Oxford University Press, 2005)

14 *Ibid.*

15 H.C. Maxwell Lyte (ed.), *Calendar of Close Rolls Edward II: vol. 3 – 1318–1323* (Institute of Historical Research, 1895)

16 *Ibid.*

17 *Ibid.*

18 Dennis Morgan, *The Cardiff Story*, 4th edition (Dennis Morgan, 2001)

19 John Hobson Matthews, 'Records of the Cordwainers and Glovers: Introduction', vol. 3 (Cardiff Records, 1901) pp. 336–341

20 John Hobson Matthews, *Charter V: On the right of the townsmen to municipal self-government* (1340) vol. 1 (Cardiff Records, 1901) pp. 19–27

21 John Hobson Matthews, *Records of the Cordwainers and Glovers: Documents to 1601*, vol. 1 (Cardiff Records, 1901) pp. 342–352

22 Gwyn A. Williams, *When Was Wales? A History of the Welsh*, 2nd edition (Penguin Books Canada Limited, 1985) pp. 98–99

23 *Ibid.*

Chapter Four

24 John Hobson Matthews, *Manorial Records: Ministers' Account of the Lordship of Leckwith* (1456)', vol. 2 (Cardiff Records, 1900) pp. 60–67

25 Stewart Williams, *Glamorgan Historian Volume Three*, 1st edition (D. Brown & Sons Limited, 1966) p. 134

26 Glanmor Williams, *Recovery, Reorientation, and Reformation: Wales c.1415–1642*, vol. 3, Oxford History of Wales (USA: Oxford University Press, 1987) p. 321

27 Glanmor Williams, *Recovery, Reorientation, and Reformation: Wales c.1415–1642* (Oxford History of Wales) vol. 3, (Oxford University Press, 1987) p. 281

28 Stewart Williams, *Glamorgan Historian Volume Three*, 1st edition (D. Brown & Sons Limited, 1966) p. 226

29 *Ibid.*

30 Eamon Duffy, 'The Queen and the Cardinal: Eamon Duffy Explores the Relationship between Mary I and Her Archbishop of Canterbury Cardinal Pole. Pole's Advice to His Queen about Attitudes to Henry VIII and in Dealing with Heretics Show He Played a Far More Energetic Role in the Restoration of the "True Religion" Than He Has Been Given Credit For' in *History Today*, May 2009

31 Stewart Williams, *Glamorgan Historian Volume Three*, (D. Brown & Sons Limited, 1966) p. 226

32 John Hobson Matthews 'The Manors of Cardiff District: Descriptions', vol. 2 (Cardiff Records, 1900) pp. 8–41

33 Glanmor Williams, *Recovery, Reorientation, and Reformation: Wales c.1415–1642* (Oxford History of Wales) vol. 3 (Oxford University Press, 1987) p. 303

34 John Fox, *Fox's Book of Martyrs or The Acts and Monuments of the Christian Church, Being the Lives, Sufferings and Deaths of Christian Martyrs*, vol. 1 (J. Woodward, 1830) p. 817

35 *Ibid.*

36 *Ibid.*

37 John Hobson Matthews, 'Church goods of Llandaff Cathedral and diocese (1558): Introduction', *Cardiff Records: volume 1* (1898) pp. 369–371

Chapter Five

38 John Hobson Matthews, 'The Municipal Charters: Introduction and Description', *Cardiff Records: volume 1* (1898) pp. 1–9

39 *Ibid.*

40 Philip Jenkins, *The Making of a Ruling Class: The Glamorgan Gentry 1640–1790* (Cambridge University Press, 2002)

41 Glanmor Williams, *The Welsh Church from Conquest to Reformation* (University of Wales Press, 1962) p. 530

42 John Davies, *A History of Wales*, 1st edition (Penguin Books, 1995) p. 271

43 Trevor Royle, *The Civil War: The War of the Three Kingdoms 1638–1660* (Abacus, 2005) p. 468

44 Trevor Royle, *The Civil War: The War of the Three Kingdoms 1638–1660* (Abacus, 2005) p. 513

45 *Ibid.*

46 Peter Gaunt, *A Nation Under Siege: The Civil War in Wales 1642–48* (Cadw Theme) 1st edition (Stationery Office, 1991) p. 32

47 *Ibid.*

48 *Ibid.*

49 Jonathan Scott, 'Sidney, Algernon (1623–1683)', *Oxford Dictionary of National Biography* (Oxford University Press, online edn, Jan 2008, first published 2004)

50 Susan Wiseman, *Conspiracy and Virtue: Women, Writing, and Politics in Seventeenth-Century England* (Oxford University Press, 2007) p. 9

51 John Hobson Matthews 'Glamorgan Calendar Rolls and Gaol Files: 1595-1702', *Cardiff Records: volume 2* (1900), pp. 166–184

52 John Foxe and W. Grinton Berry (ed.) *Foxe's Book of Martyrs* (Fleming H. Revell Co., 2003)

Chapter Six

53 *Identifying the Black Presence in Eighteenth-Century Wales, Llafur*, vol. 10, no. 1, 2008

54 G. Hall, *In Miserable Slavery: Thomas Thistlewood in Jamaica 1750–1786* (University of the West Indies Press, 1998) p. 107

55 D. Hayton, E. Cruickshanks and S. Handley (eds), *The History of Parliament: the House of Commons 1690–1715* (Boydell and Brewer, 2002)

56 John Hobson Matthews, 'Glamorgan Calendar Rolls and Gaol Files: 1703-37', *Cardiff Records: volume 2* (1900) pp. 184–198

57 William Wordsworth, *The Prose Works of William Wordsworth*, 12th edition (Echo Library, 2006)

58 Richard Watson, 'Annecdotes of the Life of Richard Watson', 1st edition, (Richard Watson, 1814)

Chapter Seven

59 Gwyn A. Williams, *When Was Wales a History of the Welsh* (Penguin Books Limited, 1985) p. 201

60 John Hobson Matthews, 'Glamorgan Calendar Rolls and Gaol Files: 1800-30', *Cardiff Records: volume 2* (1900) pp. 250–270

61 *Ibid.*

62 *Ibid.*

63 Rob Bryer, 'The Roots of Modern Capitalism: A Marxist Accounting History of the Origins and Consequences of Capitalist Landlords in England', *The Accounting Historians Journal*

64 Raymond Grant, *On the Parish* (Glamorgan Archive Service, 1988)

Chapter Ten

65 Jack Ashore, 'Seamen in Cardiff before 1914' in *Welsh History Review*, vol. 9, nos 1–4, 1978–79

66 Angela Gaffney, *Aftermath: Remembering the Great War in Wales* (University of Wales Press – Studies in Welsh History, 2000)

67 *Ibid.*

68 Elizabeth Crawford, *The Women's Suffrage Movement: A Reference Guide 1866-1928* (Routledge, 1999) p. 97

69 Deirdre Beddoe, *Out of the Shadows* (University of Wales Press, 2001) p.30

70 *Ibid.* p. 52

71 Neil Evans, 'The South Wales Race Riots of 1919' in *Llafur* (1980) pp. 5–29

72 Alun Burge, 'The 1926 General Strike in Cardiff' in *Llafur*, vol. 6, no. 1, 1992

73 John Mcllroy, 'Glowyr Cymru ym Mosgo: Welsh Communists at the Lenin School between the wars', vol. 8, no. 4, 2003

74 Will Paynter, *My Generation. Edition* (Allen & Unwin, 1972) p. 67

75 *Ibid.* p.145

76 Robert Stradling, *Wales and the Spanish Civil War, 1936–39: The Dragon's Dearest Cause* (University of Wales Press, 2004)

77 Abbie Wightwick, '70th anniversary of war being declared brings back WW2 memories', *Western Mail*, 3 September 2009

78 Mari. A. Williams, *'A Forgotten Army': The Female Munition Workers of South Wales, 1939–1945* (University of Wales Press, 2002)

79 *Ibid.*

80 Dennis Morgan, *Cardiff, a City at War* (Dennis Morgan, 1998) p. 132

Chapter Eleven

81 Alun Michael, 'Jim never forgot his constituents' in *Western Mail* (28 March 2005)

82 Gary Younge, 'American civil rights: the Welsh connection, Gary Younge' in *The Guardian* (6 March 2011)

83 Dominic Sandbrook, *State of Emergency: The Way We Were*, 2nd edition (Penguin Books, 2001) p. 74

84 Jeanne Whalen, 'U.K. Drinking Problem Gets Political', *Wall Street Journal*, 14 April 2009

BIBLIOGRAPHY

Books

Beddoe, Deirdre, *Out of the Shadows* (Cardiff: University of Wales Press, 2001)

Childs, Wendy R., *Vita Edwardi Secundi: The Life of Edward the Second* (Oxford Medieval Texts)(Oxford: Oxford University Press, 2005)

Crawford, Elizabeth, *The Women's Suffrage Movement: A Reference Guide 1866–1928* (Oxford: Routledge, 1999)

Davies, John, *A History of Wales* (London: Penguin Books, 1995)

Davies, Wendy, *The Llandaff Charters* (Ceredigion: National Library of Wales, 1979)

Foxe, John and W. Grinton Berry (ed.) *Foxe's Book of Martyrs* (Ada: Fleming H. Revell Co., 2003)

Francis, Hywel, *Miners Against Fascism: Wales and the Spanish Civil War* (London: Lawrence & Wishart Ltd, 2012)

Gaffney, Angela, *Aftermath: Remembering the Great War in Wales* (Cardiff: University of Wales Press, 2000)

Gaunt, Peter, *A Nation Under Siege: The Civil War in Wales 1642–48* (London: Stationery Office, 1991)

Grant, Raymond, *On the Parish* (Swansea: Glamorgan Archive Service, 1988)

Gregory, Frank, *Deacon's Dissenters Raise the Cross: History, Origin and Memoirs of Cross Hills Baptist Church* (Colorado: Catamount Publications, 1998)

Hall, G., *In Miserable Slavery: Thomas Thistlewood in Jamaica 1750–1786* (Jamaica: University of the West Indies Press, 1998)

Henry Hart, William (ed.), *Historia et cartularium Monasterii Sancti Petri Gloucestriae: Volume 1* (Cambridge Library Collection) (Cambridge: Cambridge University Press, 2012)

Hayes, Andrew, *Archaeology of the British Isles: With a Gazetteer of Sites in England, Wales, Scotland and Ireland* (Hampshire: Palgrave Macmillan, 1993)

Hayton, D., E. Cruickshanks and S. Handley (eds), *The History of Parliament: the House of Commons 1690–1715* (Suffolk: Boydell and Brewer, 2008)

Jenkins, Philip, *The Making of a Ruling Class: The Glamorgan Gentry 1640–1790* (Cambridge: Cambridge University Press, 2002)

Morgan, Dennis, *The Cardiff Story* (Dennis Morgan, 2001)

Morgan, Dennis, *Cardiff, a City at War* (Dennis Morgan, 1998)

Paynter, Will, *My Generation* (London: Allen & Unwin, 1972)

Royal Commission on the Ancient and Historical Monuments in Wales, *An Inventory of the Ancient Monuments in Glamorgan: The Later Castles from 1217 to the Present v. 3, Pt. 1b: Medieval Secular Monuments* (Aberystwyth: Royal Commission on the Ancient & Historical Monuments of Wales, 2003)

Royle, Trevor, *The Civil War: The War of the Three Kingdoms 1638–1660* (London: Abacus, 2005)

Rutherford, Anne, *I, Giraldus: The Autobiography of Giraldus Cambrensis (1145–1223)* (Cambridge: Rhwymbooks, 2001)

Sandbrook, Dominic, *State of Emergency: The Way We Were* (London: Penguin Books, 2011)

Stradling, Robert, *Wales and the Spanish Civil War, 1936–39: The Dragon's Dearest Cause* (Cardiff: University of Wales Press, 2004)

Webster, Graham, *Rome Against Caratacus: The Roman Campaigns in Britain AD 48–58* (Oxford: Routledge, 2003)

Williams, Glanmor, *Recovery, Reorientation, and Reformation: Wales c.1415–1642* (Vol. 3) (Oxford: Oxford University Press, 1987)

Williams, Glanmor, *The Wel.sh church from Conquest to Reformation* (Cardiff: University of Wales Press, 1962)

Williams, Gwyn A., *When Was Wales? A History of the Welsh* (London: Penguin Books Limited, 1985)

Williams, Mari A., *'A Forgotten Army': The Female Munitions Workers of South Wales, 1939–1945* (Cardiff: University of Wales Press, 2002)

Williams, Stewart, *Glamorgan Historian: Volume One* (Stewart Williams, 1963)

Williams, Stewart, *Glamorgan Historian: Volume Three* (Cowbridge: D. Brown & Sons Limited, 1966)

Wiseman, Susan, *Conspiracy and Virtue: Women, Writing, and Politics in Seventeenth-Century England* (Oxford: Oxford University Press, 2007)

Wordsworth, William, *The Prose Works of William Wordsworth* (Fairford: Echo Library, 2006)

Journals

Anon., 'Identifying the Black Presence in Eighteenth-Century Wales', *Llafur*, vol. 10, no. 1, 2008

Ashore, Jack, 'Seamen in Cardiff before 1914', *Welsh History Review*, vol. 9, nos 1–4, 1978–79

Bryer, Rob, 'The Roots of modern capitalism: A Marxist accounting history of the origins and consequences of capitalist landlords in England', *The Accounting Historians Journal*

Burge, Alun, 'The 1926 General Strike in Cardiff' *Llafur*, vol. 6, no. 1, 1992

Eamon, Duffy, 'The Queen and the Cardinal: Eamon Duffy Explores the Relationship between Mary I and Her Archbishop of Canterbury Cardinal Pole. Pole's Advice to His Queen about Attitudes to Henry VIII and in Dealing with Heretics Show He Played a Far More Energetic Role in the Restoration of the "True Religion" Than He Has Been Given Credit For' in *History Today*, 2009

Evans, Neil, 'The South Wales Race Riots of 1919', *Llafur*, vol. 3, no. 2, 1980

McIlroy, John, 'Glowyr Cymru ym Mosgo: Welsh Communists at the Lenin School between the Wars', *Llafur* vol. 8, no. 4

Scott, Jonathan, 'Sidney, Algernon (1623–1683)', *Oxford Dictionary of National Biography*, Oxford University Press, online edn, Jan 2008, first published 2004

Primary Sources

Foxe, John, *Foxe's Book of Martyrs* or *The Acts and Monuments of the Christian Church, being the lives, sufferings and deaths of Christian Martyrs*, vol. 1 (J Woodward, 1830) p. 817

Hobson Matthews, John, 'Records of the Cordwainers and Glovers: Introduction', *Cardiff Records: vol. 3*, 1901, pp. 336–341

Hobson Matthews, John, 'Glamorgan Calendar Rolls and Gaol Files: 1800–30', *Cardiff Records: vol. 2*, 1900, pp. 250–270

Hobson Matthews, John, 'Charter V: On the right of the townsmen to municipal self-government (1340)', *Cardiff Records: vol. 1*, 1898, pp. 19–27

Hobson Matthews, John, 'Records of the Cordwainers and Glovers: Documents to 1601', *Cardiff Records: vol. 3* 1901, pp. 342–352

Hobson Matthews, John, 'Manorial records: Ministers' account of the Lordship of Leckwith (1456)', *Cardiff Records: vol. 2*, 1900, pp. 60–67

Hobson Matthews, John, 'The manors of Cardiff district: Descriptions', *Cardiff Records: vol. 2*, 1990, pp. 8–41

Hobson Matthews, John, 'Church goods of Llandaff Cathedral and diocese (1558): Introduction', *Cardiff Records: vol. 1*, 1898, pp. 369–371

Hobson Matthews, John, 'The municipal charters: Introduction and description', *Cardiff Records: vol. 1*, 1898, pp. 1–9

Hobson Matthews, John, 'Glamorgan Calendar Rolls and Gaol Files: 1595–1702', *Cardiff Records: vol. 2*, 1900, pp. 166–184

Hobson Matthews, John, 'Glamorgan Calendar Rolls and Gaol Files: 1703–37', *Cardiff Records: vol. 2*, 1900, pp. 184–198

Michael, Alun, 'Jim Never Forgot his Constituents', *Western Mail*, 28 March 2005

Watson, Richard, 'Annecdotes of the Life of Richard Watson', 1st edition, Richard Watson, 1814

Whalen, Jeanne, 'U.K. Drinking Problem Gets Political', *Wall Street Journal*, 14 April 2009

Younge, Gary, 'American civil rights: the Welsh connection', *The Guardian*, 6 March 2011

INDEX

If you enjoyed this book, you may also be interested in …

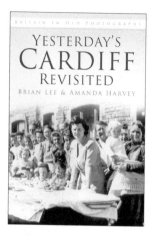

Yesterday's Cardiff Revisited

BRIAN LEE & AMANDA HARVEY

Drawing on their detailed knowledge of the city's history, the authors have collected a diverse selection of images which give a fascinating insight into how life has changed in Cardiff over the last century. Packed with over 200 charming photographs, *Yesterday's Cardiff Revisited* includes scenes of Cardiff's docks, historic pubs and visits from royalty.

978 0 7524 6529 6

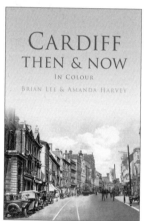

Cardiff Then and Now

BRIAN LEE AND AMANDA HARVEY

This compelling book contains a selection of fascinating old photographs of Cardiff paired with modern ones taken from the same spot as those photographers of a century or so ago. Younger readers will be able to visit the places that their parents or grandparents have told them about, while for older readers it will be a real walk down Memory Lane.

978 0 7524 7113 6

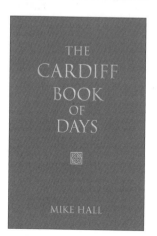

The Cardiff Book of Days

MIKE HALL

Taking you through the year day by day, *The Cardiff Book of Days* contains a quirky, eccentric, amusing or important event or fact from different periods of history. Ideal for dipping into, this addictive little book will keep you entertained and will delight residents and visitors alike.

978 0 7524 6008 6

Visit our website and discover thousands of other History Press books.

www.thehistorypress.co.uk